Women on trial

*A study of the female suspect,
defendant and offender
in the criminal law and
criminal justice system*

—Women's crimes came into my mind with a rush. Child burdened women who were left without money, without the means or opportunity or physical power to earn it, who had stolen in order to save their lives and that of their children – thieves! Women who from their childhood had been trained to physical shame, women who at their first adolescence had borne children by their own fathers under circumstances when resistence was inconceivable. Women who had been seduced by their employers. Women deceived and deserted by friends and lovers, Women employed by their own parents for wage earning prostitution, Women reduced to cruelty after being for years the unconsulted churning mills for producing in degradation and want and physical suffering the incessant annual babies of an undesired family. Women who had been stolen in their bloom and imprisoned for purposes of immoral gain. If amongst such women, such criminals, there are many who are professionally thieves, prostitutes 'by choice', immoral 'past redemption' as it is called, sodden with drink, undermined by drug taking, their maternity transfomed into cruelty, their brains worn to madness, what cause is there for surprise or reproach and what hope is there of cure by imprisonment? Before they took to these muddy lanes have they not been driven out from the fair road? What was their training, what their choice from the start? Are not the doors of the professions and many trades still barred to them? Their right to work, a fair value for their work, is it not denied to them? When they undertake the burdensome but joyous labour of maternity, is there any security to them of physical respect and choice, of economic security, of rewardful honour and social influence? Where is the recognition of the woman's great service, how is she helped to render it suitably and efficiently; does the state, the race, the family, the individual, see to it that she has her reward?

Constance Lytton (*Prison and Prisoners* pp. 62–3)

Women on trial

*A study of the female suspect,
defendant and offender
in the criminal law and criminal
justice system*

SUSAN S. M. EDWARDS

Manchester University Press

© Susan. S. M. Edwards 1984

Published by
Manchester University Press
Oxford Road, Manchester M13 9PL
and 51 Washington Street, Dover
New Hampshire 03820, USA

British Library cataloguing in publication data

Edwards, Susan S.M.
  Women on trial.
  1. Female offenders
  364.3'74   HV6046
  ISBN 0-7190-0995-2

Library of Congress cataloging in publication data

Edwards, Susan S. M.
  Women on trial.

  Bibliography: p.227
  Includes index.
  1. Female offenders—Great Britain. 2. Sex
discrimination in criminal justice administration—Great
Britain. 3. Female offenders—Legal status, laws, etc.
—Great Britain. I. Title.
HV6046.E37 1984   364.3'74'0941   83-24840
ISBN 0-7190-0995-2

Printed in Great Britain
by Butler & Tanner Ltd, Frome and London

*In remembrance
of father Bahman
and in celebration
of daughter Nadia*

Contents

List of tables and figures   *page viii*

Key to tables and abbreviations   *x*

Acknowledgments   *xi*

Introduction: The legal organisation of sex, sexuality and gender   1

Part one: Sex differences in the criminal law

1. A question of sex   25

2. The 'common prostitute' – An antecedent presumption of guilt   53

3. Medico-legal conundrums – The legal organisation of physiological
   difference   79

4. Female sexuality – Changing conceptions in the criminal law   101

Part two: Gender considerations in the administration of justice

5. Indicators of suspicion – Detecting and apprehending suspects   121

6. Sentencing negotiations – Excuses and justifications   143

7. Crimes unnatural – Some criminological social and legal questions 161

8. Individualised justice – Treatment, leniency or lessened responsibility,
   or informal state control   183

Notes and references   217

Select bibliography   227

Name index   237

Subject index   239

List of tables and figures

Tables

i:1	Custodial remand and non-custodial outcome	17
i:2	Reasons for conditional bail	18
i:3	Remands in custody	19
1:1	Prosecutions for prostitution and allied offences	27
1:2	Prosecutions for loitering for the purpose of prostitution	31
2:1	Prostitution: plea and outcome	71
2:2	Not-guilty pleas and offences	72
4:1	Outcome of contested trials	106
6:1	The function of motive in conduct: shoplifting	157
6:2	The function of motive in conduct: prostitution	158
7:1	Showing increase in number of women defendants found guilty of 'abnormal' crimes: 1969–78	164
7:2	Monthly variation in cautioning and arrest	166
7:3	Showing increase in number of women defendants cautioned for 'abnormal' crimes: 1969–78	166
7:4	Defendants proceeded against for violent crime at the Crown Court: 1981	178
8:1	Social Inquiry Reports requested according to offence and sentencing outcome	192
8:2	Agreement and diversity: probation officers' recommendations and magistrates' disposal	194
8:3	Pre-trial reports: according to offence, nature of comment and recommendation	197
8:4	Pre-trial Social Inquiry Reports requested: reasons for non-preparation	198
8:5	Medical remands: number and percentage according to offence and disposal	199

8:6	Representation and sentence	200
8:7	Mitigation and its influence on sentencing in offences of loitering for the purposes of prostitution	201
8:8	All offences committed by women according to sentence	203
8:9	Committals for sentence by type of offence and outcome	204
8:10	Sentencing of female defendants according to offence	205
8:11	Appeals: according to offence and outcome	206
8:12	Reasons for allowing or varying appeal	207
8:13	Inter-urban variations in the sentencing of prostitutes	208
8:14	All Women aged 17 and over proceeded against at the magistrates court for loitering for the purposes of prostitution by result	209
8:15	Effect of number of previous convictions for offences of loitering for the purposes of prostitution on sentencing outcome	211
8:16 a.b.c	Percentage of sentencing of prostitutes in relation to previous convictions	212
8:17	Receptions of adult women (21 and over) by age and offence, and fine default	213
8:18	Proportionate comparison between males and females aged 17 and over: subject to hospital order under the Mental Health Act 1959	216

Figure

8:1	Scale of disposals	193

Key to tables and abbreviations

BO	Bound Over
AD	Absolute Discharge
CD	Conditional Discharge
PO	Probation Order
HO	Hospital Order
AC	Appeal cases
All ER	All England Law Reports
CL	Current Law
CLR	Criminal Law Review
Cox CC	Cox's Criminal Cases
ER	English Reports
FD	Family Division
JP	Justice of the Peace and Local Government Review
KBD	King's Bench Division
LR	Law Reports
NACRO	National Association for the Care and Resettlement of Offenders
NAPO	National Association of Probation Officers
P	Probate
P & D	Probate and Divorce
QBD	Queen's Bench Division
WLR	Weekly Law Reports

Acknowledgments

The research study from which this book derives would not have been possible without the drama of those many women on trial. To them all, some of whom managed to maintain a sense of humour while others were broken, I am more than grateful for their memoirs and their invitation to enter a legal unfolding which was very much their own.

I am also grateful for the enormous goodwill of a great many people working within and outside the criminal justice system. Quite apart from the key decision makers in the various organisations to whom I am obliged for granting me the necessary access to resources and information, it is to those alongside whom I worked, who taught me some of the skills of their respective trades, introduced me to brighter and darker moments, supported, encouraged and enthused me in their curious interest in my work, that I am especially grateful. Their friendship and commitment to their own task made mine one fondly remembered.

Whilst I cannot mention them all, though equally deserving, some I recall particularly with a special affection and gratitude. Jean White, Senior Probation Officer at the City Magistrates' Court, Manchester, introduced me to social inquiries and their function in sentencing. Pat Fitzgerald did much of the work of collating those reports and provided an atmosphere where I could always rest assured of a welcome. Jean Schofield and her staff in the Criminal Records Office greatly assisted in providing information relating to bail applications and to court records. Whilst at the Crown Court, Manchester, I have to thank Ken Howe, Senior Probation Officer, and more importantly the late Alan Fryman and his assistant Muriel Pearce for their continual interest, critical comments and support. So too the staff of the listings office who let me know in advance what cases were coming up; the courts administration department, especially Kit MacDonald, the file registry staff, and all the court clerks, especially Christine Mayer and Barbara Fox, for their assistance in locating the trial, plea and appeal samples, not least of all for their friendship. I am deeply appreciative to those with whom I had many insightful discussions on matters medico-legal, particularly Mr P. Haywood, M.B., Ch.B., D.P.M., Medical Officer, Risley Remand Centre, Warrington, and Dr S. O'Brien, Nottingham City Hospital with whom I shared insights on the medical aspects of pre-menstrual tension; Keith Evans, Barrister-at-Law, helped to clarify the legal developments in this regard.

Many days were spent at the Greater Manchester Police Headquarters at their Criminal Records Office, and in this regard I am especially grateful to the entire team who even when given the vaguest of details to work on miraculously managed to locate the relevant information. I am also especially indebted to Inspector Taylor and his team of the plain-clothes department, Moss Side Police Station, Manchester, for their vigilant assistance and hospitality during this part of the study. Group 4 headquarters, Broadway, Worcestershire, invited me to participate in a training programme: I thank them for their hospitality and also a special remembrance to all my store-detective 'colleagues' on the course.

Officially, access was granted and co-operation forthcoming from:

Greater Manchester Police
Greater Manchester Probation and After Care Service
South Yorkshire Probation and After Care Service
West Midlands Probation and After Care Service
Inner London Probation and After Care Service
Merseyside Probation and After Care Service
The liaison officers and personnel working in the corresponding courts
The Chief Clerk to the Justices, Mr P. Dodd, Manchester City Magistrates'
    Court
The Courts Administrator, Mr B. Whittaker
Mr Snowden, Chief Clerk, Knightsbridge Crown Court
Mr J. Tebay, Chief Clerk, Manchester
Mr Lewis, Chief Clerk, York Crown Court

I would also like to acknowledge the Home Office, the Lord Chancellor's Department and the Prison Department for permitting me to consult court files and medical records, and to visit Styal Women's Prison, Cheshire, and Risley Remand Centre, Warrington. On a more personal level I am very grateful to both the magistracy and judiciary in Manchester for sharing some of their insights with me. And finally, I would like to thank staff of the libraries of the Home Office, the Police College Basingstoke, Institute of Advanced Legal Studies, London, the Law Faculty at the University of Sheffield, and the Wellcome Institute for the History of Medicine Library, London.

What I managed to accomplish regarding data collection, tabulation and analysis owes much to the able assistance of Liz Farrell. As assistant to the project she was indefatigable in her commitment to the task in hand, slow to take holidays, and worked all hours, though drawing a line at participant observation *à la* William F. Whyte, *Street-Corner-Society*-style, in a red-light area of Manchester, reminding me at the time that it was not part of her contract. I thank her for her endeavour.

Of course the research would not have been possible without financial support. The Social Science Research Council sponsored the study, 'The routine management of discretion in the sentencing process of female offenders', grant number HR/7588/1, upon which this book is based, and I thank them.

For intellectual support I would like to thank my colleagues at the Centre for Criminological and Socio-Legal Studies, Faculty of Law, University of Sheffield, and especially to Paul Wiles for his support throughout. Mrs Monica Walker read and commented on draft chapters and I am grateful for her observations, friendship and hospitality. Hal Pepinsky, Professor Forensic Science, Indiana University, and presently Visiting Research Associate at the Centre for Criminological and Socio-Legal Studies, has made many useful suggestions on the draft of Chapter 5, a subject upon which he is more than qualified to comment. I have also to thank the friends I met at the Second International Institute on Victimology, Bellagio, Italy, July 1982, for their continual exchange of ideas, especially Dorothy Bracey, Assistant Professor of Criminology at John Jay, College of Criminal Justice, New York, and Kathleen J. Ferraro, Center of Criminal Justice, Arizona State University.

The manuscript would not have seen the light of day had it not been for the diligence of Mrs Vera Marsh, secretary at the Centre for Criminological and Socio-Legal Studies, University of Sheffield, who was resolute in her determination to type and present it with propriety. I am more than grateful for her kindness.

Any errors whatsoever in presentation, interpretation, fact or expression are entirely my own.

Finally, a very special thank you to my close friends and family and especially to Dr Iris Gillespie for her distant but uncannily timely encouragement and Shirani Dassanaike for her never-ending practical help and philosophical wisdom. To Abdul Redha, my husband, for his encouragement and love, and to Tina, my youngest sister, who, in order that the book be completed, volunteered herself as mother surrogate to my baby daughter, who upon her return to me had clearly thrived and flourished.

May 1983

Introduction: The legal organisation of sex, sexuality and gender

It could be said that one of the paradoxical effects of feminism as a political force has been to force the recognition of the diverse and unexpected character of the organisation of sexual differences.

> P. Adams, 'A note on sexual division and sexual differences,' 1979

This is a study of the way in which ideologies of crime – who commits what and when – and theories of motivation for criminal conduct and culpability influence the location of suspects and the handling of defendants.

In the criminal justice process a central consideration is to examine how both judgments and discretion (and there is a distinction: *R v Lawrence and Another* 1977 CLR 493) are mediated by hunches, prejudices and essentially intuitive and sophistical sentiments, often extraneous to the proof of guilt. The process of detection, prosecution and sentencing is guided, *inter alia*, by theories concerning the types of persons who behave in this way. As Goffman (1970) has observed, 'Society establishes the means of categorising persons and the complement of attributes felt to be ordinary and natural for members of each of these categories.'[1] The chief aim of this study is to examine how far and in what way these considerations are informed by characterisations of gender and sex difference.

The unifying theme is to examine the validity of the proposition that women, whether as suspects, defendants or offenders, are dealt with in part in accordance with the degree to which their criminal behaviour deviates from what is expected of them in their appropriate gender role. Thus the expression 'women on trial' denotes a lived experience which is double-edged, encompassing not only a consideration of the female defendant's passage though the criminal justice system, but also the way in which *mens rea* and culpability – though issues based on fact – are nevertheless (like mitigation and the sentencing process) influenced by the degree to which the female defendant in question is a good wife, mother and homemaker, honest, decent and moral, and above all feminine.

Whilst it would be considered absurd if culpability were reduced on the grounds that the woman was a good painter and decorator, if she is said to be a good wife and mother then her crime becomes very often excusatory and justifiable as in theft of food, abstracting electricity and prostitution; yet condemnatory and baffling when crimes of burglary, violence and criminal damage are committed.

In the processing of female defendants, the courts and the criminal justice system draw on their 'everyday' assumptions of 'what kinds of people' do what kinds of things. Whether or not the woman fits into the preconceived stereotype will ultimately have some influence on the courts' perception of her. This tendency is well illustrated in work on the way in which ideologies of rape victims actually dictate the kind of justice and restitution a complainant may receive. Thus the attractive single woman was asking for it, whilst the dowdy woman's allegation must be true! Such typifications of 'kinds of offenders/victims', whilst not exactly perverting the course of justice, have profound consequences for locating suspicious persons, decisions to prosecute, to remand, and to request reports, and finally for the sentencing outcome (see Swigert and Farrell 1977: 17). And again, the way in which facts are subject to differing interpretations is well illustrated in debates over medical evidence in rape trials, where the defence often interprets evidence as indicative of passionate consenting intercourse, whilst the prosecution argues that it suggests a brutal sexual attack (Edwards 1981a: 166-7).

Forensic experts can differ widely on the interpretation they give to the same set of facts. Harold Loughans was acquitted of murder on the evidence of Sir Bernard Spillsbury, a murder to which he subsequently confessed in 1963.[2] More recently Dr Clift's interpretation of forensic facts led to wrongful conviction for murder of John Preece in 1973; Preece has now been cleared, as Clift's evidence has been discredited (*Sunday Times,* 30 August 1981). But in any event, and in sexual offences in particular, police surgeons are not adequately trained (only a handful have the Diploma in Medical Jurisprudence – see ex-Scotland Yard police surgeon Dr Arnold Mendoza's remarks (*Sunday Times* 30 August 1981)), which in the absence of expert examination leaves the interpretation of bruising to the kind of sexist assumptions which I have already described.

The basic theoretical orientation then draws in part on the perspective adopted by labelling theorists Lemert (1951), Becker (1963), Schur and Bedau (1974) and by those who have recognised the consequent impact of stereotypes of deviants for actors' passage in the criminal justice system (Sudnow 1965, Skolnick 1966, Swigert and Farrell 1977). Such theories, however, fail to account for the political reasons why certain persons' activity is normalised whilst others' behaviour is subject to punitive sanction. Indeed, Harris (1977: 3) explains how particular perceptions of women in relation to crime are a product of wider power relations within society. Thus the political implications of certain explanations for women and crime becomes particularly insidious with relation to certain offence categories and routine decisions in the criminal justice system which shore up motherhood and a biological and pathological conception of women (Rowett and Vaughan 1981). The expression of attitudes to infanticide in law is an instance of the way a particular image of motherhood is tactically perpetuated and sustained, diverting wider political questions of welfare and public support onto 'personal' and role competence.

The interest in women and crime has been a growing one, though from a variety of conflicting perspectives, since Maudsley. Until very recently the chief concerns of 'criminologists' have been in classifying female offenders according to physiological and latterly sociological antecedents. In certain respects studies of female criminality have often been guided by the prevailing paradigms that have directed theorisation within the criminological domain. Criminology, during the last twenty years, has been significantly characterised by approaches of labelling and interactionism, though this perspective has been less readily adopted in studies of the female offender, the preference persisting for some pathological vision.

The critique of women and crime, the development of an understanding of female offenders in criminological theory and their experience in the criminal justice system has been addressed by, amongst others, Smith (1962, 1965), Klein (1973), Smart (1976, 1981) and Morris and Gelsthorpe (1981). The central unifying strategy and commitment of much of this contemporary work has been with the exposure and confrontation of the institutionalisation of gender assumptions regarding criminality of women that are built into the definitions and procedures of criminal justice as well as evident in discretionary decision making. Whatever the consequences, whether some decisions are advantageous to women in the short term, nevertheless there are instances of gender ideologies at work which may lead to unjustifiable disparate treatment and in some instances to sexism (Pearson 1976). Worrall (1981) explains that the fact that women are regarded as 'out of place' in the criminal justice system affects the way in which they negotiate the various escape routes: 'This fundamental incongruity may be seen to advantage women, but it serves, in fact, to define the parameters of negotiation in a restrictive fashion and causes breaches of those parameters to be severely penalised.'[3] Scutt (1981) argues that the treatment of women offenders is an extension of their position in society,[4] and Omodei (1981) and Shacklady Smith (1978) maintain that particular stereotypes of womanhood inform female crime. As Klein and Kress (1981: 153) write, 'sexuality becomes the key to understanding the deviance of a woman, since this is supposedly her primary function'.

In Britain some of the more recent critiques of sexual difference in the application and interpretation of criminal law and in the administration of justice have been provided by Mawby (1977, 1980), Morris and Gelsthorpe (1981), and Greenwood (1981); in America, in the work of Brodsky (1975), Harris (1977), Norland and Shover (1977), Bowker (1978), Warren (1981), and Phillips and DeFleur (1982). In Australian criminology these questions have been addressed in the work of Scutt (1978), Mukherjee and Fitzgerald (1981), Hancock (1980), Mukherjee and Scutt (1981), and Edwards Hiller (1982).

The research studies have focused on some aspect of each stage of the pre-trial and trial process, although such research remains underdeveloped, particularly in

Britain. Much of the work on the impact of gender in the pre-trial process is based on American studies, particularly of bail decisions, in the work of Swigert and Farrell (1977) and Nagel (1981), whilst the most insightful studies on the decision to prosecute are provided in the work of Simon and Sharma (1978), and Bernstein, Cardascia and Ross (1979). The predilection for plea change and charge reduction is explored by Crites (1978), although the work of Shapland (1981) in England on mitigation, albeit not directly addressing gender difference, is also important.

Sentencing studies, rather than complacently arguing that women are treated more leniently, argue that women are sentenced in accordance with their perceived culpability and deviation from gender role. Thus, Warren (1981: 10) cites Sheldon who argues that for offences against morality women receive harsher sentences than men. Bernstein *et al.* (1979: 379) points similarly to the increase in severity of sentence dependent on the degree to which the offence deviates from the appropriate gender role. Other studies have also examined class, race and economic factors in mediating experiences and the type of justice of different classes of women. And certainly the 'crimes' of Joan Little and Inez Garcia must be considered in this light (see Chapter 7) – 'crimes' which might, if the defendant were white, be seen as expressions of justifiable self-defence. Lewis (1981) has already contemplated preliminary research on the racial factor, whilst Kruttschnitt's latest research (1982) explores the impact of economic independence on sentencing outcome.

Differences of sex, sexuality and gender

Instances of sex-gender division, that is occasions of the disparate treatment of 'men' and 'women' in their particular sex roles and the accommodation of men and women in their social and gender roles, are readily observable features in both criminal law and the operation of the legal justice process. For instance, some of the formal statements of criminal law incorporate fundamental biological or physical criteria as a warrant for their exclusive applicability to one 'sex-class'. The Infanticide Act 1938, and particular aspects of the criminal law relating to rape and inchoate offences, are predicated uniquely on a social interpretation of physical capability. Contingent on these biological conditions and the social construction of physical criteria are not only considerations of physical capability but also ideas relating to sexual maturity, which are often regarded as mutually exclusive categories. These concepts find a more fixed legitimation within the law governing sexual relations. The age of consent for instance is predicated on such a belief. But there is little reciprocity between the social reality relating to physical capability and the legal enshrinement – whilst a boy under the age of fourteen is deemed incapable of rape within criminal law, within civil law this rebuttable presumption has not been heeded. In a recent paternity case a boy who had fathered a child whilst under the age of thirteen was ordered to pay maintenance, the law in this instance thereby conceding his capability (see Chapter 4).

The law also draws on, and in turn manages, differences between the sexes based on presumptions of physiological incompatibility. This, largely a medical presumption, has found legal credence within the framing of the Infanticide Act, where women as a 'sex-class' are considered by virtue of a post-natal physiological incapacity to be predisposed to killing their newly born infants. Some of the principles upon which such laws are predicated remain immutable, thus only men are capable of rape within the existing statutory formulation, though some regard this category to be one amenable to change. O'Donovan (1979: 148) remarks that there is no reason why this should be linked to sex since aspects of the South Australian legislation on sexual offences have recently been amended to encompass both males and females as aggressors and victims.

In certain areas of law, however, the conventional wisdom of pristine social interpretations of the meaning and implication of biological division is now being called into question. In consequence, the medical assumption that mothers may pathologically be predisposed to killing their children is being treated with increasing scepticism and so too is the legal affirmation of this now precarious presumption. More recently it has been conceded that women are capable of committing an indecent assault on a male, where hitherto they were deemed physically incompetent.

The particular 'sex-specific' laws which fall outside any logical comprehension are those statutes which relate to prostitution, which by their very existence claim that only 'women' are capable of prostitution. This belief, enshrined in law, strangely enough has persisted with a momentum of its own, since the basic assumption on which it is predicated corresponds to no biological or cultural rule. Originating with a desire to punish women, this law now exists as a legal conundrum, seemingly capable, however, of autonomous development, though anachronic; sufficient evidence and proof that physical criteria do not always stand at the basis of disparate treatment—often it is blind prejudice!

In the context of civil law, too, the physical criteria of biological sex, physiological difference, sexual maturity and capability have been considered central to the legal validity of a marriage contract. In this event marriage is based purely on biological criteria, and on heterosexuality, with a definite view to reproductive potential. As O'Donovan (1979: 135) indicates, 'Justifications for different treatment of men and women by law . . . may rest on sex differences but usually it is gender role differences that are invoked.' Indeed it is from within the practice of criminal law that the interpolation of specific gender considerations throughout the legal continuum in the pre-trial, trial sentencing and appeal stages appears as an ever-recurrent, if not always conspicuous, action. Thus the problem of the management of sexual difference is to be considered by an examination of the various statuses, roles, rights and obligations which are ascribed to, or conferred upon particular cultural classes and to the social ascriptions incumbent on the sub-groups — that of wife, mother, daughter, etc. — and also to the corresponding gender expectations which are linked to them.

The tendency then has been to assume that cultural and social requirements follow on from basic biological differences. Yet as we shall see it is in the very social rules and meanings incumbent on these conditions that basic differences are constructed. Hence 'Physical nature is assigned to classes and held to them by rules' (Douglas 1971: 113). And perhaps more specifically social meaning is acquired within a context of social relationships both within and outside social institutions. Weeks (1981) refers to this tendency when he writes, 'it is in the family that the anatomical differences between the sexes acquire their social significance'.[5] Other authors have similarly insisted on the necessity for structurally situating such analyses. And in the context of family law, custody in particular, Brophy and Smart (1981) write, 'it is not motherhood in isolation that is revered by the courts but motherhood within a familial structure'.[6]

Characterisations relating to gender divisions inform all stages of the legal process from law in the making to the administration of justice. For instance, the parliamentary debates preceding the Acts relating to married women's property, women and the franchise and the guardianship of infants reflected the prevailing attitudes to women's status and role within the family and revealed those instances where gender functioned to exclude women from participating in public life. Moreover, the discussions which preceded the Guardianship of Infants Act 1884, for example, betray some astounding inconsistencies between social and legal reality. In home life the woman's roles as wife and mother were extolled. Yet the law refused to accord her domestic status with any legal recognition, preferring instead to confer guardianship rights on husbands and brothers whilst hypocritically glorifying maternity. However the Act conferred upon the mother the power to appoint a guardian. Of course the gender basis of legislative decision making is often overidden by a concern for the more obvious instances of gender invocation in the court process. A more recent and flagrant instance of this is apparent in *Watchel* v *Watchel* [1973], FD.72, 90) where gender role considerations were at the basis of a decision regarding the division of the family home. The justificatory rationale for the judgment betrays a fundamental aquiescence with a division of labour — domestic and work — along 'sex' lines. Lord Denning MR declared:

when a marriage breaks up, there will thenceforward be two households instead of one. The husband will have to go out to work all day and must get some woman to look after the house – either a wife, if he remarries, or a housekeeper, if he does not. He will also have to provide maintenance for the children. The wife will not usually have so much expense. She may go out to work herself, but she will not usually employ a housekeeper. She will do most of the housework herself, perhaps with some help.

It is in the arena of the criminal law and in its administration that the organisation of gender is particularly visible. Although an empirically under-researched area, studies which have investigated specific aspects of this relationship have reached similar conclusions. Research has shown that gender role has had a significant impact in shaping probation officers' understanding of clients' motivation for crime, decisions made by department stores to prosecute shoplifters, police discretion to caution, and of course judicial decisions in the sentencing process. In the process of mitigation it has been noted 'Family considerations particularly in the case of a woman and young children can have a realistic effect on mitigation' (Fallon 1975: 138). Moreover, it is with astounding recurrence that the economic needs of family members and a mother's natural predilection to provide for these demands (an intractable relationship with incumbent obligations) are considered in mitigation, if not to exonerate the female shoplifter, then to provide extenuating circumstances. It is of some interest that this particular gender rationale is not invoked with such frequency where the defendant is male and by virtue of a different relationship may waive different gender obligations. What is more recurrent in mitigatory speeches of solicitor and counsel in such cases is the plea 'My client has a job to go to on Monday' or 'My client will lose his job if a custodial sentence is passed upon him' (see Thomas 1979). Such references do not characterise mitigation when women are faced with a possible sentence of imprisonment (Carlen 1983: 63). Instead, it is the inevitable disintegration of the family unit in consequence which constitutes the major deterrent, though not sufficiently imposing or forbidding according to the Director of NACRO, Vivian Stern.

But within this recognition of relationships the law actively invades and extrudes by honouring these relationships only when certain additional moral imperatives prevail. In this sense moral judgment on the capability of a defendant to perform a particular gender role is monitored by observers working within the judicial process. Judges and magistrates currently take into consideration when passing sentence the fact that a defendant is a good or conversely a bad mother. Social and welfare workers together with legal advocates facilitate the accommodation of such facts in arriving at judgment, with the consequence that sentencers deliberate at length on the possibilities of imposing alternative forms of disposal if the penalty of custody removes a 'good' mother from her children. Such dilemmas are not in evidence when the defendant is considered to be a thoroughly bad mother. 'Good' mothering has also had an impact of quite considerable magnitude in stages of the post-trial process. Appeals against terms of imprisonment have been successfully varied on this point alone (see Chapter 8). *R v Cunningham* 1966 CLR 348 is a case in point. The appellant, who was initially sentenced to three years' imprisonment, had this reduced to eighteen months since she was pregnant and 'There was a chance that the child might be a stabilising influence.' And indeed it is a matter requiring some further investigation whether the criminal justice system at the parole stage considers whether the prisoner is a good or bad mother in examining the application (Bedford 1974: 110). Such considerations should be *non sequiturs*, but the fact that such extraneous factors are considered suggests that criminal law in the administration of justice also embodies a concept of what kind of behaviour is appropriate for whom. Thus the concept of individualised justice can be seen to be used for politically conservative ends in the maintenance of appropriate gender behaviour (see Pearson 1976: 267). It is in the maintenance of appropriate behaviour that agencies within the legal process and para-legal agencies develop a classificatory language which together with typifications of appropriateness is built insidiously into the system, with the result that certain motivatory scripts become inextricably linked with particular forms of behaviour. The presence or absence of such an association of accounting and behaviour may have a bearing on the very decisions made within the justice administration. In this way when the agents within the law are presented with a female defendant on a criminal charge considered 'typical' of women, i.e. theft from supermarkets, common assaults such as domestic rows with neighbours, it is likely that such behaviour will be 'normalised' and handled with greater leniency because the crime is committed in accordance with the requirements of the female gender role in feeding her family and protecting her territory. However, once that behaviour deviates from such expectations and becomes 'untypical', inappropriate or out of place (such as offences of malicious wounding and crimes against property), then behaviour is not so readily normalised nor scripts invoked in explanation, simply because any attempt to excuse or plead for a more lenient sentence for a woman on the grounds that she is a mother is a plea which would be unlikely to succeed since mothers do not wound or burgle. What may be observed then in the ordering of society on a gender-role basis is a corresponding ordering of men and women within the legal process according to the respective demands of the labour and the family process through specific relationships and gender alignments which the law recognises. Recently, in the much criticised sentencing decision in the case of Jasbir Singh Rai, convicted at Leeds Crown Court on 18 October 1982 for the rape of a six-year-old girl, the offender was described as a 'hardworking man'.

Considerations relating to male and female sexuality have also informed and influenced the operation of the criminal justice process. Taking the rules that govern sexuality they can be defined as patterns of activity involving sexual stimulation. Much of this sexual practice is often sex-class correlated and therefore part of gender. And the intractable interrelation of sex, gender and sexuality are expressed by Cousins (1980: 117): ' "men" and "women" are used as anchors for other categories such as "male and "female", or even "masculine" and "feminine" '. In the province of sexual offences it is with unfortunate but repeated occurrence that the behaviour or demeanour of the complainant are deemed 'contributory' in the commission of the crime. 'Contributory negligence' on the part of the victim has been suggested in cases of rape during the last decade and more recently, in the now notorious case of *Allen* in January 1982, the defendant was fined £2000 by Judge Bertrand Richards. The male defendant for his part has with interminable consistency been regarded as the misunderstood victim of his own 'uncontrollable urges'. So it was in the infamous case of the guardsman Holdsworth in 1977, who in lacerating his victim's vagina by the insertion of ringed fingers had, according to the judge, let his enthusiasm for sex overcome his normally good behaviour' (*Guardian*, 17 June 1977), and in the case of *Allen* 'male lechery' was normalised. In the latter case the defendant was exonerated with the following utterances: 'The circumstances of this case do not disclose any particular intention to rape this young lady, rather a lecherous hope that she would have sex with you' (*Guardian*, 7 January 1982).

The assimilation of particular constructions of sexuality is also built into the criminal law as it relates to loitering for the purposes of prostitution. According to the Street Offences Act 1959, section 1(1), women may be prosecuted for both loitering and soliciting in so far as 'it shall be an offence for a common prostitute to loiter or solicit in a street or public place for the purpose of prostitution'. And as stated in *R* v *Webb* (1963) 3 All ER 179, 'It cannot matter whether she whips the man or the man whips her.'

In these various instances, in both the formal statement of law and in its everyday practice, the legal process may be seen to consolidate and ratify particular conservative forces working in society for the arrangement of sex, gender and sexuality as if they were fixed and immutable entities. Thus it may be stated, though perhaps not too strongly, that in an alignment of the sexes according to biological criteria and the cultural arrangement of gender predicated on physical criteria, certain aspects of the law go beyond the mere 'ordering of society on a gender role basis' and actively organise sexual difference. As Adams (1979: 57) and Cousins (1980: 119) correctly insist, it is not the categories of 'men' and 'women' *per se* which are of central importance but the precise legal forms of agency of which mer and women may be a part. The legal forms of agency may be 'a person, a man or woman as defendant, or plaintiff; sometimes it might be a man as father or a woman as mother' (Cousins 1980: 119). In this instance the law is concerned with the female defendant as wife and mother, as a single parent, and the functional rights and obligations of these respective roles. In this context it is important to consider what effects the law and the agents within it have upon the organisation of sexual difference', and in so doing to explain how recalcitrant biologically grounded differences become a warrant for disparate treatment throughout social and legal institutions. It is not then merely a question of the control of sex-gender divisions, because this concept poses a conscious conspiracy. The mechanisms involved are indeed much more subtle insofar as the law 'manages' and maintains sexual difference.

Problems of theorising

Whilst the formation of legislation and the administration of criminal justice are processes influenced by certain assumptions predicated on sex and gender, there is no single unilinear or implacable relationship between the law and sex and gender (see Adams 1979: 57). Indeed, from within the various areas of sex–gender division which this study examines, invariably a different though sometimes mutually exclusive body of knowledge of characterisations of sex and gender is being invoked, often dependent on the legal form of agency in question. Within sex and gender beliefs, provinces of knowledge relating to physical criteria and biological sex do not, for instance, automatically correspond with those concerns relating to gender. Gender differences are frequently and erroneously considered to be inexorably predicated on biological differences, such that common-sense knowledge which relates to sex-genderisms is not necessarily incorporated into the legal reality with consistency or conviction. Inconsistencies within the sex–gender domain of an interpretive nature and inconsistencies within the legal domain render any attempt to theorise the interrelation between the two a misconceived endeavour, since to reduce sex and gender and the law to this level would be to assume that both were intransigent realities, instead of fluid, fragmentary and capricious entities.

In exploring the correspondence between sex–gender relations and the legal process this area has been characterised by a number of misconceptions. First, it has been assumed that a correspondence exists between common-sense social definitions and legal reality. Since our shared assumptions may be assigned or appropriated by different disciplines there may be a problem of the degree and extent of correspondence between social and legal reality. This has already been discussed by Taylor-Buckner (1978) and O'Donovan (1979). The second misconception is the tendency to treat 'men' and 'women' as definite categories or subjects. As

Cousins has indicated, they will be produced as definite forms of difference by the particular discourse and practices in which they appear. It becomes important to avoid treating men and women as definite categories in law. In exploring this misconception it becomes necessary to demonstrate the extent of this folly by revealing the fragmentary and piecemeal assimilation of gender in law. Thus it can be shown with some force that 'rights and equality cannot be posed in an abstract or general way'. The third fallacy relates to the belief that natural divisions inevitable underpin social divisions within society. Accordingly, natural divisions predicated on physical criteria are then regarded as the basis and cause of cultural ascriptions, with the consequence that cultural ascriptions of gender are reified. What we have instead is a fundamental conflict of meanings within laws and between them, an uneven assimilation of social constructs within the legal domain, and a measure of reification of gender.

First, there is very often a fundamental conflict of interests between criminal law, its original intended meaning and the interpretation it is given in the process of administration. The conflict arises too because of the differences between the formation of law as part of the parliamentary process and the enactment of law which is part of the judicial process. Second, legislative measures, case law and aspects of the legal process are governed by rules which are autonomous to those domains and may exist in conflict one to another. Third, there are different levels of law: 'the law itself is not a unified structure, . . . operations . . . can vary according to its different levels of jurisdiction' (Smart 1981: 44). Fourth, the administration of criminal justice itself is a process which is mediated by the discretionary decisions of para-legal professionals – social workers, etc. – who bring their private and professional ideologies to bear on the operation of the criminal justice system. In addition to the many instances the law itself poses of a fragmentary nature within the province of meaning of the cultural construction of sexual division, there are also conflicting and competing realities within this domain alone. The law for its part in an *ad hoc* fashion unsystematically adopts these conflicting concepts in its various processes, with the result that within particular legislation can be discerned the deployment of contradictory concepts of sex and of gender operating alongside one another. Consider for instance that within the wording of the statute relating to prostitution women are regarded as both loiterers (passive ascription of sexuality) and as solicitors (active formulation) (see *Field v Chapman, The Times,* 9 October 1953). The contradictory nature of female sexuality is also explicated in the law as it relates to sexual offences (and to rape in particular) where women are excluded from the legal definition or, if they are included, few prosecutions are brought, thereby enshrining the notion of female sexual passivity. The reverse is the case when women bring complaints of a sexual nature against men; they are then monitored for their participation rather than non-compliance.

From one statute to another and from one form of law to another inconsistencies are even more absurd. These differences are often more baffling when matters of interpretation are examined. Consider for instance that the self-same rationale – that of woman's weakness – inspired support for the Married Women's Property Bill and indeed was the rationale upon which opposition was founded. Thus the assumptions, rules and meanings upon which sexual divisions are based are context-bound and depend very much on the 'situations' to which they apply. Hence, as has been already suggested, whilst motherhood becomes a legitimate reason for not imposing a custodial sentence, it is this very social relationship which is often deliberately destroyed if the morality of the mother is at question. In this framework a very high proportion of those recorded on registers of children at risk are children whose mothers are prostitutes. Within the area of family law contradictions of interpretation exist. For instance whilst the President of the Family Division of the High Court, Sir Jocelyn Simon, has intimated that the use of the one-third rule in matrimonial issues is a discredited concept, Barrington Baker (1977) discovered that the majority of registrars still use it as a rule of thumb in deciding financial matters.[7] And, whilst women are generally regarded as financially and economically dependent on their husbands (see O'Donovan 1979), it is interesting that in a recent decision it was ruled by Browne-Wilkinson J that a woman's place is not necessarily where her husband's job takes him, though Dewi Evans, a Deputy Director of Social Services, did not recommend the applicant for a place on a course for reasons relating to where he thought she should be. Mr. Evans, said the judge, 'made a general assumption on the basis of her sex that she would follow her husband's job and vice versa' (*Daily Telegraph*, 23 June 1982).

But this is not a study of inconsistency in law or criminal justice or of its fragmentary nature, however important that might be. On the contrary, it is a study of consistency, when and insofar as it exists, of the way the law is informed and influenced by specific notions of sex and gender and the consequences which follow on from that assimilation for the female defendant arraigned before the court. That is not to deny or obviate the possibility of any kind of theorising whatever. It does, however, of necessity imply that we can no longer be content with the analyses of law with relation to gender that were once satisfied to pose the existence of some uniform relationship between patriarchy, gender and the oppression of women *per se*.

Instead therefore, of seeking to demonstrate that the law *en masse* is patriarchal and oppressive and in so doing to assume that in revealing instances of oppression some inner consistency is being unveiled, it is of far greater importance that the specific basis of assumptions, judgments and discretionary decisions as they are influenced by sex and gender be revealed, though not without, as Goffman (1977: 307) argues in a related context, structurally situating these specificities:'The issue, then, is not that women get less, but under what arrangement this occurs and what symbolic reading is given to the arrangement.' In exploring this arrangement it is important to regard the criminal law and the administration of justice not merely as passive agents in the reception of sexual meaning, but also as reflexive institutions in the active reaffirmation and reproduction of sexual division. In this light it becomes important to account for this reciprocity and thereby to consider 'how particular legal forms of agency are more or less implicated in the organisation of sexual difference and what effect they have upon that organisation' (Cousins 1980: 120). In examining these rules and meanings,

> It is not, then, the social consequence of innate sex differences that must be explained, but the way in which these differences were (and are) put forward as a warrant for our social arrangements, and, most important of all, the way in which the institutional workings of society ensured that this accounting would seem sound. (Goffman 1977: 302)

Thus, when we talk of the mechanisms, agencies or bases of sex-gender relations they are discussed in terms of social relationships and social institutions which provide the authorisation for such beliefs. Goffman expresses this linkage as one of 'institutional reflexivity', by which he means to analyse the way in which institutions and social organisations contain gender divisions. Thus in some legal situations motherhood in its relation to the family unit is being evoked, in others motherhood in relationship to the legal contract of guardianship.

Sex and gender in the legal process
The approach adopted in consideration of this problem will be to explore the law and criminal justice system as a process, and in so doing to examine how the organisation of sex, gender and sexuality is made possible within the legal sphere by and through the invocation of formal rules and procedures and also by the application of discretionary decision-making in informal practice. The female defendant is constituted as the legal subject for analysis, thereby defining the parameters of the field of analysis from the onset. Interest is therefore not with the offender, nor with the deviant. Instead attention is diverted to observe the sequential process of an imbalanced interaction between a suspected law breaker and the various agencies within the criminal justice system that are set in motion as a result of this suspicion. Patricia Hewitt, in opening her book *The Abuse of Power* (1981), writes, 'The central aim of a criminal justice system should be the impartial enforcement of just laws'.[8] In examining this sequence of events we look to test this proposition in observing the deployment of discretion in both its formal

and informal guises. And it is often at these junctures that the greatest interplay of social reality and legal reality is reciprocated. However, in many instances within the criminal justice process the rules are so rigid and formalised that there is absolutely no opportunity for flexibility or manoeuvre, the stage for criminal justice being set by 'iron law' procedures and precedents. The intransigence is particularly marked in certain areas. Formal rules of legality demanded at least initially that a rape case could not be heard in the absence of the complainant however seriously wounded or psychologically brutalised. Similarly, the rigidity of formal rules prevented an inquest from being held in the case of Helen Smith, though this is now after two years a matter of public enquiry (*Guardian*, 27 October 1982). The clearest statement of formal rules exists within the statutory provisions themselves. But even the invocation of formal rules depends upon interpretation since legal rules do not contain clarifications or elaborations of their meaning or indeed indications of how the legislators intended they should be interpreted. Thus, for example, it is difficult to conceive that legislators, when drafting the words of statutes in the form 'fit person of full age' intended that the word 'person' should be exclusively applicable to men, thereby excluding women from entry into the professions (Sachs and Wilson 1978). It has been necessary, therefore, to back up statutes with the Interpretation Acts, 1898 and 1978. Thus a study of law and the formation of statute involves more than a consideration of those instances wherby the sex categories 'men' and 'women' are formally or informally included or excluded from the statute on the premises already outlined. The examination of case law, at least initially, appears less problematic since it involves a consideration of 'gender neutral' or 'androgynous' laws. But case law too provides a clear instance of formal rules whose legitimacy is beyond question. Precedent is often referred to as iron law. However, such decisions are not slavishly followed, and unwise decisions are certainly far less likely to be. Thus departures from precedent which thereby introduce contradictions compel legislators to reconsider the issue of divergence in their quest for consistency.

As well as being concerned with the formal content of law, much of the study is devoted to a consideration of the administration of justice. As Bottomley and others have indicated, many of the decisions made within the criminal justice system depend upon the use of discretion including 'discretionary patterns of law enforcement and decision making by the police, courts and other penal agencies' (Bottomley 1973: 1). A defendant's passage through the criminal justice system may best be seen as part of a sequential process, since a decision at one juncture may influence the movement, direction and outcome of a defendant's progress. Accordingly, it is a fair comment that 'From illegal act to legal punishment there are numerous escape routes. It is as though the offender has to pass through a corridor of connected rooms!' (Box 1971: 167). These various junctures of decision-making have also been theorised by, amongst others, Wilkins (1963) who presents this sequential process as a 'process continuum'.[9] But the question of legitimacy is central to an understanding of how decision-making works since the use of discretion is bound by rules. There are of course instances where the use of individual discretion is formally allowed and thereby legitimate. Within this legitimate deployment discretion is routinely managed by rules regulating procedural conduct.[10]

Let us look first at what may be loosely termed routine management of discretion and the opportunites for arranging sex, sexuality and gender therein. Those instances wherein discretion is formally allowed include the discretion of the police to charge and the decision to prosecute a suspected offender, to keep a defendant in custody, and at the other end of the continuum the sentencing powers of the judge as to type and leniency or severity of sentence. Other instances of routine usage of discretion have been examined by Walker (1965), who found that the female offender was much more likely to be dealt with by means of a police caution than her male counterpart (see Chapter 7).

Decision to prosecute and bail

The decision to prosecute is another consideration which involves the use of discretion. The police are not placed under a duty to prosecute all suspected persons who come to their notice. The question of police discretion is deciding whether to prosecute was raised in the report of the 1962 Royal Commission on the Police which stated that one of the main duties of the police 'was the responsibility for deciding whether or not to prosecute'. Lord Denning MR, in *R* v *Metropolitan Police Commissioner*, ex parte *Blackburn*, decided: 'It is for the Commissioner of Police of the Metropolis, or the chief constable, as the case may be, to decide in any particular case whether enquiries should be pursued, or whether an arrest should be made or a prosecution brought' (Wilcox 1972: 11). The more recent enshrinement of this view is found expressed in the report of the Royal Commission on Criminal Procedure 1981, where regarding police decisions on prosecution it is stated that 'The officer on the street therefore takes decisions about what to pursue . . . This decision is normally ratified at Chief Inspector level' (paragraph 139).

The police may also use their powers to extend or deny bail conditions (see paras 61–7, Report of the Royal Commission on Criminal Procedure 1981). Research in this particular area has already shown that such decisions may have a very real influence on conviction rates and on the nature of the sentence imposed.[11] The proportion of women who are remanded in custody and who do not receive a custodial sentence is said to be much higher than for men.[12] There are various reasons for this. It may be that the courts consider that women should be protected from themselves or else deserve a short shock (Heidensohn 1981: 127). It may also be the case that in the final event, although the crime may be a serious one, judges are reluctant to impose sentences of imprisonment on women. In 1977, 3868 women were remanded before trial or sentence. Of these, 2393 were found 'not guilty' or else were given a non-custodial sentence (62 per cent), the remaining 953 (26 per cent) received a custodial sentence. (See table i:1 for the 1981 figures.)

For some time great concern has been expressed over the American evidence that defendants who are refused bail are much more likely to (a) be convicted and receive a custodial sentence, or (b) plead guilty. There is also evidence that a custodial remand may be used in order that an offender may be protected from herself. It is a belief that women might be more likely than men to attempt suicide or inflict harm on themselves.

In addition there is some considerable concern that many of the women remanded in custody are refused bail in order that reports are prepared more speedily, which otherwise could be prepared on bail. The Howard League has heard 'allegations of improper use of remands for punitive purposes',[13] so, too, Gibbens, Soothill and Pope (1977: 38). Furthermore, Dr Bull, Governor of Holloway, asserts

> We have a very large proportion of women remanded for medical reports and a high proportion are negative in the sense that there is no medical recommendation, and I think sometimes this is simply a device to put a woman in prison for three weeks with the supposition that a medical report might do something, or perhaps just as a punitive way, because a very high proportion are negative.[14]

There is some evidence that women are more likely to be remanded for medical/psychiatric reports than are men. Gibbens, Soothill and Pope (1977) found that in the inner London area, magistrates' courts were much more ready to remand females for medical report (18 per cent of men, 32 per cent of women p.28). Martin and Webster (1971) examined the importance of police bail in relation to the subsequent resources and outcome.[15] They found that those bailed from the onset have a much better chance of seeking legal advice, and are in a more favourable position altogether, compared with the defendant who is kept in custody overnight. It is interesting to see exactly who, or which category of offenders, the police choose to keep in overnight custody. And if proportionately fewer women receive bail than do men their chances of successfully negotiating their way through the criminal justice system are reduced.

In 1981, 2024 women in England and Wales who were refused bail received non-custodial sentence, whilst 17,607 men who were refused bail received non-custodial sentences (see Table i:1). Technically bail is refused on grounds relating to the gravity of the offence, and the possibility that the accused does not answer to his/her bail in appearing for trial. This second factor is considered to be related to living accommodation, because when a defendant has no fixed address bail is likely to be refused. Bedford (1974: 110) found parole decisions were similarly influenced by fixed residence. But since there is no dictate requiring police to state the nature of their objections considerable discretion may be exercised. Withholding bail may also be related to legal representation. Suzanne Dell (1978) found that 38 per cent of women remanded in custody and not subsequently imprisoned were unrepresented.

Table i:1 Custodial remand and non-custodial outcome: England and Wales 1981

Type of disposal	Number of persons		Percentage	
	Males	Females *	Males	Females *
Hospital order	521	152	3	7
Absolute discharge	265	47	2	2
Bound over	258	24	1	1
Deferred sentence	1,226	97	7	5
Conditional discharge	1,324	280	8	14
Probation order	3,425	618	19	31
Supervision, attendance centre and care order	305	25	2	1
Fine	3,455	276	20	14
Community service order	2,188	78	12	4
Suspended sentence	4,189	364	24	18
Freed on †	365	51	2	2
Otherwise dealt with	86	12	-	1
Total	17,607	2,024	100	100

(*) Excludes those detained under section 53 of the Children and Young Persons Act 1933.

(†) A sentence of immediate imprisonment of such length that it has already been served on remand.

Source: Prison Statistics: England and Wales 1981, Cmnd. 8654 (Table 2(e), p.47).

Schedule 1, Part 1, paras 1(3) and (7) of the Bail Act 1976, which provide respectively for the remand in custody of persons for their own protection and for inquiries to be made, may both be provisions which unwittingly discriminate against women. First, because it is commonly assumed that women are more likely than men to be unstable. Second, because it is more likely in the case of a female defendant facing criminal charges that a social inquiry will be requested.

In a study of conditional bail and exceptions to bail gender assumptions informed the decision-making process. With regard to conditional bail the interrelation of the sex of the alleged offender and the type of crime committed were significant factors in the conditions that were imposed (see Table i:2). For 25 per cent of those charged with burglary bail was conditional on a curfew. In 50 per cent bail was conditional on residence. Similarly, in offences of obstruction, in all cases a curfew was imposed. In 90 per cent of the cases involving violent crime the condition imposed was that the accused make no contact with other stated persons.

Table i:2   Reasons for conditional bail according to offence Manchester: City Magistrates' Court 1981

	Surety	*Condition of residence*	*Make no contact with certain person*	*Reporting times at police station*	*Curfew*	*Surrender passport*	*Attend hospital or Probation Office for Reports to be prepared*	*Total no. of persons*	*No. of defendants in total sample*	*Percentage of total sample*
Indictable Offences										
Violence	–	1	9	–	–	–	–	10	81	12
Sexual offence	–	–	–	–	–	–	–	–	2	–
Burglary	1	4	–	1	2	–	–	8	50	16
Robbery	1	4	–	1	–	–	–	6	13	46
Theft & handling	6	21	–	1	1	–	–	29	1112	3
Fraud & forgery	5	12	–	–	1	–	–	18	143	13
Criminal damage	1	7	–	–	–	–	–	8	81	10
Other	1	4	2	1	3	–	–	11	–	–
Summary offences										
Assault	–	–	–	–	–	–	–	–	40	–
Prostitution	–	9	–	5	1	–	4	19	299	6
Drunkenness	–	2	–	–	–	–	–	2	307	1
DHSS offences	–	–	–	–	–	–	–	–	119	–
Drug offences	–	2	1	2	–	–	–	5	50	10
Obstruction	–	–	–	–	3	–	–	3	6	50
Breach of the peace	–	–	–	–	–	–	–	–	86	–
Possessing an offensive weapon	–	–	–	–	–	–	–	–	9	–
Harbouring an escaped prisoner	–	–	–	–	–	–	–	–	4	–
Total	15	66	12	11	11	–	4	119	2402	–

In a study of those remanded in custody (see Table i:3) bail was refused, particularly in untypical female crime (although it must be conceded these crimes were more serious), including violence, criminal damage, criminal damage by fire and breach of the peace. However, the study revealed that a high proportion of the sample were remanded for their own protection. This tendency may be precicated on the assumption that self-mutilation or annihilation seem to be more common amongst women (Rowett and Vaughan 1981: 138). In 29 per cent of women remanded for violence this reason was given for bail refusal, compared to 60 per cent in criminal damage, 60 per cent in criminal damage by fire, and 50 per cent in breach of the peace cases. It is of some concern that out of a total of 299 cases of prostitution proceeded with, in 4 per cent of the cases defendants were remanded in custody, each time on the ground that the defendant would fail to answer bail or would commit further offences.

Table i:3 Remands in custody according to the relevant sections of the Bail Act 1976 (Manchester City Magistrates' Court 1981)

	If released would fail to surrender to custody	If released would commit further offences	If released would interfere with witnesses	Kept in custody for own protection	Already in custody	Not enough information obtained in the time	Has been arrested for breach of previous bail	Remanded for reports	Total no. of factors	Total no. remanded in each offence category	Total no. proceeded against	Total remanded as % of those proceeded against
Indictable offences												
Violence	5	2	–	2	–	2	–	2	13	7	81	9
Sexual offences	–	–	–	–	–	–	–	–	–	–	2	–
Burglary	7	7	–	–	–	–	–	–	14	7	50	14
Robbery	9	5	–	–	1	2	–	–	17	9	13	69
Theft & handling	18	19	6	1	–	1	–	3	48	27	1112	3
Fraud &forgery	7	6	1	–	–	5	–	1	20	11	143	8
Criminal damage	4	4	–	3	–	–	–	1	12	5	81	6
Criminal damage by fire	3	3	–	3	–	–	–	–	9	5		6
Summary offences												
Prostitution	10	7	–	–	–	–	–	–	17	10	299	4
Drug offences	4	3	1	1	–	–	–	1	10	4	50	8
Breach of the peace	1	3	–	2	–	–	–	–	7	4	86	5
Drunk & disorderly	1	–	–	–	–	–	–	–	1	1	307	–
Bilking	2	1	–	–	–	–	–	–	3	2	NK	–
Assault	–	–	–	–	–	–	–	–	–	–	119	–
Possessing an offensive weapon	–	–	–	–	–	–	–	–	–	–	9	–
Harbouring an escaped prisoner	–	–	–	–	–	–	–	–	–	–	4	–
Wasting police time	–	–	–	–	–	–	–	–	–	–	6	–
Total	71	60	8	12	1	10	0	9	171	92	2402	–

NK - Not known

Discretion and the trial process

Discretion is also formally allowed during the trial process. Legal advocates may, for instance, request that a social inquiry report be prepared to assist the court. Indeed para-legal agencies such as the probation service are responsible for report preparation and also employ their discretion. Officers are bound by two conflicting sets of rules, demands from the court, Home Office circulars and the position of their own association, NAPO. For instance, discretion is formally allowed in the Home Office's position on the preparation of social inquiry reports in not-guilty pleas. Officers do not consider this legitimate and are not prepared to be bound by the rules. Particularly in these areas where discretion is formally allowed and routinely managed, it is not questioned but is treated as non-problematic; yet even though the discretion is institutionalised it may be equally discriminating in its management of sex, sexuality and gender. Thus in knowing the rules we can anticipate the possible moves and outcomes. It is when discretion is deployed non-formally that it is not possible to anticipate.

Amongst those para-legal agencies one would include for consideration the impact on the operation of the criminal justice system of non-statutory policies, decisions and guidelines issued by the Home Office, resolutions of organisations such as NAPO and, on perhaps a more informal basis, the impact of local magistrates' committees, and the decisions of area police forces.

For instance, Hardiker (1977) in assessing the influence of the probation officer in the criminal justice process wrote, 'Probation officers have very little direct influence in the realm of criminal detection, prosecution and conviction, but the social inquiry practices can have a bearing on the type of sentence particular offenders get.'[16] Similarly, views of local magistrates may be influenced by committee decisions which may in some part go towards regional differences in sentencing.

However it is to be noted, perhaps with some consternation, that para-legal agencies are every bit as intrusive in the private life and freedom of individual citizens as the more overt state agencies. Consider, for instance, the intrusive aspect of the social inquiry report for the court, and probation. There is already a growing realisation that state agencies in non-state guises are increasingly flourishing and intervening in organising the private realm; extra-judicial agencies are also organising and limiting individual freedom and privacy. Research has focused on the increasing intervention and unwarranted interference of the state in areas of welfare, social policy, the family and psychiatry (Wilson 1978, McIntosh 1978, Procek 1981). Few studies have researched the role of extra-judicial agencies as they intrude on the processing of the criminal defendant in a systematic manner, although in the work of Yablonsky (1962), Szasz (1963) Halmos (1978) and Cohen (1979)[17] some consideration of this intrusion can be found.

Discretion is also employed when it is not formally allowed. However, it may still be managed routinely. For example, it is anticipated that magistrates and judges will refrain from sentencing a mother to a term of imprisonment; this is not formally allowed but is nevertheless managed routinely as a recurrent observable tendency in the lower courts (see Carlen's work on sheriffs, 1983: 67). However, such decision-making practices are questioned and often treated as problematic when the use of discretion is not formally allowed and when it is non-routinely managed. These decisions in particular are subject to review and criticism since this use of discretion is considered illegitimate. For instance, to the casual observer the pre-trial negotiations between solicitor/barrister and the defendant appear to constitute an occasion of the non-routine use of discretion. These negotiations as to plea are certainly not formally allowed and solicitors would in public vehemently deny the extent of their interventions whilst privately recognising them as routine strategies. Indeed plea arrangement is considered to be one important means of working the system. Contemporary research conducted into plea and bail bargaining has revealed the various pressures on defendants to plead guilty. Baldwin and McConville (1977) suggested that advice to plead guilty may come from a variety of sources: the police, the defence solicitor, family and friends. The researchers maintained that defence counsel had a considerable role to play in inducing a guilty plea, and their findings revealed that forty-eight defendants changed their plea to guilty on the advice received from counsel. Yet as the authors point out, 'the voluntariness of the plea is far from clear' (p.41). A number of more obvious factors are thought to influence this decision to plead. First, advice given by the police is thought to have some effect. Second, the decision to plead is often based on the advice that the court will be lenient. Baldwin and McConville (p.48) argue that this may give rise to a disturbing situation since a guilty plea may not result in a discount. Besides, the quantitive of the discount is not known, although Baldwin and McConville discovered that informal discussions with judges suggest 'something between one quarter and one third' (p.50). Third, defendants may be influenced by the promise that it will be over quickly. Baldwin and McConville maintained that many pleas were negotiated and the pressures included the promise that a defendant would soon be free again.

From these preliminary statements, it becomes evident that it is in both the formal and informal stages of the criminal law and administration of criminal justice that sexual divisions in their various constitutions are organised or reaffirmed. That in certain areas of law and justice administration 'women' may fare better than 'men', more specifically when as a form of legal agency of wife and mother, may well be true. But the instances where the treatment of women, as a sex class or gender class, has restricted and in some cases controlled their activities are indeed far more apparent. In observing these influences it is of greater import to identify not merely the 'clusters of consciousness' that accompany these ideas but the 'institutional linkages'[18] which locate these influences in a social context.

Part One · Sex differences in the criminal law

1 · A question of sex

> Prostitution is really the only crime in the penal law where two people are
> doing a thing mutually agreed upon and yet only one, the female partner,
> is subject to arrest.
>
> K. Millett, *The Prostitution Papers* (1975:146)

Introduction

One of the more manifest instances of the 'organisation' of sexual difference
within the criminal law is visibly observable in the regulation of loitering and
soliciting for the purposes of prostitution. The visibility of such legislation is
evidence of the extent of discrimination against women as a 'sex class'. The sex-
specificity of laws governing this particular activity are ever more difficult to com-
prehend and therefore more absurd, since the regulation of this activity, unlike
other legislation of a sex-specific nature, is not predicated on physiological rules,
anatomical disparity or difference of sexual capability. At least, the invocation of
such 'essentialist' criteria as a basis for differential treatment of the sexes renders
other such legislative measures and procedures intelligible, even though such
justifications are rationales not altogether wisely held. Indeed, more recent discussions relating to issues of consent presented for instance in the Working Paper
on Sexual Offences rested on such basic physiological tenets (1980: 4–5).
However, the matter of singling out this prelude – namely 'loitering and soliciting'
– to a particular activity for the purposes of prostitution', and thereby prosecuting
women alone, is considered to be unjustified (Smart 1976, Greenwald 1969,
McLeod 1982). From the onset a legal anomaly is betrayed; since prostitution of
itself is no offence, it seems erroneous that certain designated ways of pursuing
this activity if committed by women are considered to be so.

   The basis then for this dissimilar treatment is, and can only be, moral. Such an
assessment is as applicable to contemporary legislation as it was of nineteenth-
century regulation, in spite of more recent claims that the primary objective of
present-day legislative measures, after all, is to rid the streets of a public nuisance.
We would do well to bear in mind that it is not that simple. And to remember that
in the next breath the Report of the Wolfenden Committee (1957: 79) remarked,
'Prostitution is an evil of which any society which claims to be civilised should
seek to rid itself.' The argument for the moral basis of such legislation becomes increasingly evident in that there is no correspondence between the extent of this activity pursued in everyday life and the legal reality. If it were the case that only
women loitered or solicited for the purpose of prostitution, then the one-sided
application of criminal sanction might be deemed logical and consistent. As it is,

men also provide similar sexual services to other men. In addition, heterosexual men in their receipt of sexual services, and by virtue of their participation in this 'prelude', are parties in the criminal act of pursuance. To coin a phrase, the law will not recognise that it takes two to tango. More pertinently it is more often the case that heterosexual men actively pursue women for the purpose of prostitution. Yet none of these activities is considered illegal. These are only some of the areas of inconsistency and confusion within the legislature. It becomes exceedingly difficult to understand the motivation for criminalisation of a 'prelude' to an activity which involves consent and no concept of victim, with the possible exception of the offender herself. The National Association of Probation Officers, amongst others, support this sentiment, since they stress that they can 'see no reason why the penal system should be involved in the control and suppression of an activity which is not in itself illegal and in which there is no victim'. (See also Schur and Bedau 1974, James 1978 b). And indeed since the Street Offences Act 1959, this has been particularly starkly revealed, because the effect of the Wolfenden Report was to abandon the requirement that prostitution and soliciting need be 'to the annoyance of passers by'.

The warrantability for this exclusive treatment must be examined in the context of women's gender and sexual role and relation to the social institution of marriage and the family. I want first to explore in some detail the pristine origins of state policy of the regulation of prostitution, the particular debates from which such policies emerged and the justificatory rationale legitimating such control measures. Since

> We need to know precisely how and why a particular law was made, how it relates to differences in the wider social structure, how it relates to the distribution of normative structures, and what kind of typifications of meaning it includes.[1]

The legislative measures – England and Wales
The focus of this investigation is on the state regulation of prostitution, a regulation which defines as illegal those activities which encourage or assist in its occupation. Amongst these are the activities which encourage others to become prostitutes (section 22(1), Sexual Offences Act 1956), allow under certain circumstances premises to be used for prostitution (section 33, Sexual Offences Act), a man living on the earnings of prostitution and a woman exercising control over a prostitute (sections 30 and 31, Sexual Offences Act), together with the offence of loitering or soliciting for the purposes of prostitution. With the exception of the last offence both men and women are liable to prosecution or else similar behaviour is covered by different statutory sections. See Table 1:1.

Table 1:1 Prosecutions for prostitution and allied offence since the Street Offences Act 1959 (England and Wales)

Offences	1959	1960	1961	1962	1963	1964	1965	1966	1967	1968	1969	1970	1971	1972	1973	1974	1975	1976	1977	1978	1979	1980	1981
Procuration (M)	32	15	13	18	18	5	12	20	11	58	59	38	42	39	40	36	45	44	66	70	225	362	322
(F)	3	11	11	8	7	5	5	7	3	9	5	4	6	6	23	10	9	10	4	8	25	17	19
Brothel-keeping (M)	68	42	72	41	41	41	51	35	69	63	52	32	29	29	16	16	22	31	25	38	33	30	47
(F)	130	108	121	122	145	103	126	130	161	152	120	132	120	157	116	85	95	141	83	118	115	95	113
Male living on prostitute's earnings (M)	283	235	277	325	275	304	300	321	267	355	358	371	276	344	239	226	231	233	202	223	–	–	–
(F)a	8	8	11	18	22	1	22	4	1	0	2	0	0	0	1	0	1	0	0	1	–	–	–
Female living on prostitute's earnings (M)	121	29	0	0	0	0	0	1	1	0	0	0	0	1	2	0	0	0	0	0	–	–	–
(F)a	578	28	0	0	0	12	14	10	2	4	5	5	6	1	6	22	10	9	7	7	–	–	–

aAmbiguous cases due to opposite sex aiding and abetting the principal offender, latterly errors in recording or more possibly transsexualism.

Within the context of the criminal law women alone are defined as prostitutes and thereby prosecuted for offences of loitering and soliciting in pursuance of that activity. No male or transsexual male is liable to prosecution for loitering or soliciting, though men who offer a sexual service to other males are liable to arrest for 'importuning' in the pursuit of an 'immoral' activity (see table 1:1). Despite the various ways of pursuing prostitution, it is indeed curious that the legislators and legal administrators have been primarily concerned with further tightening up existing legislation as it affects the street prostitute. This is nowhere more evident than in the Street Offences Act of 1959, whose main object was to drive the nuisance off the streets. The aftermath of the Act was characterised by the almost triumphant proclamation that the diminished visibility of street activity and the decline in prosecutions was evidence of its overnight celebratory success, though this was a shortsighted analysis. There was no apparent concern for the inevitable increase in prostitution in other areas nor their undetected increased exploitation, which was a certain consequence.

The origin of the criminalisation of certain activities of prostitutes has a long and complicated history. Insofar as contemporary legislation is concerned the nineteenth century has been regarded as an appropriate point at which to start. The detection and apprehension of this activity because of its intractable association with police resources and deployment has inevitably risen and fallen with policing strategies. As police powers grew and developed, so too did the surveillance strategies and prosecution of women for offences relating to prostitution. Indeed, with the introduction of the 1824 Vagrancy Act local police forces were granted wide discretionary powers enabling them to arrest any woman for loitering or soliciting who in their view was 'acting suspiciously', or behaving in a 'riotous or indecent manner'. These earlier unbridled powers were given further rein in the legislation which followed. The Metropolitan Police Act of 1839 allowed a constable to arrest prostitutes and nightwalkers soliciting 'to the annoyance'. And section 28 of the 1847 Town Police Clauses Act empowered the courts to imprison prostitutes for a period of fourteen days. These statutory provisions remained in force until 1959.

There was however considerable variation in the interpretation of the statutory measures, and the deployment of police resources and personnel within and between forces. In certain regional areas police activity was largely determined by an independent jurisdiction. In the Manchester area for example police powers were circumscribed under the Manchester Police Regulation Act 1844, section 99 and 102. In regulating the activities of prostitutes the arrest and prosecution of 'Every "common prostitute" or nightwalker loitering or being in any thoroughfare or public place for the purpose of prostitution or solicitation to the annoyance of any inhabitant or passenger' was provided for. In addition the City of London

Police Act of 1839, paragraph 11, regulated activities relating to prostitution in the London Area.

Since the invocation of legislative measures in this area has depended since 1824 on whether a constable considers a woman to be 'acting suspiciously' the women of the street were a particularly defenceless group against state control and oppression. This feeling of vulnerability and powerlessness extended beyond those women who provided a sexual service to all women of the working class who used the streets and thoroughfares for social activity or simply for going about their everyday business. It is worthy of note that since 52 per cent of the labour force in the 1850s was composed of women and children, it is not hard to envisage how many women must inevitably have come under police suspicion in their routine travel to and from their place of work.

By the 1860s a second wave of state control over prostitution began. The legislative measures which provided the police with the greatest power over prostitutes and working-class women were contained in the provisions relating to the checking of the spread of contagious diseases to the civil population. The Contagious Diseases Acts of 1864, 1866 and 1869 institutionalised the double standard of morality and control over sexual behaviour as a central tenet of state policy. Women alone were regarded as the 'civil population' in respect of contagious diseases and the Acts enshrined the belief in the 'active' and 'precipitating' sexuality of all women, founded on the erroneous principle that unchaste women were wholly responsible for transmitting the disease, whilst unchaste men, unlucky for them, fell victims and contracted it. Deborah Gorham (1978) in her perceptive study of child prostitution[2] observed that females *per se* were not always cast in this pariah role since child prostitutes[3] were invariably regarded as the victims, though often of corrupt older women who procured them. State legislation in the 1880s reflected this predilection and adopted a protectionist stance in its central endeavour, namely the Criminal Law Amendment Act 1885 (an Act to make further provision for the protection of women and girls, the suppression of brothels and other purposes).

But the Contagious Diseases Acts had no place for such view of women or young girls. Police discretionary powers were widened and women left defenceless as the nineteenth-century 'sus' law monitored their every move (Edwards 1981a: 56). The policeman had only to report to a magistrate that 'he had good cause to believe . . . ' and the poor woman who was the subject of his suspicion would be arrested, forcibly inspected and instrumentally raped. Although the objectors to the Acts clearly made their opposition heard from its inception the measures remained unrepealed for twenty years to dog and blight the lives of all women, the poor in particular, such that 'Any woman can be dragged into court, and required to prove that she is not a common prostitute'.[4]

In the case law, *de Munck* (1918) 1 KB, 635 has been generally accepted as the precedent for asserting amongst other matters the sex-specific nature of the prostitute. Darling J in providing a definition, described such a person as '*a woman* who offers her body for acts of lewdness for payment' (my emphasis). There are however earlier instances in the case law which iterate this sex-specificity. For example, consider the dictum of Lawrence J in *Lawrence* v *Hedger* (1810) ER 128 at 7, who in a reference to the prostitute said, '*A woman* walking up and down the streets to pick up men, a nightwalker, may be apprehended' (my emphasis). More recently the sex-specificity was reiterated in Webb (1963) 3 All ER at 177; (1964) 1QBD at 357, where an appeal was held on the ground that masturbation of a man by a woman did not amount to an act of prostitution. Lord Parker CJ said in delivering judgment that whether she was an active or passive party in the proceedings, it made no difference. 'The essence is that she offers herself as a participant,' a ruling approved in later cases *Abbot* v *Smith* (1964) 3 All ER 762; *Donovan* v *Gavin* (1964) 2 All ER 611) Nonetheless (and this will be discussed in some detail later) neither the 'participator' so central to the decision in *Webb*, the acceptance of solicitation nor the propositioning of women has resulted in the prosecution of that other participant – the punter, or soutineur.

With the introduction of the Street Offences Act of 1959, a contemporary stamp of credence was given to an Act, which in essence reaffirmed the legislative measures it had superseded.[5] Police powers were restored to their former nineteenth-century glory, since section 1(3) provided, 'A constable may arrest without warrant anyone he finds in a street or public place and suspects, with reasonable cause, to be committing an offence under this section.' The colloquial terminology, anachronistic procedures and moral prejudices of the nineteenth century were in fact all retained, despite the claim of the Wolfenden Committee that their only concern was to rid the street of a public nuisance. Yet prostitution was not merely regarded as a public nuisance, for what other nuisance has attracted so much discussion, aroused so much indignation, resulted in the vast proliferation of legal measures, demanded such resources and legitimated the wasting of police time? The moral questions and condemnation were inexorably linked – thus prostitute, prostitution, common prostitute, were strongly evocative terms. The Wolfenden Committee could not pretend that their own feelings of moral indignation did not skew their vision. Commenting on prostitution they described it as 'as social fact deplorable in the eyes of moralists, sociologists and the great majority of ordinary people'. The provisions in the Act for increasing fines and the length of imprisonment resulted in greatly strengthening state control.

Whilst the number of prosecutions and convictions for offences relating to prostitution declined drastically from 19,663 before the introduction of the Act to

2726 in 1960, this by no means reflected a real diminution in police activity or in prostitution, though the media in its eagerness for selling copy carried the headlines 'Vice Girls Vanish' – 'Street Girls are Driven into Hiding' (*News Chronicle*, 17, 18 August 1959). First, the apparently dramatic decline resulted from the implementation of the cautioning system following the guidelines issued in Home Office Circular 119/59 (see Chapter 5). Yet if both prosecutions and cautions are taken together for 1960 then the difference between the pre- and post-1959 numbers is of considerably smaller significance. Second, any real decline in street prostitution did not reflect any real diminution in prostitution. Quite the reverse, since the passing of the Act actually paved the way for its commercialisation, and the greater exploitation of prostitutes in saunas, massage parlours, hotels and clubs. The Act actually forced many women to find and pursue other means of advertising themselves and contacting clients. This was an inevitable consequence admitted by the Wolfenden Committee at the time, but, as they explained, the risk of extending the call-girl system was one worth taking in order to reduce the offence to the public. But again in the drafting of the statute as in case law such delicacies and sensitivities of the committee were not sufficiently imposing to result in any legislation to prohibit the nuisance of the kerb crawler.

Table 1:2   *Prosecutions for loitering for the purpose of prostitution*

	Total prosecutions*	Withdrawn or dismissed	Otherwise dealt with	Total found guilty	Absolute discharge	Conditional discharge	Probation	Fine	Community service order	Suspended sentence	Up to 1 month imprisonment	Over 1 month and up to 2 months imprisonment	Over 2 months and up to 3 months imprisonment	Over 3 months imprisonment	Other disposals
1968	2,714	76	202	2,436	25	305	245	1,197	—	406	35	28	181	—	14
1969	2,619	69	241	2,308	34	329	270	1,125	—	272	71	19	166	2	20
1970	2,655	69	255	2,330	28	346	268	1,117	—	280	59	18	187	—	27
1971	3,229	125	244	2,856	29	428	323	1,403	—	346	73	20	193	—	41
1972	3,466	110	271	3,084	42	547	392	1,380	—	367	82	19	163	1	91
1973	3,133	146	98	2,976	66	553	407	1,443	—	202	46	10	124	1	124
1974	3,090	113	153	2,964	68	525	375	1,421	—	255	46	10	95	1	168
1975	3,455	152	228	3,292	48	568	336	1,651	—	272	49	12	98	1	257
1976	3,995	182	57	3,794	30	610	338	2,141	36	334	57	19	151	2	76
1977	3,988	131	24	3,839	37	617	314	2,232	51	332	66	12	126	1	51
1978	3,911	118	11	3,774	19	540	323	2,192	67	346	105	20	119	1	42
1979	3,167	142	14	3,014	14	518	279	1,609	82	295	78	29	85	2	33
1980	3,482	140	8	3,336	25	513	324	1,880	116	254	108	32	64	1	19
1981	4,324	182	7	4,127	39	686	379	2,389	115	288	145	26	31	3	26

Thus the legal surgery made effective under the 1959 Act was no more than cosmetic, reducing the visibility of the problem from inner-city street life, yet at the same time diverting girls and clients into other avenues of contact. In so doing the sluice gates were opened for an almost overnight proliferation of prostitution in saunas and clubs. And since this eventuality was not adequately provided for in law it was permitted to go unchecked with only a modicum of interference. As for the girl who continued to use the street to make contact with clients, she was left even more vulnerable. The prohibitory onslaught was launched on two fronts and the countervailing currents of deterrence and rehabilitation vied for its control for the next twenty years. The threat of imprisonment stood as the Scylla, moral reformism in the guise of probation as the Charybdis, which street girls steered hard to avoid. The probation officer, cast in the role of prima donna in this moral reformation drama could rapidly be seen as redundant as girls objected to the personal intrusion and the benevolent attempts to change their way of life.

Other codes

Whilst laws relating to loitering for the purpose of prostitution could be seen to tighten up in Britain, other codes were ready to take preliminary steps towards decriminalisation. Some jurisdictions favoured the relaxation of state control in this area whilst others introduced new legislation which extended to men also. In Canada for instance, the term 'common prostitute' has been in disuse since the removal of section 175(1) (c) of the Criminal Code. On 4 August 1982, the Canadian House of Commons passed a resolution, by amending subsection 179(1) of the Criminal Code to remove gender differences: '"prostitute" means a person of either sex who engages in prostitution'.[6] But it must be conceded that public opinion in Canada is less concerned with the treatment or sentencing of prostitutes than it is with the difficulties of obtaining conviction. In 1978 the Supreme Court of Canada in *Hutt* v *The Queen* held that soliciting must be pressing or persistent. In response the City of Calgary went so far as to pass a municipal by-law which sought to control this type of behaviour.[7] Montreal and two other cities have also responded in involving municipal jurisdictions. Proposals for law reform presented for consideration by the House of Commons Standing Committee on Justice and Legal Affairs, July 1982, are not dissimilar to those discussed here by the Criminal Law Review Committee, December 1982, insofar as the Library of Parliament in its submission to the House of Commons Standing Committee on Justice and Legal Affairs proposes a fourfold coverage. First, soliciting need not be 'pressing or persistent' to be criminal. Second, any definition of prostitute may include both males and females. Third, the prostitute's client may be prosecuted. Fourth, the meaning of 'a public place' may be clarified.

In New Zealand prostitution is regulated according to the 1961 Crimes Act, section 148 — though it is section 46(*a*) Police Offences Act 1927 which is invoked. This provision was amended by section 26 of the Summary Offences Act 1981, which like Canadian legislation applies equally to female and male prostitutes. The Act did not include any provision which would prosecute the client, though a much greater effort has been made to regulate the commercialism and institutionalisation of prostitutes with the introduction of the Massage Parlours Act 1978, whereby such premises have now to be licensed (but it allows the police to have a considerable influence in determining who will be licensed to operate a parlour, a provision which is obviously open to abuses of all kinds). Laws worldwide remain discriminatory, whilst changes seem only cosmetic, doing little to alter the muscle of state control.

The legislative omissions

If 'the law and legal rules incorporate and build upon perceptions of reality',[8] this particular aspect of legislation in its preclusion of men persists as something of an absurdity for two very important reasons. First, men also offer sexual services for payment. The existence of the male prostitute outside the law has been widely observed and documented; Bowker 1978: 156–8, Honoré 1978 and Hill 1981 have discussed the existence of at least two kinds of male prostitute, those who provide sexual services to homosexual clients, and those — though usually transvestites — who provide services to heterosexual males. But in neither of these instances is the male provider of the sexual service regarded as a prostitute for the purpose of the law, nor is he subject to the peculiar law enforcement and cautioning procedures and penalties that 'her' activity sets in motion.

The law as it relates to offences of loitering and soliciting for the purposes of prostitution exists as a supreme example of a non-correspondence between social and legal reality, and reveals how instances of social reality are partitioned off from legal reality in order that other imperatives, in this case moral ones may be imbued with greater compunction. Similar activities engaged in by men are said to be adequately covered by section 32 of the Sexual Offences Act 1956 which provides, 'It is an offence for a man persistently to solicit or importune in a public place for immoral purposes.' The essence of this section is that the activity has to be 'persistent' and it must be for immoral purposes. This measure which has its origin in the Vagrancy Act 1898, section 1(1), was used primarily for prosecuting men soliciting other males, though, more importantly perhaps, it was on occasions extended for the purpose of prosecuting men soliciting women. This observation can be supported in the meaning of the Act itself, since section 1(1) stated:

Every male person who — (a) knowingly lives wholly or in part on the earnings of prostitution; or (b) in any public place persistently solicits or importunes for immoral purposes, shall be deemed a rogue and vagabond within the meaning of the Vagrancy Act of 1824 and may be dealt with accordingly.

Further this application is revealed in the Report of the Royal Commission Upon the Duties of the Metropolitan Police, 1908, where it was stated, 'it must not be taken as certain that section 1(1)(b) does not apply to the case of men persisting in soliciting or importuning women for immoral purposes'.[9] And as Cohen (1982) concludes, since the 1928 Street Offences Committee stated that 'The great majority of such charges (i.e. soliciting) are made against women', then we can safely assume that there must have been a minority of cases where men were being charged with soliciting women.[10] Such cases he suggests must have been brought under section 1(1) (b) of the 1898 Vagrancy Act, a view also held by Winn LJ in *Crook* v *Edmondson* (1966) 2 QB 81. It is worthy of some note that the City of Manchester Police Force for instance considered that a man found having sexual intercourse with a prostitute in a public thoroughfare should be charged, under section 5 of the Summary Jurisdiction Act 1848, with aiding and abetting her in the commission of the said offence, though presumably in the aiding and abetting of loitering and soliciting.[11]

The occasional if infrequent practice of prosecuting men for soliciting women ceased altogether with the interpretation of 'immoral purpose' delivered by Lord Parker CJ and Winn LJ (Sachs J. dissenting) in *Crook* v *Edmondson* 2 QB at 81. The defendant in this case while kerb crawling in Preston was observed on two occasions to approach known prostitutes. When he was later stopped and questioned by the police he was unable to provide a satisfactory explanation of his conduct. The magistrates however found there was 'no case to answer' and on appeal their decision was upheld. Winn LJ, in delivering judgment, explained that a purpose is not 'immoral' unless it is prohibited in law. Thus whilst it may well be immoral in the widest sense of the word, the purpose must be immoral in respect of particular sexual conduct, as in (a) unnatural acts which outrage decency – homosexual acts; (b) exploitation of women and girls for the purpose of prostitution – as in procurement. Thus insofar as the application of section 32 of the 1956 Act was concerned a clear distinction and legal division between homosexual activity and heterosexual activity with a prostitute was demarcated. As a result of this decision, though prostitutes had never had protection of the law in the arena of sexual offences and assault (since it was assumed they had participated, deserved it, or their suffering was not worthy of much concern), precedent now affirmed with considerable muscle that they could be harassed without legal redress. And whilst women who welcomed such solicitations were liable to prosecution, men who made such overtures were beyond the law. Shortly following this wildly controversial decision the Street Offences Bill was introduced, designed to amend those overtly discriminatory aspects of the 1959 Act and with a view to introducing legislation which could effectively deal with men such as Crook. Whilst its main objective was to remove the double standard inherent in the law it is perhaps ironic that its failure revealed another double standard. The Earl of Arran, the chief opponent, was especially concerned that clause 1(5) as it stood would bestow wide powers on the police to arrest men with impurity for kerb crawling. The Bill was therefore defeated.

The debate over this legislative omission was once again refuelled by a court case in 1977, *R v Dodd, 66 CAR*. On this occasion the case against the appellant was that in driving past three fourteen-year-old girls and lewdly inviting them to have intercourse ('Are you coming with me, love?', 'Come here, I want to screw you'), it was considered that he had contravened section 32 of the 1956 Act. Appealing on the basis of the decision in *Crook* v *Edmondson* he maintained that his solicitation was not for an 'immoral purpose', i.e. for homosexuality or procuration. This conviction was upheld, however, but for quite different reasons. First, because his conduct was considered in itself immoral, since the girls were fourteen years of age, and, second, because his purpose was to commit an offence of unlawful sexual intercourse with a girl under the age of sixteen. Nevertheless it gave protection only to girls under sixteen. Thus men who persistently and offensively propositioned women aged sixteen or over, whilst a matter of much condemnation and debate, have never been the subject of effective legislation. One of the issues currently under discussion by the Criminal Law Revision Committee in its deliberation on the law as it relates to offences of prostitution is whether the judgment in *Crook* v *Edmondson* was correctly decided since a variety of organisation in their submissions of evidence to the Criminal Law Revision Committee maintain that it was erroneous. In dissenting Sachs L.J. had said that the problem rested with whether a man can be said to solicit a woman who is herself soliciting. Thus, on this point, the man who buys the services of a prostitute may, in actively seeking a sexual encounter, solicit women, and, in being passively desirous of being approached with a view to sex, loiter, but this is not the view of the legislature. Indeed in seeking a prostitute he commits no offence. Similarly, in his role as receiver of a sexual service he remains outside the law and is at liberty in his search for gratification to harass and intimidate women, both those who sell sex and those who don't. It seems an illogical turn of events that whilst a woman may commit a crime by soliciting or loitering, a man in 'accepting' and being a party to her unlawful solicitation does not. The law, desirous of consistency in other realms, prosecutes the receiver of stolen goods — the punter, happily for him, is beyond the law.

The framing of legislation in these areas has been a matter of some considerable criticism, especially since the passing of the 1959 Act. Since then Bills, Working Papers, legal and civil liberties organisations and women's collectives, as well as collectives of prostitutes, have pressed for reforming measures which amongst other changes would enable the effective prosecution of the kerb crawler. It is to be noted also that the situation prior to 1959 has changed a great deal, as any observer of night life, particularly in red-light zones, will be aware. The difference is dramatic: streets are now littered with the nuisance of the motors cruising almost nose to tail in an effort to contact a prostitute, when often there is no girl in sight. Moreover, it is frequently the kerb crawler who makes the first move in soliciting a street walker; it is then 'she' who 'accepts his solicitation' and not the other way round. Negotiations have very much changed from the pre-1959 encounter, where the woman might have put her arm into the man's as in the case of *de Ruiter* (1880) 44 JP 90. Residents in particular red-light areas, exasperated with the ineffectiveness of the law, have taken it upon themselves to deal with the nuisance of the kerb crawler. Vigilante groups have started waging their own campaign against this nuisance in certain areas of inner cities. They have started by taking down car numbers and then later resorted to strategies of a more aggressive nature, firing home-made water pistols at annoying punters and throwing bricks at vehicles of persistent offenders.

In response to this unsatisfactory legislative omission, it has been suggested that a new offence of 'accepting unlawful solicitation' be created. This has recently been mooted by the Justice Clerk's Society and has won considerable support. It has also been suggested that the decision in *Crook* v *Edmondson* be overruled. The present situation is far from satisfactory; police, prostitutes and the legal profession are unhappy. When the plain-clothes division interviewed in the Manchester study were asked to respond to this particular criticism: 'The police are charged with interpretation of the law where, as in offences related to prostitution, a double standard applies: their harassment of prostitutes and reluctance to pursue kerb crawlers is revealing' (Barrett 1980: 236) they replied unanimously that the kerb crawler was a nuisance. One officer summed up the view of them all: 'kerb crawlers are a thorn in our side, they are worse than the prostitute!' In the words of one patrol officer, 'there might be one girl out there, but for every one, there are ten to twenty punters'. When asked whether there should be a specific law to enable the police to deal with this nuisance, again in all cases they were unanimous in expressing this sentiment: 'we have to implement the law, if a statute was implemented tomorrow we would bring them in'. In a more detailed response to the problems posed by the kerb crawler 36 per cent were concerned with the traffic problems created as a result of the presence of kerb crawlers in residential areas. One officer alluded to the very real problem created, since he had particular knowledge of a punter knocking down a six-year-old, because he was not paying sufficient attention to the road. All expressed dissatisfaction with the present statutes which do not allow them to deal effectively with the problem, and it is difficult to obtain convictions for breach of the peace. Other methods or strategies for dealing with the problem have been mooted. In this direction the Medical Women's Federation have suggested the introduction of a cautioning system, similar to that in operation for street prostitutes.[12]

Anomalies – the transsexual

The absurdity of this rigid sex-specific law, of the biological criteria by which it is operated but which form no part of the presumptions upon which the criminalisation of this activity is predicated, is further dramatically highlighted by the processing of the transsexual prostitute in the criminal justice system. The need for immediate and serious consideration of the issues involved has been emphasised by a recent court case. On 29 September 1982 Gloria Greaves – a transsexual male – was prosecuted and jailed for eighteen months for living off immoral earnings (a charge applicable only to men) – and the earnings were her own! Ironically perhaps her husband at the same time was gaoled for living off the immoral earnings of prostitution – his 'wife's' though of course 'she' was regarded in law as a man and therefore incapable of prostitution. The court which heard the case was faced with a Chinese puzzle sufficient to flummox Aesop, not so much because of legal reluctance to acknowledge sex-change status, but because of the existing law, and its resolute determination to place men and women in conceptual boxes dependant upon physical criteria, and in this case because of the rigid nature of sex-specific law. (See *The Lancet*, 16 April 1983 at 885, *R* v *Tan* and Others, Court of Appeal, Criminal Division, 10 February 1983.)

Other similarly confusing cases reflect the problem posed for the courts – the transsexual. In 1980, a transsexual defendant was committed for trial at Knightsbridge Crown Court on a charge of importuning, though 'she' had gone through a ceremony of marriage in 1976 as a female. Indeed, this confusion has characterised and dogged the processing of transsexual males in court cases ever since sex-change surgery has been possible. In these cases the difficulties have arisen over which charge to prefer. Cases where transsexuals have been charged with loitering have been characterised by defendants appearing before the court on importuning charges also. Such legal conundrums are the creation of a law which is predicated solely on the biological sex of the actor rather than on the activity he/she commits. Thus, loitering for the purposes of prostitution is not merely a quality of an act a person commits, but rather a quality of the physical criteria of the actor. The case studies which follow provide some illustration of the way in which physical boundaries are drawn according to rules and meanings and then given a pre-eminent significance within the legal domain.

During recent years an increasing number of transsexual males appeared in court facing charges of loitering/soliciting for the purpose of prostitution. Indeed, the present research has revealed that magistrates in Manchester, Birmingham, London and Wolverhampton are not unfamiliar with such cases. During 1980–2, magistrates at the City Magistrates' Court in Manchester could speculate of a handful of such cases, where defendants were arrested and initially charged with the female offence of loitering for the purpose of prostitution. These cases were not surprisingly characterised by a high number of adjournments reflecting the considerable legal confusion they generated for advocates. Subsequent court appearances promised to be even more complicated as defendants were further charged, as males, with importuning. Seemingly, the decision as to their legal sex and the correct charge to be arraigned was a matter to be left to the legal expert, who responded by hedging his prosecution bets. Consider the insuperable difficulties which are presented in the following abstracted transcript. The value of which is to cast some light, first, on the rigid nature of precedent, second, on the difficulty in arraigning the defendant on either charge, and third, the need in law to recognise the new sex of the inter-changed sex person.

Case 1: Transsexual male charge – importuning for an immoral purpose

Court clerk: You have previously stated that you want the matter dealt with summarily.

Defendant: Yes.

Court clerk: The charge is that on 10th March 1981 that being a man you did persistently importune for an immoral purpose in a public place, namely Canal Street.

Defendant: Not guilty.

Prosecuting solicitor: You've heard the charge and will see that the prosecution have to prove certain elements. Firstly, that the defendant is a man and, secondly, that he was importuning. The first element: I refer you to the case of *Corbett* v *Corbett*, the defendant otherwise known as April Ashley. The decision in that case was 'once a man always a man'. I will bring before the court evidence to prove that this person is a man, and therefore he remains a man. The second part of the charge is quite easy to prove. Plain-clothes detectives will give evidence to prove they saw the defendant standing in the doorway of the Union Hotel. They saw him move over to a car, get into it and start shouting across to lone males, 'Hey do you want to have a good time?'

[To first prosecution witness]

In April 1978 were you a plain-clothes officer attached to Green Police Station?

Police sergeant: Yes.

Defending solicitor interrupts: The rest of the evidence he will give is inadmissible. I have seen a statement of his evidence. He will be referring to two connected matters.

Pros. sol.:   On April 26th 1978 did you search someone at Green Police Station?

Def. sol. interrupts: I think this is a waste of time. The prosecution cannot refer to any circumstances where a person has appeared before the court on a previous occasion and been acquitted.

Magistrate: We don't know that this is what he is going to say yet.

Def. sol.:   But the search was done at a police station.

Mag: Allow the officer to give his evidence.

Pros. sol.:   Did you search someone, somewhere on a date in 1978?

Pol. serg.:   That is correct.

Pros. sol.:   Will you tell the court where it took place and who the person was?

Pol. serg.:   I had occasion to search a person whose sex was in doubt at Green Police Station. The person was asked whether he was male or female. The person stated he was a male so accordingly that search was conducted by me.

Pros. sol.: Do you recognise that person?

Def. sol.:   I hope my friend isn't going to ask for a dock identification. You have to direct yourself as to the law on an occasion in 1978.

Pol. serg.:   The person I searched has the name Muriel and uses an alias of Margaret.

Pros. sol.:   Have you seen that person since then?

Pol. serg.:   Yes. I would recognise that person again.

   Def. sol.:   I'm not going to object to this although I could.

Pol. serg.:   Bearing in mind the defence approach to this I would prefer not to answer that.

Pros. sol.:   Have you seen that person since on more than one occasion?

Pol. serg.:   Yes.

Pros. sol.:   How many times?

Pol. serg.:   Between then and now, on six occasions.

Pros. sol.:   Would you say that person's face is well known to you?

Pol. serg.:   Yes.

Pros. sol.:   When and where have you seen that person?

Pol. serg.:   Within the precincts of the court twice.

Pros. sol.:   When was the last occasion?

Pol. serg.:   28th July 1981 [after referring to his notes].

Pros. sol.:   Have you seen him today?

Def. Sol. objects. (*Magistrates* rule that the question be answered.)

Pol. serg.:   Yes, the person sitting opposite in the dock.

Pros. sol.:   You say you searched the defendant in April 1978 because of some doubt as to his sex. Who made this assertion?

Pol. serg.: I did.

Pros. sol.: Did you ask the defendant what sex he was?

Pol. serg.: Yes.

Pros. sol.: What was the answer to that question?

Pol. serg.: The answer was 'Male'.

Pros. sol.: On that understanding you carried out the search?

Pol. serg.: Yes.

Pros. sol.: What sort of search?

Pol. serg.: Complete strip search which revealed a fully developed female bust and a penis.

Def. sol.: I think I ought to make this assertion now. I still object to the evidence given by this witness for two reasons. (1) He has said he has seen her in the precincts of this court, but hasn't given a reason why she is here. She may be a witness, but I am not going to ask. (2) He has referred to his notebook about a previous appearance in court. You must then consider this. Both these points still indicate the fact that the person the officer searched has a criminal record. Therefore the evidence is inadmissible because it is a veiled allegation that the defendant has a previous record.

Mag.: When a case has been remanded to another date there is no objection on the second appearance to the mention of the defendant's first appearance in court.

Def. sol.: In 1978 did you make any notes of what was going on?

Pol. serg.: I can't remember.

Def. sol.: Would it be correct to say that there would have been some report put before your senior officers?

Pol. serg.: Not necessarily.

Def. sol.: At that time you were a police constable?

Pol. serg.: Yes.

Def. sol.: No one would have gone into Green Police Station without a record being made of their arrest?

Pol. serg.: With respect to the procedure of the Greater Manchester Police, there are occasions where a person can be fully searched without a full report being forwarded to senior officers.

Def. sol.: But there would be some written confirmation in the precincts of the police station of the search?

Pol. serg.: It would be recorded somewhere.

Def. sol.: One thing you do recall is that there was some concern of someone you searched whether the person was male or female?

Pol. serg.: Yes, it was decided that we needed a search to establish the sex of the person I know to be the defendant.

Def. sol.:   When did you last refer to any notes made of that incident?

Pol. serg.:   I haven't referred to any notes. It is purely from memory.

Def. sol.:   So you haven't referred to any notes to refresh your memory of something that happened three years ago?

Pol. serg.:   It was the only time I have ever had to do that kind of search.

Def. sol.:   If the person gave the answer 'Male', why was there any confusion as to his sex?

Pol. serg.:   If I answer that question . . . may I have a word with the prosecution? . . . The reason why there was doubt was that he was dressed as a female.

Def. sol.:   As the defendant is dressed today?

Pol. serg.:   Yes.

Def. sol.:   So the confusion was in the mind of the police officer, rather than in the defendant's mind?

Pol. serg.:   There was an element of doubt because the person was dressed as a female and the figure resembled that of a female.

Def. sol.:   If you were so confused, why wasn't a doctor called?

Pol. serg.:   No doctor was called because of the statement by the defendant to the effect that he was a male, and because the results of the search which showed he was a male. Had there still been doubt a doctor would have been called.

Def. sol.:   And this is the only occasion you have had to do this kind of search?

Pol. serg.:   I conducted three searches that day to establish the same thing.

Def. sol.:   So you searched three people? Why are you so sure that the answer 'Male' was given to your question by this defendant?

Pol. serg.:   Because we asked the three people the same question.

Def. sol.:   Are you aware that it is not unknown for people to have attributes of both sexes quite naturally?

Pol. serg.:   The terminology used was 'Keep taking the pill'. I'm not a doctor.

Def. sol.:   No, you're not a doctor. I would like to know why a doctor wasn't called.

Pol. serg.:   By my observations that person was a male and by his own admission he was a male.

Def. sol.:   Do you have any medical qualifications?

Pol. serg.:   None.

Def. sol.:   Were you at White Street Police Station when this defendant was arrested?

Pol. serg.:   I wasn't at White Street at any time when the defendant was there.

[to second prosecution witness].

Pros. sol.:   Where were you at 10.20 p.m. on March 10th 1981?

Pol serg.:   I was on plain-clothes duty in the Union Hotel with P.C. Bolton.

Pros. sol.:   Did anyone attract your attention?
Pol. serg.:   Yes, the defendant.
Pros. sol.:   What was the defendant wearing?
Pol. serg.:   Fur coat, red dress, tights, high-heeled shoes and a wig.
Pros. sol.:   So, very similar to what the defendant is wearing today?
Pol. serg.:   Yes.
Pros. sol.:   Where was the defendant situated?
Pol. serg.:   He was standing at the exit door onto Canal Street.
Pros. sol.:   What was the defendant doing?

(*Magistrates* interrupt to ask whether *P.C. Bolton* can listen to the evidence-in-chief in order to save time. *Def. Sol.* disagrees as a lot of the evidence may be from memory.)

Pros. sol.:   Do you remember the incident without referring to your notebook?
Pol. serg.:   Yes
Pros. sol.:   Tell the court as much as you can remember without your notebook.
Pol serg.:   The defendant was standing at the side of the bar, we were standing close by. Whilst we were there we saw the defendant speak to males as they were going out of the pub. Spoke to four men in all. After a short while the defendant left the pub. We followed. We saw him sitting in his own car. Our car was parked fifteen to twenty yards further up Canal Street. Could see the defendant quite clearly.
Pros. sol.:   What did you see then?
Pol. serg.:   Saw several males leave the pub. As they did the defendant beckoned or shouted across the road. None of them took notice and walked away.
Pros. sol.:   Did you hear any conversation?
Pol. Serg.:   To one man the defendant asked, 'Do you want a good time?' This was about 10.40 p.m.
Pros. sol.:   How long had you been sitting in your car?
Pol. serg.:   About ten to fifteen minutes.
Pros. sol.:   Did the male react?
Pol. serg.:   He ignored him and walked away. At this point we approached the defendant and said we were arresting for loitering for the purposes of prostitution. He replied, 'I'm only waiting for my boyfriend.'
Pros. sol.:   How many people do you think were approached by the defendant?
Pol. serg.:   I would say four inside the pub, and three to four outside.
Pros. sol.:   You have just told the magistrates that you arrested the defendant for loitering for the purposes of prostitution. Why?
Pol. serg.:   Because we were under the impression that Muriel was a female.
Pros. sol.:   Yes. Did you take the defendant to White Street Police Station?
Pol. serg.:   Yes. It was there that we ascertained he was a male.

Pros. sol.: You say ascertained . . . (*Prosecution* has a word with *Def. Sol.* and then decides not to ask this question). Did you later formally caution and charge this defendant?
Pol. serg.: Yes.
Pros. sol.: On what charge?
Pol. serg.: Importuning.[13]

In another similar case before the court in 1982 the defendant was charged with both the offences of loitering and of importuning. Amid the confusion this case was also adjourned for matters to be sorted out'. At the later hearing the prosecution decided to offer no evidence on the loitering charge proceeding with the charge of importuning. The defendant, confused and bemused, most reluctantly pleaded guilty. Interestingly, the prosecution evidence offered on this charge was the very same evidence offered in case of prostitution: ' . . . the defendant was seen to be bending and peering into passing motor vehicles, paying particular attention to those driven by lone males, on Westwood Street, an area frequented by prostitutes and their clients'. The defence solicitor then asked the magistrates to consider it as a similar offence to loitering, but of a different gender rather than treat it as an offence of importuning, adding, 'The defendant has asked me to stress to the court that she had a sex-change operation ten years ago and that she considers herself a woman. The mention of her past convictions as a man distresses her.'

Such appearances of transsexual prostitutes before the courts are bizarre but are by no means unique. French (1976)[14] recalled such a case before a London magistrates' court where a female defendant pleaded guilty to 'soliciting to the annoyance' (used prior to the introduction of the Street Offences Act 1959). In advising the woman to seek probation assistance the case was adjourned. However, when the defendant appeared at a later date the charge had been amended accordingly, ' . . . that you being a male person did in a public place persistently importune other male persons for an immoral purpose'. Another such case was that of Rachel Gosling who was arrested for soliciting and prosecuted under section 1 of the Street Offences Act 1959. The defendant was subsequently remanded in custody for the preparation of medical reports and it was discovered that she had undergone an operation for sex-change surgery. In the light of these facts Miss Gosling was finally charged as a male under section 32 of the Sexual Offences Act 1956, and fined £10.

The debate over the legal definition of sex determination has confronted the law for some time. The definition of sex and gender within it has its origins in a judgment in civil law – in fact in the Family Division. The particular case which established this precedent examined the validity of a marriage contracted between a male and a transsexual male. The ramifications of the deliberations therein were not only far reaching and extensive throughout the various levels of jurisdiction but also stand as a statement of the way civil law, at least, regards sex-determination as immutable. Whilst in other academic fields the traditional classification of sexual determination is being questioned, the law continues to enshrine sex differences and to pronounce the pre-eminence of physical criteria over all other.

Some consideration of the legal case in question is warranted for two reasons. Firstly, because it exists as a definitive legal statement on matters relating to sexual determination. Secondly, because the case in question clearly exemplifies the way in which the anatomical distinction between the sexes gains credence from within a specific institutional framework. Thus sex determination is not a category suspended in time and space but finds its meaning within the family and marriage and the legal rules that bind that union together with the social conventions which organise that institution.

In the case of *Corbett* v *Corbett* (1971) P83, it was decided whether a wife (registered male at birth, following the amputation of external genitalia and accomodation of an artificial vagina) could be considered a woman for the purpose of marriage and whether 'she' would be considered capable of consummation. The definition of marriage has always followed the dictum of Lord Penzance rendered in *Hyde* v *Hyde and Woodhouse* [1886] 1 P & D at p. 133: 'I conceive that marriage, as understood in Christendom, may for this purpose be defined as the voluntary union for life of *one man and one woman,* to the exclusion of all others' (my emphasis).

In September 1963 the petitioner Arthur Corbett and respondent April Ashley went through a ceremony of marriage; when the marriage faltered, however, Corbett petitioned for a decree of nullity on the basis that his wife was in fact of the male sex. The wife responded by maintaining that 'she' was not male and was indeed capable of consummating the marriage which 'she' claimed had faltered through the 'petitioner's incapacity or his wilful refusal'. In the course of deciding whether the respondent was of the female sex and whether capable of consummation conflicting versions of the nature of sex and gender were discussed at some length. James Comyn QC and Leonard Lewis QC, for the respondent, maintained,

> Manhood and womanhood is not decided on the presence or otherwise of a penis or other sex organs. Sex is the sum of a number of things both external and internal and pertaining to both body and mind. Consideration must be given to hormonal make up, the person's psychological condition and chromosomal factors.

Ormrod J did not agree. He held that marriage 'is the institution on which the family is built, and in which the capacity for natural heterosexual intercourse is an essential element', arguing that the submissions confused sex with gender, and marriage was a relationship which depended on sex and not on gender.

The wife in this case he considered to be no more than a 'castrated male' and declared the marriage void *ab initio*. But the determination of sex within the law still remains far from clear. In the case of *S.Y.* v *S.Y.* (Orse W) [1962] CA(P)37, where attempts at consortium had failed, due to the wife's congenital vaginal defect (vaginal astresia), sex at birth was the pre-eminent factor. The wife was willing to undergo an operation for the creation of a complete vagina (vaginoplasty), but the operation never took place since the husband left his wife. In this case it was held: 'If there be a reasonable probability that the lady can be made capable of vera copula, of the natural sort of coitus though without power of conception, I cannot pronounce this marriage void.' And again in *E* v *B* [1954] 3WLR 237, a similar point was at issue. On this occasion the wife was born without a vagina or uterus. Following the creation of an artificial vagina whilst the husband was working abroad the vagina closed up. The point at issue was whether the marriage had been consummated. It was decided that connection had taken place, but the court was not satisfied that it amounted to consummation. Karminski J stated, 'In my view it is possible to have a marriage consummated in the case where a woman has had created for her an artificial vagina.' These cases, especially that of *Corbett*, reveal the organisation of sex in law with relation to particular social institutions and their predominant functions. In this event the function of marriage is natural heterosexual intercourse and reproduction.

The nature of the legal precedent in respect of this case reflects how physical nature becomes masticated as the law demands consistency. As Ormrod J makes so clear,

> The fundamental purpose of law is the regulation of the relations between persons, and between persons and the state or community — for the purpose of this case, legal relations can be classified into those in which the sex of the individual concerned is either irrelevant, relevant or an essential determinant of the nature of the relationship.

The decision as to sex determination in *Corbett* was discussed and followed by the Law Commission 1973,[15] and a provision included in the Nullity of Marriages Act 1973. 1(*c*) declared that the marriage is void if the parties are not respectively male and female.[16] This too was echoed in s.11(*c*) of the Matrimonial Causes Act 1973. However there have been many dissidents who have not agreed that the human race can be divided into two separate compartments.[17] Smith (1971) for one found the decision 'disturbingly simplistic',[18] whilst other critics have asserted that the necessity of 'normal heterosexual intercourse' cannot always be maintained in marriage due to senility, sickness and accident.[19]

It is also worthy of some note that heterosexuality founded on sexual determination at birth is not an essential determinant of marriage in all societies.[20] A.S. Diamond found 'a case where a wife usually barren marries a woman (Nuer Kipsigis Peristiany 1939 81 206) who will, through the help of some male, raise issue to her husband and father with the rights belonging to that status, including the right to inherit property and receive bridewealth on the marriage of children'.[21]

Although the transsexual can change name by deed poll and for National Insurance purposes, any substantive legal transformation in sexual status is not permitted. However, regarding the question of legal rights, other jurisdictions appear to be less rigid, some even treating the transsexual as an independant social and legal category.[22] Most courts in the United States for instance issue new birth certificates.[23] This is a question under consideration in many European countries. In West Germany a Bill has been presented to Parliament pressing for a change of name on birth certificates. More recently in Italy the Minister of Justice has drawn up a preliminary draft Bill providing for the rectification of civil status for those who have undergone sex-change surgery. Moreover, the European Court of Human Rights was called upon to consider this question in the Van Oosterwijck case, regarding the applicants appeal for the rectification of civil status as a man.[24] At present the European Commision of Human Rights is considering a particular application made by a British subject, judgment to be delivered sometime in 1983; the British transsexual community eagerly awaits the outcome.[25] With regard to the marriage question the marriage of transsexuals has been permitted for some time in Sweden.[26] And in a recent United States case the judge concluded that if sex-reassignment surgery was successful he could see 'no legal barrier, cognisable social taboo or reason to prevent a marriage'.

As transsexualism becomes an increasingly world-wide conundrum, it may well be that the courts will be persuaded to accede a new status to those who are socially of a different sex, and medically different at least to some intents. However, Australia and Britain remained unmoved as the corresponding appeal courts addressed the question. In January 1982 in Australia, two transsexual males were charged, as men, with attempting to procure two other males. The defendants claimed that they could not be charged with the offence because they were women (*Age*, 25 September 1982). Phillis McGuiness and Vicki Harns appealed against the finding that they could be pronounced guilty of an offence when they solicited two policemen; it is not an offence for a female to solicit a male, but it is for a male to solicit a male (*Sydney Morning Herald*, 4 January 1983)

Similarly, on 10 February 1983 the English Court of Appeal reaffirmed the legal presumption that men who undergo sex-change surgery are still biologically men. In rejecting the appeal, Parker J, May LJ and Staughton J, although agreed that 'philosophically, psychologically and socially' the appellant was a woman, rejected the submission that the appellant was 'biologically' a woman, a decision which, they declared, was based on common sense and had regard to the institution of marriage (*The Times*, 11 February 1983).

Transsexuals who seek sex change surgery are fundamentally unhappy about their bodies and about the gender role considered appropriate to that body. In consequence they see the only real solution to their conflict and dilemma in a visible alteration of their physical bodies, thus permitting them to live in their chosen gender role with a greater viability. Billings and Urban (1982: 226) in their study of transsexualism are quick to point to the political implication of this drastic solution to a problem which should be solved elsewhere. They write, 'Sex-change surgery privatises and depoliticises individual experiences of gender-role distress.'

Exegesis and explanations

In the exclusive prosecution of women as 'common prostitutes' and in the criminalisation of loitering and soliciting, the law actively 'organises' sex difference. This organisation is rooted in history, and present-day justificatory rationales for the prosecution of women only, bear a surprising similarity to the rationales which provided either the motivation for, or the rationalisation of, the Contagious Diseases control measures of the nineteenth century. Some of these rationales have remained unchanged, namely that women are the source of vice and without the prostitute there would be no men to consort with them. The predilection echoed in Mercier's work in the 1890s – 'In women sexual vice has to be judged by a standard, different from that which applies to men'[27] – has persisted to this day. A number of crucial theoretical and analytical questions remain unanswered. First, why has legislation in this area applied exclusively to women'. Second, why in the 1950s and 1960s was the new legislation, so long overdue, apparently so retrogressive? Third, why did it fail from the outset and in which direction does impending reform promise to take us?

Sex, or so it has been thought, in excess has always led to degeneracy, socially, psychologically and physiologically, with the consequence that the free unbridled expression of the sexual impulse has been kept in check by a series of stringent moral, medical and legal controls. With this object in mind, medical men, psychologists and eugenicists have unified in the pursuit of the control of sexual expression. Whenever sexuality has promised to break loose from its tight rein, the moral crusaders, fear-mongers and watchdogs have come to the fore.

It is not altogether surprising that throughout history the ebb and flow of sexual repression has paralleled the ebb and flow of sexual expression. In the 1880s in response to the desire to prevent the spread of venereal disease, Manchester and other cities introduced sluice toilets in public conveniences. Very quickly after their introduction this cleansing facility was closed, since it was thought it would actually encourage immorality. Marie Stopes's endeavours to educate the civil population on contraceptive matters were also feared as a positive inducement to immorality.[28] And Mercier (1918: 195) feared any relaxation in sentences for infanticide since at present the law was 'one of the strongest safeguards of chastity'. Even Rowntrees and Lavers in discovering antibiotics in 1951 conducive to the treatment of venereal disease were considerably concerned about the impact the drugs might have on encouraging sexual promiscuity (see Comfort 1967: 136–85).

Latterly, the trend in adolescent sex has prompted a number of research studies, some of which indicate the frequency of cervical cancer in adolescent girls, which has been interpreted as the consequence of a too early indulgence. It might also be worthy of note that endometrial cancer has been observed to be also related to diet (Armstrong 1977 in Hiatt *et al*). Of recent discovery too is the new disease, AIDS (Acquired Immuno-Deficiency Syndrome). This is purported to be sexually transmitted and, so it has been reported, has claimed a number of lives. We might do well in this context to remind ourselves of Foucault's remarks (1978: 36) on the control of sexuality:

> sexual irregularity was annexed to mental illness; from childhood to old age, a norm of sexual development was defined and all possible deviations were carefully described; pedagogical controls and medical treatments were organized; around the least fantasies, moralists, but especially doctors, brandished the whole emphatic vocabulary of abomination.

In this respect note John Scales's excellent letter to the *Guardian* (16 March 1983) where, after producing evidence which positively rejects any association between sexual intercourse and AIDS (*Lancet* 1981, 1162, 2132, 2598; 1982, 1184; *New England Journal of Medicine* (1923) 308, 940), he concludes, 'Syphilis was widely believed for centuries to be God's punishment for those who sinned sexually. It is small wonder that latter-day moralists dressed in doctor's clothing have had to invent new lethal forms of V.D.'

Even lesbianism and its relation to gynaecology has been the subject of recent research. Findings reported in *American Journal of Obstetric Gynaecology* ((1981) 140, 20) suggest that it was significant that a number of women had a diagnosis of trichomonas when they were engaging in homosexual activity only, though venereal disease and cervical dysplasia were uncommon. It is not merely sexual freedom in itself which is feared but the degree to which the sex act becomes separated from the socio-cultural meanings which constrain it within a

familial context. Thus the casual relationship is frowned upon whilst the dissocia-
tion of the sex act from any relationship whatever and the recasting of sexual
gratification as a pleasure which can be bought is regarded as reification of body
and soul in the extreme (Reiman 1979: 64). Neverthless, such arguments do not
explain why women particularly are condemned for promiscuity and why women
alone are regulated for their part in the prostitute contract.

Historically, 'she' has been criticised, derided and punished through medical
discursive practices, by judicial procedures and indirectly by discriminatory
policies of welfare agencies. From the nineteenth century onwards women who
engaged in too frequent intercourse were said to be liable to cancer of the uterus.
This discourse in its various forms had a most impressive following from Colom-
bat de L'Isère onwards (see Graham 1950: 433), E.J. Tilt remarking that connection was considered to have a poisonous influence on the generative organs of
some women. He went further and added that sexual connection was also the
cause of sub-acute ovaritis wherein 'Marriage may give an additional impulse to
the morbidly disposed ovaries'.[29] This was a view which won support in the work of
Thomas, who in *Diseases of Women* stated that the very act of intercourse
became a positive source of disease, whilst Grailly Hewitt (1872) maintained that
sexual intercourse was a predisposing element in cancer of the uterus. Even more
recently, as McLeod (1982: 56–7) has shown us, medical studies of prostitutes
have concluded that such women are more likely to suffer from carcinoma of the
cervix.

Female sexuality has also been controlled, and still is in certain parts of the
world and in countries to which immigrants have brought their cultures (hence the
necessity for Lord Kennet's Bill on circumcision), by surgical means (see also
Cranfield and Cranfield 1983). As Weeks (1981) and Daly (1978) point out,
clitoridectomy was used in Britain, America and Europe for the control of female
sexual behaviour in the nineteenth century. Other almost equally perverse
methods of surgical intervention was performed by the grand master – Baker-
Brown – in the control of women. A surgical operation to the tongue known as
glossodoctomy resulted in an immediate cure for the woman who talked,
whilst the woman who danced was victim to a surgical horror of similar
magnitude.[30]

It is clear then that the oppression and control of female sexuality in the law as
it relates to prostitution is an extension of the sexism and sexual harrassment
(Sedley and Benn 1982: 8) rife in society, sexism, which is manifest in all areas of
law, family, civil and criminal, and at all levels of jurisdiction. This is a tendency
apparent in pre-capitalist economies though not in so codified a form and it is
best explained via an analysis of patriarchal attitudes and precedents, relating to
birthright, inheritance and paternity (Figes 1972, Coward 1983), all assured
through virginity before marriage and fidelity within. Hence, all societies at some

time have been guilty of the barbarism of female genital mutilation in their desire to ensure virginity and fidelity and the exchange of money and commodities in brideprice and dowry (Sadaawi 1980). Thus mode of production, at least insofar as control of sexuality is concerned, is not of primary importance to an analysis of prostitutes, though it of necessity must be contemplated within the following framework. As Engels (1972 maintains: 'with the conversion of the means of production into social property, wage labour, the proletariat' also disappears, and therewith, also, the necessity for a certain – statistically calculable – number of women to surrender themselves for money.'[31] And Davis wrote: 'Prostitution embraces an economic relation and is naturally connected with the entire system of economic forces'.[32]

Sex has always been a matter for legislation. More recently, the Court of Appeal decided that sex once a week for a husband was enough. The husband had protested that his wife's unreasonable behaviour of permitting sex only once a week entitled him to a divorce. Ormrod LJ said, 'It seems to me quite impossible for any court to find that a wife's refusal to have sex more often than once a week is unreasonable' (*The Times*, 5 December 1980).

The present laws which legislate against loitering for the purposes of prostitution are considered unjustifiable, a further expression of the extent of sexism within the law (Scutt 1981, Klein and Kress 1981, and of the exercise of power within society, Roby (1969), and Bujra (1982). More specifically prostitution reflects an economic interest linked to division of husband and the household economy (Reiman 1979, Jaget 1980, Bujra 1982, whilst James (1978b) and Bujra (1982) argue that prostitution is an institutionalised occupational choice related to the viability of economic opportunities for work. James found that the prostitutes in her study were in low paid low-status jobs. Certainly history has shown in times of economic crisis, when women's opportunities for paid work are restricted, that a certain proportion will be diverted into forms of prostitution in order to generate the necessary income. The main analytical problem is as Bujra (1982: 145) suggests: 'prostitution is both theoretically and politically problematic. It does not fall neatly into any existing model of sociological explanation, whether this be in the field of development, deviancy, feminism or class analysis.'

Whilst the legal control of prostitution betrays a double standard between men and women, the existing state of sexual exchange, particularly its institutionalisation since 1959, is equally undesirable. Women must be free, as the English Collective of Prostitutes claim, to do as they please with their own bodies, though in the light of the existing relations of prostitutes to society such a claim may have negative repercussions. A recurrent problem for feminists lies with its ambiguous enclosure of sexual freedom with sexual exploitation (Bujra 1982: 145). Indeed the writings of Klein and Kress (1981), Millett(1975) and McLeod (1981: 69) assert that prostitution is a natural result of the traditional subserviency of women. It seems difficult to see how, given the nature of our society, even if women were in total control, free from state coercion, the activity could be elevated into one of real self-determination and equality with men, though Bujra shows how prostitution can be made to work as a way of life in Nairobi. Even so, social stigmas die hard, as one magistrate commented, 'You are the type of woman who should be removed from the city' (p.160).

During the last few decades, with the relaxation in sexual attitudes, the greater exploitation of sex and of women in particular, attitudes to prostitution have similarly relaxed. This has had the effect of increasing the numbers of women visibly plying their trade, and in response to this visibility the 1959 Act received Royal Assent. One of the reasons for this repressive legislation was as Smart (1981: 49) suggests, a concern for family life based on 'the power of prostitution to corrupt the vulnerable nuclear family' (p.53). The visibility of the problem had struck a very personal and resonant chord in every breast. Almost everyone had an interest in moral entrepreneurism, condemning the flagrancy with which the activity went on unbridled. Male moral crusaders openly criticised the activity which a part of them desired, whilst a part of them feared the temptation. Women moral crusaders were also forced to consider the obvious parallels between their 'respectable' sexual relations and exchanges with those blatant monetary exchanges of the women they condemned. Consequently the brash openness of prostitution disrupted and disturbed peace of mind, generating a sense of personal unease which could not be tolerated.

The law: which way now?
In December 1982, the Criminal Law Revision Committee, assisted by the Policy Advisory Committee, published the Working Paper on Offences Relating to Prostitution and Allied Offences. This is the fourth such review in the last fifty years, its predecessors being the Street Offences Report of 1928, the Wolfenden Report (1957) and the Working Papers on Vagrancy and Street Offences of 1974 and 1976. The recommendations mooted in 1974 and 1976 were soon to gather dust as rape reform seemed a more urgent issue. It is unlikely that the present proposals will meet with such a fate. Already, there are ripples on the waters indicating that the tide is about to turn. As from 31 January 1983, and in accordance with Home Office Circular 2/1983, following section 71 of the Criminal Justice Act 1982, the sanction of imprisonment for loitering and soliciting is abolished forthwith (for further discussion on imprisonment in relation to fine default see Chapter 8). Nonetheless the extent to which this move reflects an endeavour to liberalise existing laws, or instead and perhaps more realistically mirrors a piecemeal attempt to solve the general problem of prison overcrowding, is a matter of contention. In this respect a number of experimental adjustments have been made, including the introduction of the partially suspended sentence, as

from December 1981. Pressure for reform of the laws relating to prostitution has also attracted the support of local government. The Greater London Council, in response to requests from the English Collective of Prostitutes, appointed an observer to assess and monitor the implementation of the cautioning system in the King's Cross area (*Guardian*, 21 January 1983; *Observer*, 23 January 1983). In addition the GLC, accepting that the rise of prostitution is a direct result of increasing unemployment, have set up a number of women's information and employment centres throughout the Greater London area. It was within this climate of opinion that the Criminal Law Revision Committee delivered its working Paper.

The disagreement of its members regarding many of the reform proposals is encouraging as it will mean that they will be more amenable to diversities of public comment. So far the Committee have agreed that the term 'common' should go, though they have suggested that 'being a prostitute' is a term that should be retained (3: 13). Whether the cautioning system should be abolished or retained is a matter over which agreement could not be reached, though they conceded that the present system did not deter and the role of the probation service was singularly ineffective (3:17). Members remained divided over the impact of cautioning in the court, declaring, 'there can be no doubt that cautioning facilitates the conviction of the guilty' (3:15).

Their suggestions for the prosecution of the kerb crawler are to be welcomed, though the tripartite decision may be difficult to administer. They propose that it shall be an offence, first, for a man to accost a woman from a motor car for sexual purposes so as to put her in fear; second, for a man to accost a woman from a motor car for sexual purposes so as to cause annoyance; and third, for a man to accost a woman from a car for the purpose of prostitution (p.50).

The paper also proposes to tighten up the law relating to the commercialisation and institutionalisation of prostitution (2:7, 2:10). The restriction of advertising services (2:10) unless newsagents get a cut is not to be welcomed; neither is licensing of massage parlours or saunas (2:28).

Whether any of these proposals become law will not be known for some while. If the law-makers do not opt for decriminalisation, and it seems clear in the absence of any such discussions that they will not, a half-way house may be a step in the right direction and a certain improvement on the legal situation to date. In this respect it is curious why existing legislation in the Town Police Clauses Act (section 28), the Public Order Act 1936 s.5, and the Road Traffic Act 1976, all viable alternatives, has not been invoked more readily. One thing is certain, that until loitering and soliciting for the offence of prostitution is struck off the statute book, prostitutes' organisations, women's groups and feminists will not cease in their agitation for its decriminalisation. Sooner or later their arguments must be taken seriously.

2 · The 'common prostitute'
– An antecedent presumption of guilt

'No, no! Sentence first – verdict afterwards!'
The Red Queen in Lewis Carroll, *Through the Looking Glass*

Introduction

The term 'common prostitute' derives from a society where women were defined and categorised by men who made law, administered justice and controlled property. Judith R. Walkowitz (1980), in her historical study of the state regulation of prostitution, records the case of one such woman who echoed this self-same sentiment:

> It is *men, men only men,* from the first to the last, that we have to do with! To please a man I did wrong at first, then I was flung about from man to man. Men police lay hands on us. By men we are examined, handled, doctored and messed about with. We are had up before magistrates who are men, and we never get out of the hands of men.[1]

The epithet arises too from a society which was overtly class-ridden and where taxonomisation had become a near obsession. But though references to the 'common prostitute' found in social, legal and medical sources were numerous they were as confusing as they were contradictory, an ambiguity that has been inherited into the present day.

Perhaps the main area wherein categorisation and definition were most apparent was in the medical field, where Dr William Acton, the notorious Victorian physician, is considered the major proponent. He distinguished between three classes of prostitute: the 'kept woman' who resides with a paramour, the common prostitute who is at service with slight reservation of the first comer and attempts no other means of life, and the woman whose prostitution is a subsidiary calling. One of his chief purposes however, was to humanise the prostitute and to persuade the Victorian public, who viewed her as a 'pariah' or 'social leper', that the main cause of prostitution was 'cruel biting poverty' and 'the lowness of the wages paid to workwomen in various trades'[2] The visiting surgeon of the Devenport Lock Hospital, in his evidence to the 1869 Select Committee, said of the 'common prostitute', I would define them as women who habitually gain their livelihood partly or wholly by the proceeds of prostitution'.[3] The term 'common prostitute' was also widely used in gynaecology and in medical jurisprudence. For instance, in a chapter which deals with rape, J.G. Smith in *The Principles of Forensic Medicine,* first published in 1824, wrote:

> The crime is not only equally atrocious, whether committed on the person of a virgin or of a married woman but also if the subject be of ill fame . . . even a common prostitute . . . but the strongest corroboration is required if she is unchaste or a strumpet.[4]

Victorian social critics used the term in various ways. W.R. Greg remarked that the term 'common' was widely considered to mean 'poor'.[5] To add to an already abundant confusion what is perhaps of greater import is to contemplate the relative impact such definitions had upon the codification of law and upon legal practice. Whilst the term 'common prostitute' had been used in law since 1822, classes or types of prostitute continued to be differentiated as the predilection for distinguishing between levels of morality prevailed. In the Report of the Metropolitan Police, London, 1857, three classes of such women were carefully demarcated; there being well-dressed prostitutes, well-dressed streetwalkers, and prostitutes infesting neighbourhoods.[6] The bootlegging of this construct into twentieth-century statute and case law is an anachronism which is difficult to explain.

The 'common prostitute' in law

Under British criminal jurisdiction the prostitute is not only exclusively female but is also regarded as a 'common prostitute'. However, the precise meaning of this term has never been defined in statute, and attempts at such a clarification in case law, such as they are, have been unsatisfactory. It is interesting that this democracy with its high value and regard for sexual equality continues undeterred to employ this label with a tenacity which competes well with Victorian morality. And it is to be noted with some consternation that the application of the term has persisted whilst many other criminal codes, with notably few exceptions (Western Australia Police Act 1892–1972, and New Zealand's criminal statutes, for example), have for some time abolished the use of this flagrantly condemnatory label. It is an offence for a ' "common prostitute" to loiter and importune passengers in or upon a public place for the purpose of prostitution' (Police Offences Act, section 46), and in Western Australia an offence is committed by 'Any "common prostitute" who shall solicit, importune or acost any person or persons' (section 59) and 'Every "common prostitute" wandering in the public street or highways' (section 65(8)). In Canada, however, moves are presently underway to secure the abolition of the term (Working Paper on Vagrancy and Street Offences 1974).

The term in British law makes its first appearance in the Vagrancy Act 1822, the later consolidating Vagrancy Act of 1824 providing for the prosecution of 'every common prostitute' wandering in the public streets or public highways, (and behaving in a riotous or indecent manner) . . . shall be deemed to be an idle and disorderly person within the true intent and meaning of the Act'. Subsequent statutes similarly referred to such women as 'common prostitutes'. Section 54(11) of the Metropolitan Police Act 1839 also introduced the prosecution of 'nighwalkers', although as was the case with the term 'common prostitute' no statutory definition of 'nightwalker' was provided. However within this statute the regulation of particular behaviour was more specifically defined, thus providing for the prosecution of a 'common prostitute' or 'nightwalker' for loitering or being in a public place for the purpose of prostitution or soliciting, and this particular use and application of the term 'common prostitute' is evident in later statutes (Town Police Clauses Act 1847, section 28).

Later legislation in the guise of the Criminal Law Amendment Act 1885 and the Vagrancy Act (1898) played a marginal role in regulating their activities. Already conflicting interests in the desire to control were in evidence. In the various stages of the Criminal Law Amendment Bill a move was made to abolish the term 'common prostitute' and 'nightwalker' and to insert 'person' in its place. It was a move which did not succeed.[7] Instead when the Act came into force police powers were considerably extended despite much opposition to the clause, expressed amongst others by the Marquess of Lothian who asserted that as the clause stood any lady speaking to a lord in the street would be at the mercy of policemen. The Earl of Milltown similarly opposing the clause maintained that it placed injudicious power in police hands.[8]

In the case law, *de Munck* [1918] 1 KB 635 is generally accepted as the first attempt at a definition of the term. The presiding judge in his deliberation had this to say:

> The term "common prostitute" is not limited so as to mean only one who per-mits acts of lewdness with all and sundry, or with such as have [*sic*] her, when such acts are in the nature of ordinary sexual connection. We are of the opinion that prostitution is proved if it be shown that a woman *offers her body* com-monly for lewdness for payment in return.

The application and meaning of the phrase came up for some further discussion in *Webb* (1963) 127 *JP* 516, [1964] 1 QB 357, 3 *All ER* 177–9, where the judge explained that the behaviour of girls in a 'massage parlour', part of whose job was to masturbate men, constituted acting as 'common prostitutes'. Thus the meaning of the term was widened to include not only those who offered their body but those who actively did something to the client. The appeal is interesting since it turned on the proper meaning of the term 'common prostitute'.

Whilst the law has used the term to denote a woman who sells her body to all in common, the social definition of a 'common prostitute' as a woman who is low and of bad character has been allowed to persist uncontested. And it seems clear that whatever the legal meaning announced in *de Munck* the fact that the very different social nuance has persisted reveals the desire to maintain its policing function. The continued stigmatisation of this group of women by the use of this pejorative label has performed a clear social control function. Yet in this dualistic attempt of enforcing law and enforcing a standard of morality the law has overstepped its mark, with the result that the continued application of the concept constitutes a legal impropriety of the grossest kind. For this is the only occasion within criminal law, with the exception of the use of the label 'incorrigible rogue' under the 1824 Vagrancy Act, (James 1951: 33) where a defendant is branded as 'guilty' even before the case is heard. Whatever the legal meaning of the concept, since it is clear that its usage implies an acquired status where one act of prostitution would constitute 'acting as a "common prostitute" ',[9] the intransigent reluctance to abandon the concept reveals a moral function above and beyond the function of law itself. This acquired status is also expressed by women themselves: 'It's as if — you did it once, you become it' (Millett 1975: 65). It is hard to believe that when the Wolfenden Committee needed a term to describe the streetwalker they once again made use of this label, 'finding no evidence that injustice results from its use in legislation'. (Smith and Hogan 1965: 316.)

On the contrary, there is a growing mountain of evidence that whatever the term may be taken to mean gross injustice flows from its application, the nature of which opponents of the Street Offences Bill preceding the 1959 Act were acutely aware. For instance, during discussions of clause 1 of the Standing Committee consideration of the Bill ('loitering or soliciting for the purpose of prostitution'), Mr. A. Greenwood moved an amendment to omit the term 'common prostitute' and to put 'any person' in its place. It was a valiant attempt which fell on stony ground and the 1959 Act opened with relentless vigour: 'It shall be an offence for a "common prostitute" . . . '. However, this legislative implementation did not silence the many critics who persisted in voicing their dissension. The misappropriation of the term came up once again for debate in the discussions central to the Street Offences Bill of 1968. The Bill strove to amend the Street Offences Act first by substituting the term 'other person' for the words 'common prostitute', and second by abolishing the phrase 'for the purposes of prostitution' substituting in its place 'immoral purposes'.[10] Criticism of the term has been stepped up during the last decade and objections submitted to the Working Party on Vagrancy and Street Offences professed that the term was 'at best derogatory and at worst prejudicial'. More recently certain evidence submitted to the Criminal Law Revision Committee 1982 has been particularly concerned that the term has been construed to imply an acquired status. In this respect, the Justices Clerks' Society have suggested that the term implies she was a person of previous bad character, and not, as the legal connotation intimates, that she is one who hands out her services to all in common.

Since 1976 we have witnessed an increasing politicisation of the prostitute who, supported by prostitutes' collectives and by women's organisations and no longer prepared to pay lip service to the courts, can amongst other things be seen to refuse the offer of probation assistance and openly to challenge police evidence. Consider the abstract from the following transcript of a case heard at Highbury Corner Magistrates' Court.

Case 1 : Not guilty, unrepresented
Defendant (upon entering the courtroom):   Can I just say something?
Court clerk: (Explains procedure.)
Police constable: I saw a woman who I know to be a common prostitute . . . she was walking slowly . . . bending at the hips and looking into a vehicle [car registration number read out in court] . . . the woman continued to walk north . . .and approached a second vehicle [car registration number read out]. This vehicle had only one male occupant. I saw the woman wave her right hand in the air and appear to wave the driver . . . [third car registration number given] . . . I then saw Miss X walk up to the car, I saw her lean into the car and appear to speak to the driver. She then walked briskly away. I stopped the woman and arrested her for soliciting. She replied 'It's not fair; I get nicked more than the other girls.'
Magistrate: Do you wish to ask any questions?
Defendant: I disagree with it all [sighs]. You don't wave to people, it's silly!

During the last few years the formation of PROS (Prostitutes Reform of the Law on Soliciting). PLAN (Prostitution Laws Are Nonsense) and ECP (English Collective of Prostitutes) reflects the growing politicisation of prostitutes as a group whose key demands are to abolish imprisonment for offences of loitering and soliciting (and so section 71 of the Criminal Justice Act will be welcomed) to abolish the term 'common prostitute', and most importantly ultimately to remove the activity from the jurisdiction of the criminal law.

An administration of injustice — 'that you being a "common prostitute" did solicit . . . '

The main concern arising from the judicial application of the term is that it results in the administration of injustice and not justice. The Working Party on Vagrancy anc Street Offences (1974: 74) remarked that one of the main criticisms of the present law and administration of justice within it 'is that to brand an accused person as a "common prostitute" when she first appears before a court applies to her an offensive label which may confirm her in her way of life or predispose the court against her'. Indeed, one of the two objectives of the Imprisonment of Prostitutes (Abolition) Bill (4 April 1981) was to abolish the use of the term 'common prostitute'.

The administration of criminal justice in this country is founded on the judicial principle of an *a priori* presumption of innocence, though certain critics maintain that this is no more than a quaint concept no longer practicable since public safety must be balanced against this clandestine right. Thus in not-guilty pleas defendants may be refused bail if for instance the offence is serious or there is reason to believe that the defendant will not be present for the court appearance. The rules regulating the conduct of British criminal procedure are then only more or less based upon this notion of due process. The system incorporates many safeguards to ensure that this fundamental civil liberty is not undermined. In order that this cardinal principle may be honoured the accused is presumed innocent until guilt is proved beyond reasonable doubt. The accused is also protected from character assassination by certain rules of evidence, and matters relating to antecedent criminal record are rendered inadmissible. This has been a principle of long standing. According to Lord Herschell (*Makin* v *Attorney-General of New South Wales* [1894] AC 57 at p.65), it is inadmissible to show that the defendant may have a propensity to commit that sort of crime.

But as Sanders (1979) observes, 'the criminal process in action systematically deviates from these rules in practice'.[11] The persistent use of the phrase 'common prostitute', both at the police station and in the court is a flagrant abuse of these cardinal principles, a glaring instance of this systematic deviation. Its usage perverts justice and abrogates the fundamental rights of defendants. Moreover, the consequence of the use of this term, as I will .later demonstrate, is to undermine one of the most impelling of all rights in the criminal justice system, the exercise of choice as to plea. This right is conspicuously threatened since the very application of the pejorative and condemning label strongly influences the defendant's perception of the partiality of the legal process, thereby often inducing a plea of guilt. The substantial forfeiture of right of trial is a significant feature of this offence.

A sample of prostitutes was interviewed in April 1982 in Moss Side, Manchester, with the precise objective of assessing whether a prostitute is condemned before she is heard when addressed in court '. . . that you being a "common prostitute" did solicit'; and whether this wording of the charge in any way at all influences the defendant's free choice as to plea. The results were overwhelming if not altogether surprising with all the interviewees sharing the view that their's was a condemned case, whilst 80 per cent provided more specific objections to the application of the label. Some maintained that it was unfair whilst 27 per cent thought it embarrassing and unnecessary. A smaller proportion of 25 per cent considered the label perverted the course of justice and actually affected the way in which the magistrates arrived at their judgment. Some resisted the use of the term altogether, declaring most emphatically that they were not 'common'!

Certainly any seasoned and experienced observer of court procedure in cases involving female defendants appearing on charges of loitering or soliciting for the purpose of prostitution will be only too aware of the constant reference to the defendant as a 'common prostitute' from the onset of the court hearing. In the course of the research a total of fifty-one such cases were observed at Manchester City Magistrates' Court, over a period of nine months and a handful of cases observed at an Inner London Magistrates' Court. Before proceeding to assess the effect on the impartial administration of such application of this label as perceived by defendants, let us first examine its viability and recurrent usage in the context of the court process, as is demonstrated in the following abstracts of recent cases.

Case 1: Highbury Corner Magistrates' Court, (Inner London), not represented
Court clerk: You Ms X on 22 January 1982, being a 'common prostitute' did loiter in — , in the borough of Islington, for the purposes of prostitution. What do you plead, Guilty or Not Guilty?
Defendant: Guilty!
Court clerk: Guilty.
Police prosecution witness: At 1.30p.m. Miss X a common prostitute was seen paying particular attention to passing vehicles with lone males inside.
Antecedents: The defendant has eight previous convictions . . . and her four children are in care.
Stipendiary Magistrate: Were the victims in the offence her children? [The defendant was walking with two children when she was arrested for soliciting]
Pol. pros. wit.: No.
Stip. mag.: Have you got anything you would like to say to the Court?
Def.: I've got nothing at all to say. I don't believe in living on social security so I do the only thing I can.
Stip. mag.: What about finding a job?
Def.: I can't get work. I'm supposed to be registered disabled, but I'm not.
Stip. mag.: Very well, pay a fine of £20.
Def.: Can I have time to pay?
Stip. mag.: No! You don't need time, you have it on you.
Def.: I have nothing on me.
Stip. mag.: You will go back out to pay.
Def.: Well, I won't be going out tonight!

Case 2: Manchester City Magistrates' Court, unrepresented

Court clerk: You, Ms Y, on 23rd June 1981, being a 'common prostitute' did
  oiter in Great Western Street in the City of Manchester for the purposes of
  prostitution. Guilty or Not Guilty?

Defendant: Guilty

Prosecution: At 11.30p.m. on Wednesday 23 June two policemen were on duty
  in Great Western Street, Moss Side, and observed the defendant who was bending and peering into passing motor vehicles, especially those driven by lone
  males. At 11.35p.m. a yellow Hillman Avenger stopped. The defendant had a
  short conversation with the driver through the open window before the car
  drove off. She continued her previous actions. At 11.40 p.m. a second car
  stopped. She appeared to be about to get into the car when the policemen approached her and informed her of what they had seen. She replied 'Guilty'.
  The defendant was taken to the police station where she was cautioned and
  charged to which she made no reply.] The defendant is divorced and lives in a
  rented flat with her two children. She is in receipt of Social Security Benefit.
  [Her previous convictions were then read out in court, the last conviction for
  loitering for the purpose of prostitution being 21 February 1980 for which she
  was given a conditional discharge.]

Chairman of the Bench of Magistrates: Is there anything you have to say?

Defendant: I have just moved into a new house and I needed the money to buy
  some furniture.

Chairman: Conditional discharge for 2 years and £10 costs, because the conditional discharge seems to have worked last time.

In the transcript that follows the defendant was represented and probably
therefore had a better opportunity to put forward mitigating circumstances in
negotiation of sentencing outcome.

Case 3: Manchester City Magistrates' Court, represented

Court clerk: You, on 22 June 1981, being a common prostitute did loiter in a
  certain street called Range Road, in the City of Manchester, for the purposes
  of prostitution. Guilty or Not Guilty.

Defendant: Guilty.

Prosecuting solicitor: On Tuesday 22 June 1981 at 10.15 p.m. two police officers commenced observations in Range Road, Whalley Range – a road frequented by prostitutes and their clients. They observed the defendant bending
  and peering into passing motor vehicles, paying particular attention to those
  driven by lone males. A number of cars slowed down as they passed the defendant. After ten minutes had passed a blue Vauxhall car stopped. The defendant

had a conversation with the driver of the car, and opened the passenger seat door when the two police officers approached her, informed her of what they had seen. She was cautioned and charged when taken to the Police Station and made no reply.

The defendant had £3.70 in her possession when arrested. She is in receipt of Social Security and Child Benefit, and lives in Council accommodation with an eighteen-month-old-son. Four previous convictions for similar offences and in breach of a conditional discharge given on 9 March 1981.

Defence solicitor: [Stresses that the defendant's attitude has been one of complete co-operation with the arresting officers.] There are various reasons why girls commit this offence. It is not easy as one might think to bring up a young baby as a single parent. The father of the child pays no money to the defendant and he has an appalling criminal record. Her total income is £40.20 p.w. and she pays £18 per week rent and £2 for items on hire purchase. She tells me the reason she committed the offence was that she had a gas bill of £125 to pay. She doesn't find it easy to make ends meet and I urge you to deal with her as leniently as possible.

Magistrate: You will be fined £20 and £10 costs plus £20 for breaching conditional discharge.

The greatest impropriety can be observed in the use and application of this term, particularly in contested cases where the rights of the accused should be protected. Consider the prejudicial application of the label in the contested cases that follow.

Case 1.1. Manchester City Magistrates' Court, contested, dismissed

Court clerk: That on 14 September 1981 you, being a common prostitute, did loiter on a certain street, namely Alexandra Road South in the City of Manchester, for the purposes of prostitution. Guilty or Not guilty?

Defendant: Not guilty.

Prosecuting solicitor: The prosecution case is that at 11.10 p.m. on Monday 14 September two policemen on plain-clothes duty in Alexandra Road South saw the defendant bending and peering into vehicles driven by lone males. One car slowed down but didn't stop. One car stopped. The defendant had a short conversation with the driver and got into the passenger seat. The two policemen stopped the car and informed her of what they had seen. She replied 'guilty'. [Before the two police witnesses gave evidence a statement was read out from a policeman who was in court when the defendant received a conviction for an earlier loiter prostitution charge.]
[The second policeman was allowed to be in court when first police officer gave his evidence-in-chief.]
Give evidence to the court of what happened on that day.

First police witness (referring to his notebook):   At 11.10 p.m. on Alexandra
   Road South in Whalley Range I commenced observation on the defendant who
   was standing close to the pavement bending and peering into passing motor
   cars paying particular attention to those driven by lone males. At 11.12 p.m. a
   Ford Escort came along the road from the direction of Moss Lane East. It
   slowed down. The defendant moved towards the vehicle — but it did not stop
   continuing along Alexandra Road South. At 11.15 p.m. a Volkswagen slowed
   down. She commenced a conversation with the driver through the passenger
   window. P. got into the front seat. The car was about to drive off, but we approached the car, arrested and cautioned her. She replied, 'Oh no you can't'.

Defending solicitor: Most of what you have said is not denied, so I have only a
   few questions to ask. Can you remember what the weather was like?

1 pol. wit.:   Possibly it was raining.

Def. sol.:   You agree that the evidence and observation is reasonably standard in
   these matters.

1 pol. wit.:   Yes

Def. sol.:   You say she was peering into all vehicles.

1 pol. wit.:   Yes, but especially those driven by lone males.

Def. sol.:   Isn't it the case that she appeared to be thumbing a lift?

1 pol. wit.:   No, not in the usual manner.

Def. sol.:   Couldn't you accept that she was trying to get a lift on a rainy night?

1 pol. wit.:   She could have been but in my opinion she was loitering for the purposes of prostitution.

Def. sol.:   Don't you think you could be jumping to conclusions because she is a
   known common prostitute?

1 pol. wit.:   No.

Def sol.:   I also put it to you that when she was charged she did not say 'Guilty'.

1 pros. wit.:   She did.

Pros. sol.:   Is the evidence given by the first witness right to the best of your
   knowledge?

Second prosecution witness (referring to the same notebook):   Yes.

Pros. sol.:   Did you have the defendant in your field of vision all the time?

2 pol. wit.:   Yes.

Pros. sol.:   At no time was she thumbing a lift?

2 pol. wit.:   No.

Pros. sol.:   Was it raining?

2 pol. wit.:   I can't remember.

Pros. sol.:   If it was an extremely bad night would you have remembered it?

2 pol. wit.:   Yes.

Def. sol.:   You would agree that in cases of this kind that the evidence you give is standard.

2 pol. wit.: Yes.

Def. sol.: You didn't hear any of the conversation that took place between the defendant and the driver of the car.

2 pol. wit.: No.

[That is the case for the prosecution]

Def. sol.: On this particular day can you remember where you had been during the afternoon?

Def.: I had been to your office.

Def. sol.: Was your appointment at 4.30 p.m?

Def.: Yes.

Def. sol.: Did you leave at 5.30 p.m?

Def.: Yes.

Def. sol.: And you visited three pubs?

Def.: Yes.

Def. sol.: Had you had a lot to drink?

Def.: Not really. About 3½ pints of bitter.

Def. sol.: Were you with Mr Granada until 9.30 p.m?

Def.: Yes.

Def. sol.: Where did he go at 9.30 p.m?

Def.: He went home. I had to go to my friends in Alexandra Park Estate to get some clothes because I was soaking wet. It was like a monsoon.

Def. sol.: Was anyone in at your friend's house?

Def.: No. So I went to the Great Western.

Def. sol.: Did you leave at closing time?

Def.: Yes.

Def. sol.: Did you make a telephone call?

Def.: Yes.

Def. sol.: It's accepted that you have previous convictions and that you were in the area on that particular night, but did you have any intention of loitering for prostitution that night?

Def.: No.

Def. sol.: How long have you been living with Mr Granada?

Def.: About ten months.

Def. sol.: What does he think of your past behaviour?

Def.: He says, 'Everyone has done something wrong in their lives'.

Def. sol.: So after the phone call what were you doing?

Def.: Trying to get home. One car stopped, he said, 'Are you doing business? I said, 'No, but can I have a lift home please?' He said, 'No.' Then another car stopped and he agreed to give me a lift. I got in the car and it was then that the police stopped me.

Pros. sol.: I don't wish to appear unkind but you have had a drink problem?

Def.: Yes.

Pros. sol.: And regarding the weather. It seems to have had a lasting impression on you. It's therefore surprising that neither of the police officers can remember it.

Def.: Well, I had no coat and only sandals on.

Pros. sol.: You say you were going home. How far is Alexandra Road South from where you live?

Def.: About $\frac{3}{4}$ hour walk.

Pros. sol.: How was it that you only managed to stop cars driven by lone males?

Def.: I've got very bad eyesight in the dark. It could have been a woman with short hair. And I don't have to bend to look into cars.

Pros. sol.: So you were hitching a lift were you, Mrs Poulton?

Def.: Yes.

Pros. sol.: No further questions.

Def.: I'm really annoyed. I used to be a clerk/typist but no one calls you that for the rest of your life.

Def. sol.: You live with the defendant?

Second defence witness: Yes.

Def. sol.: You know about Mrs Poulton's previous convictions?

Def. wit.: I do.

Def. sol.: You have lived with her for some time. During that time are you aware that she has gone back 'on the game'?

Def. wit.: Not that I know of.

Def. sol.: You spend most of your time together.

Def. wit.: Yes.

Def. sol.: That night you were with the defendant to about 9.30 p.m.

Def. wit.: Yes, at the Snooty Fox. Then I went home. She went to see a friend because she was wet through and she wanted to get changed.

Def. sol.: And when at home you had a phone call from Mrs Poulton to say she was on her way home?

Def. wit.: Yes.

Pros. sol.: You weren't with the defendant at 11.10 p.m.?

Def. wit.: No.

Pros. sol.: No further questions.

Def. sol. [summing up]: The facts are that if you are going to convict her you must question that she made that phone call to her cohabitee. This would be unusual if she was going to loiter for prostitution.

You cannot either convict her on the evidence of the conversation that took place between the defendant and the driver of the car because there are no witnesses to say that the conversation wasn't as she said. It is a great shame that the man in the car can't come along to give evidence on her behalf. If you convict her you will have to say that any woman walking through Moss Side at that time of night is likely to be arrested for loitering. I have to say that there is some reasonable doubt and for that reason you cannot convict her.

Magistrates (who did not retire in order to decide):   There is some doubt in our mind. Case dismissed.

Case 2: Manchester City Magistrates' Court contested, convicted
Court clerk: That on 8 May 1981 you, being a common prostitute, did loiter on a certain street, namely Newton Street in the City of Manchester, for the purposes of prostitution.
Defendant: Not guilty.
Prosecuting solicitor: The case involves two police officers. The defendant, prior to the 8 May, had been cautioned on 23 March and 17 April by the same officers who took up observations on her on the night in question in Newton Street. She kept stopping males and talking to them. She didn't stop any women passers-by. She also flagged down cars driven by lone males. When the police officers approached her her reply was, 'I won't do it again if you let me off.' When cautioned she said 'What about all the other girls who are doing it?' and when formally arrested said, 'I wasn't loitering.'
Pros. sol.:   On 8 May at 10.05 p.m. were you sitting in an unmarked police car in Newton Street?
First police witness (referring to his notebook):   Yes
[Second police witness listened to evidence-in-chief]
Pros. sol.:   On plain-clothes duty?
1 pol. wit.:   Yes.
Pros. sol.:   When you parked your vehicle at the junction of Newton Street and Dale Street what did you see?
1 pol. wit.:   I saw the defendant outside Papas' Club.
Pros. sol.:   Was she known to you?
1 pol. wit.:   Yes.
Pros. sol.:   Had she been cautioned twice previously?
1 pol. wit.:   Yes.
Pros. sol.:   You know she has fourteen previous convictions which date back to 1965?
1 pol. wit.:   Yes.
Pros. sol.:   What did you see?

1 pol. wit.:   I saw the defendant stop a white male. She appeared to have a short conversation with the man. He shook his head and walked quickly away. A few minutes later she had a second conversation with another male. This ended in the same way. This happened three more times. I then saw her flag down a car.

Pros. sol.:   During all this time where was the other police officer?

1 pol. wit.:   He was in the car with me.

Pros. sol.:   Could you hear any of the conversation which the defendant had with the men.

1 pol wit.:   No.

Pros. sol.:   What happened then?

1 pol. wit.:   P.C. Buxton drove the car up the road toward her. She began to walk away very quickly. I got out of the car. She started to run. I caught her by the wrist, identified myself, cautioned and charged her. She replied, 'Give us a chance, officer. I won't do it again.' She was arrested and taken to the Police Station where she said, 'I'm sorry I did it.' I said, 'Do you admit it?' She said, 'I will if you give us a caution.' I said, 'I am arresting you,' so she said, 'I'll plead not guilty then, you sod.'

Def. sol.:   Is it right that you went into a public-house, the Wheatsheaf, where you were seen by the defendant?

1 pol. wit.:   I don't remember seeing her.

Def. sol.:   She remembers you from years ago and she went out of the pub quickly to get away from you.

1 pol. wit.:   I don't remember seeing her in the pub.

Def. sol.:   You remember seeing someone called Big Bertha. And you know that where she is the defendant usually is.

1 pol. wit.:   Yes, they do go around together.

Def. sol.:   You arrested her because you wanted to arrest her – not because she was loitering for the purposes of prostitution.

1 pol. wit.:   No.

Def. sol.:   Have you asked her on several occasions since the arrest what she was going to plead and that if she pleaded not guilty you said you would arrest her every time you saw her?

1 pol wit. :   No, I did ask her what she was going to plead, but nothing else.

Pros. sol.:   To clarify the point – have you in fact arrested her since May for loitering offences?

1 pol. wit.:   No.

Def. sol.:   You have heard what your colleague has said. You made the the notes together. Do you think they are a true version of the account?

Second police witness: Yes.

Def. sol.: Before the arrest took place did you stop outside the Wheatsheaf public house?

2 pol. wit.: I don't remember.

Def. sol.: I am not asking you for a massive feat of recall.

2 pol. wit.: I don't recall my colleague going in to the Wheatsheaf.

Def. sol.: I put it to you that he did go in the pub.

2 pol wit.: As far as I remember I do not think so.

Def. sol.: So you say I'm wrong in saying this.

2 pol. wit.: I don't know. I don't remember.

Def. sol.: I put it to you that you had decided to go out that night purposefully to look for the defendant.

2 pol. wit.: No.

Def. sol.: All right, you had gone out to look for Big Bertha.

2 pol. wit.: No.

Def. sol.: Had you seen Big Bertha?

2 pol. wit.: I don't recall.

Def. sol.: Did she come up and talk to you in the police car?

2 pol. wit.: I don't remember.

Def. sol.: You can't remember very much.

2 pol. wit.: Only the bare facts of the case that have already been referred to by the other police officer.

Def. sol.: I put it to you that you can't remember anything other than parroting what is in your notebook.

2 pol. wit.: The event did happen.

That is the end of the prosecution case

Def. sol.: On the night in question you had been out with a friend.

Defendant: Yes. Bertha. I had been in the park and I met her there. We went to the Wheatsheaf. I saw the first officer in there. He had been at Bury a few years ago when I lived up there. I said to her, 'He keeps staring at me.' I don't like people staring at me so we went out of the pub.

Def. sol.: So you were loitering in the street?

Def.: No, I just walked round the corner and they got hold of me and pushed me in the car.

Def. sol.: You made a statement at the police station.

Def.: Didn't make any statement because I hadn't done anything wrong.

Def. sol.: Would you flag cars down?

Def.: No, I'm too frightened. I wouldn't go in a car with a strange man.

Def. sol.: Had you spoken to any passers-by?

Def.: No. I stood on the corner of Newton Street for a second, but I only spoke to Bertha.

Pros. sol.: Is Bertha in court?

Def.: No. She had a letter to appear but she didn't come.

Pros. sol.: You have been cautioned twice before?

Def.: Yes.

Pros sol.: You have fourteen previous convictions?

Def.: Yes.

Pros sol.: But you say you wouldn't stop strange men?

Def.: I would have to know who they were.

Pros. sol.: You stopped four men walking and one in a car.

Def.: I didn't get the chance. I had just come out of the pub.

Pros. sol.: The police officers couldn't have been mistaken. They knew you. They kept a careful watch on you.

Def.: I didn't stop no fellas.

Pros. sol.: When arrested didn't you say 'Give us a chance'?

Def.: No. I never did. He came and spoke to me in the park.

Def. sol. (submission): I find it difficult to see how the court could be impressed with the two police officers' evidence. The second officer was intent on not saying any more than what was written in his notebook. I would ask you to look with some compassion at this case. It is a matter for you to decide – but if you look at the practicalities of the matter, would you sleep with this woman? What sort of prospect has she as a prostitute?

[Magistrates retired to decide and returned to find the case proved. Previous convictions given.]

Def. sol. (mitigation): The defendant has suffered from various medical complaints. I submit a doctor's note to the court. You may think realistically that her career as a prostitute is at an end. She is in receipt of £40 a week social security and pays £7 a week rent plus large gas and electricity bills. I ask you to deal leniently with her.

Magistrates: Fined £20 + £5 costs.

Inducing guilty pleas

The application of the term 'common prostitute' in criminal proceedings has had a much greater and more profound influence on the criminal justice system than to be merely discriminatory, to challenge such self-definitions of women or to disadvantage their case before presiding magistrates. The belief that the application of the term 'common prostitute' is regarded as an acquired status and biases their case before it is heard is a fact which influences both the defendants' choice as to plea, and magistrates' conviction and sentence.

It has been stated elsewhere in more general terms that a defendant's decision as to plea is the single most important aspect of decision-making in the penal process (Bottomley 1973: 105). Whilst any efficiency in the administration of criminal justice would cease if all defendants in exercising this right pleaded not guilty, it is perhaps of some significance that any prostitute challenges the system and pleads not guilty at all.

Regardless of the offence, defendants are exposed to divers inducements to plead guilty which vary from bail conditions or an earlier hearing to a sentencing discount. Defendants may be persuaded to plead guilty to a lesser, often alternative charge or simply to plead guilty. The pay-offs in administration terms are obvious since the backlog of cases is cut down considerably and the administrative process speeded up. But over recent years injudicious tampering with this justice mechanism has produced much criticism since such machinations are not always in the defendants' best interests.

Baldwin and McConville (1977) in research into the question of plea bargaining found that unfair pressure was put on defendants which led the researchers to conclude that in some cases defendants who pleaded guilty might not have committed the offence in question. But defendants have always been subject to pressures, and this has been a particularly sensitive area following the decision in *R v Turner* (1970) 54 CAR 352.

The negotiations principally revolve around questions of sentencing discount where the defendant pleads guilty and it is well known that defendants are given 'credit' for their admission. If however lawyers bend justice to conform to their administrative or personal requirements and if judges offer deals on the basis of factors extraneous to justice this is a real cause for concern and since much of the plea bargaining takes place between the prosecution, defence and judge in chambers the question of 'in whose best interests' becomes unanswerable.

Indeed as the *Sunday Times* writers Phillip Knightley and Elaine Potter discovered, the £2000 fine imposed in the notorious *Allen* rape case was in fact the result of a thirty-minute plea bargaining session in the judge's chambers. But as Michael Zander points out (*Guardian,* 12 July 1982) 'plea bargaining is an integral, necessary and, on the whole beneficial part of the system . . . Well over 90 per cent of the two million or more cases dealt with by the criminal courts end with a guilty plea. If it were not so the system would grind to a halt.' However, in some cases defendants are subject to unfair pressures to plead guilty. In a trial for a trivial offence at Manchester Crown Court the judge after the first day of hearing said to the defending counsel, 'Mr. X, could you have a word with your client? We could clear this up very quickly. I have in mind a fine.' The defendant did not capitulate, and could be heard outside the courtroom during the adjournment protesting her innocence and refusing to change her plea.

Suzanne Dell (1978) in a study of female defendants found that certain kinds of offences were particularly associated with inconsistent pleas – that is cases where women pleaded guilty but in fact privately protested their innocence. An immediate concern was to what extent these defendants had, indeed if they had, been subject to unfair pressures. Of Dell's sample of 527, 106 denied having committed any offence yet of those denials 56 actually pleaded guilty. A comparison was then conducted between the 47 consistent and 56 inconsistent pleaders. Three main ways in which the two groups differed related to the type of offence. for which they were charged, whether defendants were remanded in custody and whether they had representation. Among the inconsistent pleaders, offences like soliciting and drunkenness were more frequent, and legal advice was noticeably less evident amongst this group.

Dell found that soliciting was particularly associated with inconsistent pleas of fifty-nine girls charged with this offence – all but one unrepresented. There were twenty-seven denials whilst eighteen pleaded guilty. The majority of the inconsistent first offenders – nine out of fourteen – gave police advice or pressure as their reason for pleading guilty. Some said police had threatened them that they would be 'sent down' if they pleaded not guilty. Others said that they had been told that they would 'get off' with a fine or probation. Others had been told that it was the simplest way to get the case over with quickly. Zander (*Guardian*, 12 July 1982) maintains that plea bargaining takes place in three different stages of the process: 'By far the most frequent and the least studied is in the police station.'

Inconsistent pleaders

In interviewing prostitutes outside the court process at the pre-trial caution/arrest stage in Moss Side, Manchester, an alarming proportion of the sample were clearly inconsistent pleaders. Whilst not denying that they were prostitutes they certainly denied that they were committing an offence at the time they were cautioned or arrested. In order to cast some light on these admissions of legal guilt the interviewees were asked in general terms whether they preferred guilty pleas because they considered the system against them. 22 per cent of those interviewed said that the invocation of the label 'common prostitute' induced a plea of guilty. 18 per cent said they pleaded guilty to 'get it over'. 13.6 per cent pleaded guilty because they believed it had certain advantages for being granted bail, and 50 per cent said they pleaded guilty because the stakes were stacked against them. Of course these accounts were rendered by a very small sub-sample of defendants, representing only 12.7 per cent of the total number of defendants appearing on this charge before the City Magistrates' Court in 1981. But the findings interestingly compare with the results of Dell's study.

Prevaricate pleaders

In the Manchester court study, out of a total of 299 cases of loitering for the purpose of prostitution proceeded with, 273 defendants said they were going to plead not guilty from the onset (see Table 2:1, cols 1,2,5). Of these seventy three, only fifty (17 per cent) actually pleaded not guilty on the day the case was dealt with (cols 1.2). Twenty three of the seventy-three defendants initially pleading not guilty entered pleas of guilty on the final day. Thus a total of 8 per cent of cases changed their plea at the last moment. Of those who elected for summary trial from the onset 8 per cent changed their plea to guilty on the day fixed for the hearing. In all these cases a considerable number of adjournments had provided defendants with the opportunity to reconsider the appropriateness of their plea. What then were the reasons for this last-minute change of heart? It has been suggested that plea changes of this nature may be indicative of defendants being subject to unfair pressures. Unfortunately the scope of this study did not allow for consideration of the exact proportion of the plea changes which may have been of this kind.

Table 2:1 *Prostitution: plea and outcome (showing the distribution of pleas and contested cases involving loitering and soliciting offences before Manchester City Magistrates' Court, 1981)*

Sentence	All defendants by representation and plea					All defendants by age			
	1	2	3	4	5				
	NG R	NG NR	G R	G NR	NG to GR	20	21–39	40+	Complete total
Absolute discharge	1		7	3		3	7	1	11
Conditional discharge	5	1	31	21	3	15	42	4	61
Fine	9		46	46	8	31	74	4	109
Probation order	3		20	7	3	6	26	1	33
Hospital order									
Community service order	1		6	1	3	2	9		11
Suspended sentence	5		20	4	2	6	20	5	31
Imprisonment			12	1	4	4	10	3	17
Total	24	1	142	83	23	67	188	18	273
Committed to Crown Court for trial									
Committed for sentence			1				1		1
Already in. Deferred sentence	2		15		1	5	13		18
Case withdrawn									
Case dismissed	22	3				2	22	1	25

Indeed, the findings reveal contrary tendencies which suggest that for this offence at least the last-minute plea change is not an indication of indecision, capriciousness, or confusion, instead it is a deliberate strategy of 'working the system'. However, in this as in other areas the same question — whether it is in the best interests of the defendant, or her representatives – arises. Of those who changed their plea at the last possible moment, 17 per cent had adopted this strategy on more than one occasion during that year.

Table 2:2 shows the proportion of defendants pleading guilty in each offence category. The highest proportion of defendants contesting their case was for assault and crimes of violence where presumably there was conflicting evidence of who did what to whom. Sixteen per cent of the Manchester sample of defendants on charges arising from offences related to prostitution contested their case; half of this percentage was the result of plea changes.

Table 2.2   A comparison of the proportion of not-guilty pleas in each offence category of female defendants before Manchester City Magistrates' Court, 1981

Offence	Final pleas by %		Plea change total	
	Guilty	Not guilty	% of sample	Sample number
Violence	76.6	23.4	2.0	98
Burglary	90.8	9.2	3.7	54
Theft/handling	92.8	7.2	3.2	1,156
Fraud/forgery	87.4	12.6	2.5	158
Criminal damage	86.3	13.7	6.8	87
Drug offences	90.6	9.4	3.7	53
Drunkenness	93.3	6.7	3.2	309
Assault	48.4	51.1	8.8	45
D.H.S.S.	96.6	3.4	1.7	117
Breach of the peace	93.5	6.5	2.1	89
Loitering/soliciting	84.1	15.9	7.7	295

Regional disparities

The choice as to plea, whether not guilty, guilty, inconsistent/unequivocal or prevaricate is a decision which is influenced by diverse factors other than those immediately apparent in the criminal justice system. These decisions may be influenced by local magistrates' attitudes, and by local policing strategies, possible sentencing outcome and prosecution practice. In examining the regional differences in sentencing patterns of magistrates at the City courts in Manchester, Liverpool, Sheffield, Birmingham, and in one Inner London court, the disparities proved to be revealing in ways not originally anticipated. Consider for instance that 16 per cent of defendants before the Manchester City Magistrates' Court pleaded 'not guilty' on the day, whilst a much higher proportion of defendants, 22 per cent, before Highbury Corner Magistrates' Court (both samples over 100) entered pleas of 'not guilty' (see Table 8:13). This difference, though not part of the sentencing exercise, was too significant to go unexplored. And some light promised to be cast on the problem via an examination of the informal procedures which impinged upon the various stages of the prosecution process. Observations of contested cases, informal discussions with probation officers and with the police, led to the following disclosures. First, there was a major difference between the recording procedures adopted by the police in the two areas, which had a central bearing on the prosecution case. In the Inner London area, at that time (1981), car registration numbers were being recorded, together with names and addresses of car owners. This information was also on occasions part of the evidence given in open court. In the Manchester area this was not a procedure adopted as this abstract from the following transcript from 1981 demonstrates.

Defending solicitor: Did you take the number of the Escort?
Police witness: It is not our policy.
Def. sol. Wouldn't it have been at that time . . . in December (1980) in Moss Side because of the Ripper?
Pol. wit.: No, we had stopped doing that a few months before.
Def. sol.: But it was only a few weeks before then that the Ripper was caught in the same kind of situation.
Pol. wit.: I know.
Def. sol.: Don't you ever take names and numbers?
Pol. wit.: As far as I'm concerned it was an ordinary punter.
Def. sol.: But that was the sort of person the Ripper turned out to be. The man you were trying to catch.
Pol. wit.: Yes.

Second, at Highbury Corner Magistrates' Court, the registration numbers of cars approached by women were systematically disclosed in court as part of the prosecution case. In addition, in one particular contested case in September 1981, the owner of the car in question was called before the court to give evidence, the content of which was that the women charged had approached him asking for a lift home after a party. Despite his account the case was found proven. This particular procedure was introduced in mid-1981 by a stipendiary magistrate in an attempt to deal with the particular nuisance of the 'kerb crawler'. In this clean-up campaign he proposed that a system be adopted by the local police force whereby the car registration numbers of punters be read out in court and car owners called upon to give evidence.

This was not a system adopted in Manchester, though many certainly saw something along these lines as highly desirable, as the following abstract from a transcript of a contested case reveals.

Defending solicitor: Why is it that the punters' names are never taken when they could be prime witnesses in a trial?

Police witness: They are very reluctant to come forward.

Def. sol.: Isn't it right that they are more of a nuisance than the prostitutes?

Pol. wit.: I don't make the law or have the power to bring them in. People are very reluctant to come forward to give evidence against them.

However, it was very soon realised in the London area concerned that such a system was ineffective since in this event, the punter if called upon as a witness to give evidence is likely to declare that he was doing no more than giving the woman a lift home, safe in the certain knowledge that the defendant would not impeach herself, and not betray his predilections.

Indeed, since the desire to remain a 'secret punter' is particularly evident amongst those who have a real grievance against a prostitute – those who have been robbed of sometimes quite substantial amounts – it is not surprising that the punter who has no grievance whatsoever wishes to remain silent. This shroud of silence is certainly one of the reasons for the higher proportion of contested cases. And it would be true to say that defendants probably feel secure in the knowledge that if punters are called upon to give evidence they would be more likely to provide an alibi advantageous to their own reputation, and also to the case for the defendant with the result that the system of deterring 'kerb crawlers' fell flat on its face.

Other courts and legal personnel have made similar efforts to deal with the nuisance of the kerb crawler. Tim Flynn, a Bristol solicitor, said recently, 'If you believe these girls should be prosecuted, and I don't, then it is hypocritical to allow clients anonymity' (*Sunday Journal*, 1 November 1981). However, police in the Bristol area have criticised this solicitor's procedure for announcing car registration numbers and names in court since it would be difficult to convict such girls if men thought they would be named. Some Bristol prostitutes also fear that it might put them out of business.

Another factor of some considerable importance in influencing choice of plea is the time the court takes in disposing of contested cases. It is well known that regardless of the offence, defendants frequently plead guilty to 'get it over with' (Bottomley 1973, Baldwin and McConville 1977). With regard to this particular offence, and also in view of its trivial nature, the number of adjournments called for in contested cases is highly disturbing. Generally speaking, cases are adjourned for a number of obvious and very important reasons, but the adjournment is also used for illegitimate purposes. Legitimate reasons may be the preparation of a social inquiry report, or a medical report, or in order that the defendant may seek advice and legal representation. However, cases are also 'put back' for reasons related to administrative efficiency rather than justice, or more typically in order that a number of offences may be dealt with in one court appearance, occasionally in order to create additional work for the legal advocate (though this is hotly denied). Where adjournments clearly benefit the defendant there is less cause for concern, but the question remains open as to whether its use of an adjournment in every event is actually in 'their best interests'.[12]

It is clear that legal representatives benefit financially from the number of adjournments, since solicitors are paid on the basis of each court appearance they make. In Manchester, where a duty solicitor scheme has been in operation for some time, two firms of solicitors vied for business. In the opening remarks of a transcript of a contested case where there had been a significant number of adjournments the defending solicitor provided his reasons for handling the case in this way.

> Before the proceedings begin, I wish to make an application that three of the matters be dealt with together, that is matters relating to 5th December, 16th and 17th January. The reason for this is that they are similar charges and similar areas — where the evidence is virtually identical. It would take less time and therefore it is more economic to deal with them in this way.

'Common prostitutes' — contests and verdicts

The application of the epithet 'common prostitute', together with magistrates' knowledge of the cautioning system, apart from inducing guilty pleas, either at the onset or on the day of the hearing, may also have a considerable influence on verdicts delivered in contested cases. In the Manchester study the acquittal rate as a percentage of those who pleaded not guilty amounted to 50 per cent, a favourable proportion which at least initially does not suggest that magistrates are biased against defendants arraigned on loitering and soliciting charges. However, unfortunately no information was obtained which could indicate at what stage of the hearing cases were dismissed, which would have cast some further light on this difficult area. Included in this acquittal rate are those dismissed cases, where no prosecution evidence has been offered, those adjourned *sine die,* cases where some prosecution evidence has been offered, and those cases where magistrates have achieved a verdict in open court or retired in order to consider their verdict. And since loitering and soliciting for the purposes of prostitution is non-indictable it is important to consider attitudes of magistrates to the offence and the defendant and the relative credibility given to police and the evidence of the prostitute. In this context it is important to ascertain whether magistrates actually render 'a true verdict according to the evidence', or whether verdicts are influenced by other variables independent of the prosecution case.

For instance magistrates interviewed by Burney (1979) pointed out that it was on the whole reasonable to believe the police since 'in recording and giving evidence a policeman is doing a job for which he is trained'.[13] And Williams (1979)[14] commented that magistrates rely upon the word of the police officer against that of defendant. Police evidence in contested trials for loitering and soliciting offences has an embarrassingly familiar and recurrent ring. Each account is guaranteed to be of this nature: 'I was on duty in — Street and observed the defendant standing on the corner of — and — Street bending and peering into passing motor vehicles, paying particular attention to those driven by lone males.'

Research studies have suggested that the credibility of the defendants's explanation is likely to be a major consideration in decisions made by magistrates. The opportunity defendants have for explanation varies widely from one court to another. Some clerks are meticulous in alerting the defendant regarding her right to 'say something'. And motivatory explanations in mitigation are nearly always influenced by whether the defendant is represented or not. And finally, since evidence of the defendant's good character is another factor likely to have a bearing on the outcome, a slur is inevitably cast on the character of any defendant referred to as a 'common prostitute'.

The sentencing discount in guilty and prevaricate pleas

The choice as to plea is, as has already been suggested, influenced by the sentencing discount. But the professional prostitute stands in a unique position regarding this choice. For the professional prostitute court appearances represent an occupational hazard which many take in good humour as an inevitable consequence of their trade. For the professional, the use of the prevaricate plea and its implication for sentencing outcome is a calculated premeditated consideration. The professional woman can either plead guilty on each occasion as charged and have each offence considered separately, and separate sentences given accordingly, or the charges can be dealt with collectively and one sentence given to cover all of them. The differences in sentencing between the separate and collective charge make regional comparison, at this level of analysis at least, almost impossible. However, it is clear that a defendant charged, convicted and sentenced on six separate occasions is likely to be dealt with overall more severely than the defendant who has six charges preferred against her on one hearing. Since this is the case, pleading not guilty from the onset provides defendants who are likely to be charged on a number of occasions with the opportunity of having them dealt with simultaneously. The sentencing advantage is an obvious one as magistrates tend to give concurrent sentences regardless of the number of charges. Whilst a prostitute may be fined up to £50 on one charge it would be unrealistic and irresponsible to fine her £300 for six charges which were considered together. This offers itself as an inducement to the professional prostitute to plead not guilty from the onset, facilitating several adjournments, the collection of additional charges, to be followed on the final day by a plea change to one of guilty.

Equal – but unequal

Throughout history the prostitute as defendant on charges of soliciting or loitering and as victim/complainant in trials of violence or sexual crime has been regarded as unworthy of legal protection. As defendant or witness she has been considered untruthful and deceitful. W.R. Greg, writing in the nineteenth century, reveals the way in which doubt is cast on their testamentary capacity. 'Their oaths are seldom regarded in a court of justice, scarcely ever in a police court . . . In America or Holland, if you strike a woman of this class, she will take the law of you: in England her evidence might be rejected, or at all events would not be believed. "Gentlemen of the Jury", the counsel for the accused would say, "this charge rests on the evidence of a common (meaning poor) prostitute . . ." '[15]

The handling of the Yorkshire Ripper inquiry together with the media coverage was a salutary reminder, as Hollway (1981: 39) points out: 'the distinction between prostitutes and "totally respectable" women victims clearly testified to a value that the lives of prostitutes were worthless and that Sutcliffe's mission in wiping them out was somehow justifiable. Thus, Sir Michael Havers [the Attorney-General] said of Sutcliffe's victims, "Some were prostitutes, but perhaps the saddest part of this case is that some were not" ' (*West Indian News,* 6 June 1981).

The prostitute then is seen to personify all that is unworthy and untruthful, and in the court situation where her testimony is juxtaposed with the evidence of the moral, upright and law-abiding copper her testimony is doubted and his preferred. A conflict of interests is observed similar to that conflict discussed by Becker (1963) and later Young (1971) between the police and the deviant group. In addition to their law-enforcement role they are also seen as moral crusaders enforcing a law which is very often not seen as punitive but really in the best interests of all concerned, including the prostitute, who may therefore be saved.

3 · Medico-legal conundrums — The legal organisation of physiological difference

The crimes committed during the menstrual period are generally of a more violent character than those centring round the change of life, e.g. murder, arson, breach of the peace; contrasting with libel, perjury, minor crimes against property, and procuration. But there is also an inclination to violence shortly after child-birth and during lactation'.

Buschan, quoted in Ploss, Bartels and Bartels, vol. 1, 154.

Introduction

In this chapter I turn to the problem of physiological difference between the sexes as expressed in its various presentations in the law itself, and as it influences the administration of criminal justice. In so doing I have three objectives in mind. First, I wish to identify the precise social connotation of specific physiological differences in the context of gender or more specifically the biological role in which such differences find justification. In this sense, there is no pre-menstrual syndrome or tension without femaleness, and there can be no puerperal psychosis of childbirth without the gender role of motherhood. Second, I want to examine the varying assimilation of these characterisations of physiological difference in the divers levels of criminal jurisdictions and to reveal and explain the inconsistencies and contradictions. Finally, I will argue that the real predisposing factors in the following 'women's' crimes are indeed socially induced, and that the state obscures this reality in favour of the physiological imperative which is a politically expedient strategy. Women too, imbued with ideologies of perfect and natural motherhood, deny the fact that eternal childcare is an impossibility. When something goes wrong and the only available explanations are failure or sickness, they opt for the latter. At this present time when women in particular are being forced to take up once again caring tasks which were performed by the welfare state such as care for the old, handicapped and young, we can expect that the physiological model will be elevated to its former glory as a political diversion tactic.

Physiology – its role in criminal explanation

Deviant behaviour of both men and women has been frequently explained with reference to physiological imbalance. These particular explanatory models are more typically invoked in sex-related crimes, and since men are considered more likely to commit crimes of sexual assault and violence than are women, sex-specific physiological imperatives are rendered in attribution. The most commonly presented explanation has its basis in the 'drive reduction' theory, predicated on a biological presumption that man is an animal unable to control and abate his urges once sexually aroused.[1] Indeed in the administration of criminal justice we find articulated such assumptions of male physiology which function to exonerate or at the very least mitigate acts of sexual deviance.[2]

By contrast, almost all crimes committed by women have been traditionally regarded as a reflection of some internal physiological imbalance (Pollak 1950, Klein 1973). The reluctance to accept that women may actively choose to break the laws sets such a model in motion; female crime is then considered rather as the result of impulses beyond their immediate control, with the result that the aetiology of female crime, like that of mental illness, has been considered intrinsic to sex and not to gender.

This biological positivist vision has its pseudo-scientific origins, so called, in classical positivism and the physiological and gynaecological paradigms of the nineteenth century. These pristine perspectives on the deviance of women have not only persisted in various forms unto the present, but have also undergone a number of significant and alarming revivals in the present day which demand some explanation. The significance presently attached to pre-menstrual tension (PMT) in its relation to violent crime for example is illustrative of this resurgence. A recent proposal for research, presented to the Centre for the Study and Reduction of Violence, read: 'The question of violence in females will be examined from the point of view that females are more likely to commit acts of violence during the premenstrual and menstrual periods' (Klein 1973: 28 nb.1).

Perhaps it is the immutable and peculiar fact of certain physiological processes which account for the hold of 'biological positivism' in defining female deviance. Certainly menstruation, pregnancy, childbirth, lactation and the climacteric are undeniable stages in the developmental cycle of women. The curious and as yet unanswered question is why these 'normal' processes have instead most typically been regarded as 'pathological', and why such processes have been considered to play a contributory or precipitatory role in destructive acts as in female crime rather than contributing to creativity. The reinvocation of PMT, pregnancy, childbirth and the climacteric as explanations of female deviance in the present day owe much to nineteenth-century views of the nature of women generally. And from the early nineteenth century the presumption that female criminality was pathological is a supposition which has been assimilated at various levels of criminal jurisdiction. In statutory measures, in case law, as a contributory factor in crime and in mitigation of sentence these physiological considerations have variously come to influence the processing of the female defendant within the criminal justice system. But it also to the political ramifications of physiological characterisations of conceptualising conduct that we must turn.

Biological positivism and the Lombrosian myth

The belief that some women because of a physiological imbalance may be predisposed to criminal activity has erroneously been regarded as having its origins in classical positivism and the work of Cesare Lombroso (1895) in particular. There has been an overwhelming proclivity of a cumulative nature amongst criminologists, both conservative and radical, to regard this particular branch of pseudo-scientific theorising as one of the most influential in shaping criminological theory and the law, when really its potential in influencing legal decision-making was far more modest. In the mainstream of criminological theory Mannheim (1962), Taylor, Walton and Young (1973) and, in studies of female criminality and criminology, Pollak (1950), Smith (1962), Smart (1976), have to a greater or lesser degree taken Lombroso's writings as a starting point for their historical reconstruction of criminology. This preoccupation with Lombroso as 'godfather' is due to a perhaps complacent over-reliance on secondary sources, and secondly to the problems inherent in the tendency to engage in cumulative paradigm-building in the pursuance of knowledge. Consider for instance that Jeffrey Weeks[3] in his most recent analysis of nineteenth-century influences on sexuality draws very different conclusions indeed, concentrating on the role of medical professionals in this terrain. What we are presented with in the historical reconstruction of criminology is an empire of myth, the tendency in searching for origins to attribute all to Lombroso, and the unfortunate total omission of any consideration of the role of medical theories which had a very real impact on the formation of statutes and the administration of criminal justice. This mythologising leaves the historical critique of women and crime very incomplete.

Lindesmith and Levin, in accounting for this interpretive reconstruction, maintain,

> The growth of the Lombrosian myth is to be accounted for, basically, not so much in terms of the acceptance or rejection of theories or methods of research as in terms of changing personnel . . . The Lombrosian myth arose, therefore, as a result of the 'seizure of power' so to speak of the medical profession. Medical men compiled bibliographies and traced the history of criminology as a branch of medicine through the work of Gall, Lavasier, Pinel, Morel, Esquiral, Maudsley . . . [4]

This interpretation of the power of the medical profession was a view found echoed in the later work of Szasz (1970), Illich (1976) and Foucault (1978) amongst others. Szasz in looking at mental illness talks of the therapeutic state and the possession of power by medical men. Illich in his brilliant critique of the medicalisation of life, *Medical Nemesis* (1976), discussed the political implications of the growth of the power of the medical establishment. He talked of the 'expropriation of health' and the need for a political programme aimed at the limitation of professional medicine. And Foucault rather more recently has spoken of the power of the medical profession in talking about and defining sexuality.

Criminological theorising, on the other hand, with one or two notable exceptions, namely Foucault's study of the prison (1977), have largely ignored the very considerable impact of these features of biological positivism on medical thinking and theorising. Moreover, evidence shows conclusively that the thinking of Lombroso and his school, whatever its impact, was very shortlived. Lombroso wrote one of his most influential texts, *The Female Offender,* in 1895, and within less than two decades he had been discredited both in Britain and on the continent. By 1913 Goring in England declared there was no such thing as the criminal type and in France and Germany criminologists had persistently opposed and criticised the view of his school.[5]

Physiological medicine

The real and pragmatic influences on the criminal law and the administration of justice during the nineteenth century were in fact medical and gynaecological theories on women and crime. They too were based on the tenets of biological positivism but were exerting an influence in the courts well before the advent of Lombroso's work on the female offender and, indeed, long after. From the beginning of the nineteenth century, medical practitioners, mental health physicians and gynaecologists conceded rather more specifically that criminality in women could be explained by the physiological episodes to which they were subject. Thus menstruation, pregnancy, lactation and the climacteric were regarded as 'crisis periods' when women might behave erratically or criminally.

On the continent practitioners like Icard, Krafft-Ebing and Krugelsten, and Ellis, Maudsley and Mercier in England, agreed that normal menstruation as well as abnormalities of the menstrual function might precipitate, or be a contributory factor in, criminal behaviour. In 1882 Richard von Krafft-Ebing wrote in his classic *Psychosis Menstrualis:*

> The menstruating woman has a claim to special consideration by the judge because she is at this period 'unwell' and more or less psychologically disturbed. Abnormal irritability, attacks of melancholia, feelings of anxiety, are common phenomena. Inability to get along with husband and domestics, ill-treatment of otherwise tenderly cared for children, emotional explosions, libellous acts, breach of peace, resisting authority, scenes of jealousy, craving for alcoholic beverages because of physical pain, neurotic and anxiety conditions are everyday experiences with innumerable individuals.[6]

Icard in *La Femme pendant la periode menstruelle* similarly argued that the responsibility of women for crimes committed at these physiological stages was ever diminished.

> La menstruation faisant partie de l'état puerpéral, mieux encore, constituant à elle seule *un* état puerpéral, en petit (Pajot), peut, au même titre que la grossesse, l'avortement, l'accouchement, la lactation, engendrer un état mental, et mérite en conséquence toute l'attention des juges.[7]

Research studies conducted on convicted women also display a belief in the relationship between menstruation and crime,[8] of which work by Lombroso and Ferrero is significant. In 1895 they studied a group of eighty women who were arrested for resisting public officials, to find that seventy-one of the women alleged that they were menstruating at the time of the offences.[9] Buschan in *Geschlecht u Verbrechen* (1908) made a similarly extensive study of the physiological life cycle and criminality in women, finding that the crimes committed during the menstrual period were generally of a more violent nature, though he also noted a tendency towards violence shortly after childbirth. Ploss and Bartels in this context maintained that it was possible to speak of 'physiologically, defective, unbalanced and potentially criminal women'.[10]

Whilst Ellis, working in England, one of a number of medical men, who recognised that women were susceptible to mood variations during this time, declared, 'There are other mental and emotional signs of irritability and instability which tend to slightly impair complete mental integrity, and to render, in some unbalanced individuals explosions of anger or depression, in rarer cases crime, more common'.[11] But Ellis was particular in emphasising the relationship between menstruation and violence. And in *Man and Woman,* this view finds further expression: 'Whenever a woman commits a deed of criminal violence it is extremely probable that she is at her monthly period.'[12]

In rejecting the mystical arguments, he wrote, 'Menstruation is no longer a monstrific state requiring spiritual taboo, but a normal physiological process not without its psychic influences on the woman herself and those who live with her.' Nor was he unaware of the political consequence this might have for their social position. In a chapter entitled 'The influence of menstruation on the position of women' he asserted, 'A question of historical psychology which, so far as I know, has never been fully investigated is the influence of menstruation in constituting the emotional atmosphere through which men habitually view women.'[13] Maudsley, Mercier and Savage, amongst others, spoke of the relationship between menstruation and crime. Lawson Tait, a most influential police surgeon and gynaecologist of the day, referred to the special dangers that await women at this time.

Towards the end of the nineteenth century and the turn of the twentieth century the work of George Savage and Charles Mercier was of enormous importance in the impact it had upon credibility and testamentary capacity. In exploring the issues of crime and insanity women were considered lacking in responsibility and credibility with relation to crime. In 1884 George Savage in *Sanity, Insanity and Allied Neuroses* spoke of the puerperium: 'Medico-legally this condition is of great importance, because during this period of excitement the mother may commit infanticide'.[14] Similarly, Mercier (1918: 195), expressed the view, 'The time of childbirth is one of the occasions in which insanity occurs in women, and of all the features of the insanity of childbirth, none is more difficult to account for, than a fury of destructiveness directed against the helpless infant.' The climacteric perhaps more than any other stage has been of medico-legal importance in precipitating a wide variety of crimes. It has however been more typically invoked in relation to petty theft than to crimes of violence. Research at the turn of the century reveals that the menopause is a period notable for the occurrence of sudden death, as well as for a high percentage of suicide.[15] Such medical perceptions were seen to have a significant impact on law, judicial policy and the operation of justice. Referring to their impact on the trial process itself, E.J. Tilt in 1882 noted, 'judges have admitted the doctrine of uncontrollable impulse by allowing the plea in cases of puerperal insanity; the view is that it should also be allowed during puberty, pregnancy, lactation, etc.'.[16] And more specifically with reference to sentencing policy, Sir W.C. Hood in *Criminal Lunacy* (1850) argued for the release of women who commit crimes during the crisis stages and after the change of life.

Contemporary criminological and legal writers have similarly advanced the physiological differences between the sexes as a reason and exculpation for crime, thereby echoing earlier sentiments. McClean and Wood (1969) write: 'There is evidence, too, of a link between some offences committed by women and physical conditions associated with menstruation, pregnancy and menopause.'[17] And Devlin, commenting on sentencing, wrote in 1970,

in view of the suggested links between some offences and the existence of physical conditions associated with menstruation, pregnancy and the menopause as well as other evidence which has indicated the deep-seated nature of the emotional and mental disorders which are frequently associated with delinquency in women, it is obvious that imprisonment should only be used with great care.[18]

This characterisation of women is similarly shared by the New Zealand legislature. The Department of Justice, in a recent publication *Crime in New Zealand* (1968), announces with overwhelming conviction:

> only in periods of unusual stress is a woman likely to break the law . . . during adolescence, pre-menstrual or menstrual periods, at menopause or during pregnancy and for a short time after the birth of the child. (p.270)

The pre-menstruum in law

That a relationship exists between certain manifestations of criminal behaviour and the pre-menstruum is considered an interconnection of recent discovery only. Dr Katharina Dalton has earned a reputation as pioneer in this field although many oppose her theories, finding her work retrogressive. But however regressive her research may be considered to be her theories and diagnoses have nevertheless influenced the administration of justice in several recent legal cases. The sentences passed in *Owen* (1978), *Craddock* (1980), *Smith alias Craddock* (1981) and *English* (1981) reflect the extent to which the courts are prepared to acknowledge the pre-menstrual tension factor in mitigation. Until 1982 the precise legal standing of pre-menstrual tension had remained unclear, when the Court of Appeal decided that PMT was 'wholly unacceptable' as a defence to any crime. Under British law evidence of PMT can only be introduced as an extenuating factor or in mitigation of sentence or as evidence of diminished responsibility (1982 CLR 531) (Brahams 1983: 807–13. L. Taylor and K. Dalton 1983: 269–87).

The recent introduction of PMT as a contributory factor in crime may seem to some a novel innovation whilst to others it represents a retrogressive step. Its appearance however is neither new nor peculiar to British legal jurisdiction. On the contrary, PMT is presently being considered on the continent and in America and Canada. During the summer of 1982 an American mother reputedly became the first person in the US to plead PMT as a defence for beating her child (*Guardian*, 29 September 1982). But the final outcome of the case confirmed that American attorneys are adamant that it is a defence without merit (*New York Times*, November 1982, *New York Monthly*, 1 November 1982, 37–42). Santos, the defendant, in the final stage of the proceedings pleaded to a lesser charge of harassment thereby dropping the pre-menstrual defence, mirroring what Wallach and Rubin (1971) had predicted sometime earlier, namely that PMT would be useful in plea bargaining where a defendant might plead guilty to a lesser charge. It seems likely that European criminal jurisdictions will similarly be forced to resolve this question as PMT in relation to crime promises to come up for public and legal debate. It has been reported already that PMT is recognised in the French legal system as temporary insanity.

Whilst it is generally regarded as a consideration of recent origin the relationship of PMT to crime is to be discovered in legal thinking as early as 1833. In that year a case of pyromania committed by a woman was said to have been caused by her 'ill-health', that ill health being recorded as the non-appearance of the catemenia or menstrual period. The court was called upon to consider to what extent this illness might be a contributory factor. A more widely reported case in the annals of medical jurisprudence is the case of Brixey in 1845. Martha Brixey, the defendant, was charged with the 'wilful murder' of an infant in her care. It was part of the case for the defence that at the time the crime was committed she was receiving medical treatment of 'a disease' (amenorrhoea), and medical evidence was adduced to this effect. In this case the jury were left to decide whether the defendant was suffering from a derangement of mind which meant that she could not be held responsible for her actions. In a later case recorded in 1851, Amelia Snoswell was indicted for the 'wilful murder' of a child. The evidence adduced on her behalf declared that she was suffering from a constitutional irregularity likely to affect the brain. The irregularity was disordered menstruation and in consequence the defendant was found not guilty on the ground of insanity (Edwards 1981a: 94).

Disorders of the menstrual function were also admitted as contributory or extenuating factors in non-violent crimes during this time. In the case of *R* v *Shepherd* (1845) the defendant was charged with the theft of a fur boa. Evidence was submitted for the consideration of the court relating to the fact that at the time of menstruation she underwent 'personality changes and eccentricities'. Mr Ramshay, the defending counsel, in his address to the jury pleaded:

> for some years the prisoner had laboured under irregularities which occur in the health of females, which the medical evidence would show were the source of great eccentricities of conduct, and delusions, by which he thought it must be concluded that the prisoner's acts could not be deemed felony, as was often the case with drunken men, who might take property under some temporary delusion, and yet all felonious intent might be absent.[19]

The defendant's brother speaking on her behalf said, 'I have known her under delusions at such times, supposing things to have happened, which I believe had not happened. In three or four days she would get better.' Dr James in presenting the medical evidence explained that women were likely to suffer from such irregularities at these times that they were not conscious of what they were doing until the 'paroxysm' had passed. And so it was abundantly clear that in a variety of criminal offences, both violent and non-violent, PMT and related disorders of menstruation were invoked as extenuating factors. It was widely held amongst medical men that menstruation was related to crime. The medical profession were responsible for the promulgation of such a belief, and in Britain, America and on the continent the belief was advanced with conviction.

But is PMT fact or fiction, physiological, psychological or socio-political, and what is the nature of the evidence which supports the PMT crime theory? The use of PMT in court as an extenuating factor or in mitigation stands on a very uncertain medical foundation; in 1983 we are no nearer a medical consensus on the aetiology and diagnosis of the condition than we were a century earlier. Since there are diverse views on the aetiology of the condition, treatment similarly varies. The predominant and most widely publicised version is that PMT arises from a progesterone deficiency. This particular theory has been advanced in Britain by Dr Dalton. The symptoms accompanying this condition may be both physiological and psychological. Somatic symptoms are indicated by swelling of the breasts, oedema, a general feeling of bloatedness and pelvic pain. In the more extreme cases where psychological symptoms are also present, irritability, fluctuations in mood and sudden outbursts of temper are considered to be not uncommon. And it has been argued that these symptoms may become considerably aggravated when the sufferer goes for long periods without food as this may result in an increased production of adrenalin, thereby creating a hypoglycaemic condition.

Whilst PMT is no defence to crime, hypoglycaemia has been recognised in *R* v *Quick* [1973] QB 910, [1973] 3 WLR 26, where automatism was presented in defence as being caused by hypoglycaemia. In a later case, *Powell* 1980 CLR 39, hypoglycaemia was admitted as impairing concentration and judgment. (See *The Lancet*, 9 April 1983 at 832, *R* v *Bailey*, Court of Appeal Criminal Division, 11 March 1983.) Interestingly, in this same context, a New York professor of law in 1953 argued strenuously for the recognition of pre-menstrual syndrome as a legal defence on the basis that the hypoglycaemic factor of the pre-menstrual can account for the impairment of self-control (Oleck, in Morton 1953: 492–501).

According to the progesterone deficiency theory, the presence of such a progesterone–oestrogen imbalance can be measured by a test known as radioimmunoassay (*British Medical Journal*, 29 January 1979), although critics claim that there exists no reliable test that can establish the kernel of Dalton's theory. Treatment for the condition, where progesterone is considered to be in a deficient state, is given, via replacement therapy, often using a combination of injections, suppositories and tablets in the form of natural progesterone or in its chemical form retroprogesterone or duphaston, Dalton preferring natural progesterone to synthetic formulations where it is administered in dosages of between 50 and 100 milligrammes daily.

But not all researchers working in the field agree that the cause is one of progesterone deficiency. On the contrary, Dalton's physiological approach has been fiercely challenged. For instance, in a recent study of PMT sufferers conducted by O'Brien, Selby and Symonds, the researchers did not find that their patients suffered progesterone deficiency (*British Medical Journal*, 10 May 1980: 1161). And research conducted by Sampson in 1979 discovered a 40 per cent success rate in self-declared sufferers when treated with a placebo (*British Journal of Psychiatry* 155: 1979: 209). But as Trimmer points out, 'Always bedevilling the assessment of the disease . . . is the criticism that such studies . . . are the result of work carried out on a self-selected group of patients' (*British Journal of Sexual Medicine*, April 1979: 52).

As a result of the conflicting views as to its aetiology and diagnosis treatment varies accordingly; where psychological rather than somatic symptoms appear predominant, pyridoxine (Vitamin B6) is usually prescribed. Kerr in 1977 used pyridoxine in seventy patients with real benefit for 50–60 per cent of them. And Drs Brush and Taylor treated 2000 women with a 70 per cent success rate, using between 20 and 100 milligrammes of Compoment (*Sunday Times,* 10 May 1981).

The courts, and the law for all its wisdom, cannot discriminate between one school of thought and another on this medical debate. It is therefore of considerable interest and significance that it is the positivist progesterone deficiency theory which has captivated public attention and been so readily advanced in the courts. Is the 'success' of this theory related perhaps more to a judicial process which is structured to the accomodation of discernible qualifiable diseases in mitigation rather than to the validity of the debate?

Since 1978 PMT has been advanced in British courts as an extenuating factor in certain crimes. The first recorded case of this kind was heard before the Central Criminal Court where the defendant had set alight the family home. Nicola Owen was placed on probation for two years with the condition that she attend hospital for treatment as a psychiatric outpatient. Soon after this conviction she started yet another fire and was on this subsequent occasion remanded in custody for the preparation of a medical report. The prison medical officer, P.T. D'Orban, sought the assistance of Dr Dalton, who in giving evidence at her trial claimed that she was a 'classic case of PMS'. The judge agreed, declaring 'there is no doubt in my mind that this girl is suffering from pre-menstrual tension'.

In a case observed by the researcher in 1981 at Manchester Crown Court, PMT was advanced as an extenuating factor. The case in question contained all the medical and legal difficulties imposed by such a consideration. The defendant appeared before the court on charges of abusive behaviour contrary to section 5 of the Public Order Act 1936, and for the possession of an offensive weapon contrary to section 1(1) of the Prevention of Crime Act 1953. In the attempt to establish whether any medical condition existed and more specifically to determine whether the defendant was subject to pre-menstrual tension, she was remanded in custody for a total of thirteen weeks, a prison sentence itself! The judge explained, 'This delay is amply justified. We have got to know and the doctors have got to know . . . It could be very beneficial in these circumstances and it would be quite wrong not to have an adjournment. One is very much in the hands of doctors in this sort of case.' Medical evidence in this case was inconsistent and conflicting though after lengthy deliberations it was agreed by all that she was suffering from PMT.

To complicate legal matters further, sometime in 1980 PMT was advanced not only as a contributory factor in crime, but as a substantive defence to murder because of diminished responsibility. Sandra Craddock appeared before the court on a murder charge; the particulars of the offence were that she had stabbed a fellow barmaid to death. It was discovered that at the time of the crime the defendant was suffering from PMS. The Recorder, James Miskin, put the case back for three months to give the doctor the opportunity to prove what she claimed. During these three months the defendant underwent a marked improvement said to be due to the administration of progesterone. Her plea of not guilty to murder but guilty to manslaughter on the grounds of diminished responsibility was accepted by the Crown. Judge Miskin imposed a probation order with the condition that she continue to receive treatment *R* v *Craddock*, 1 CL Jan. 1981: p.49, 1982 CLR 531.

In a rather more recent case PMT functioned similarly in the assistance of the reduction of a murder charge to one of manslaughter on the ground of diminished responsibility. In 1981 Mrs Christine English was charged with the murder of her lover, whom she had knocked down and run over in her car. Purchas J accepted her plea, satisfied that she had committed the offence in 'wholly exceptional circumstances since evidence was adduced that at the time of the offence she was suffering from pre-menstrual tension (*Guardian*, 12 November 1981).

In another incidence of violence PMT was invoked as a defence. Smith alias Craddock was charged with twice threatening to kill a police officer. She pleaded not guilty. Her counsel, Mr Keith Evans, explained to the court that after killing a barmaid the previous year she was put on probation and given progesterone. On the occasion in question the dosage was reduced. Mr Keith Evans appealed against the decision on the ground that the defendant was suffering from PMT and therefore could not be held responsible for her action. Mr Evans argued that her condition constituted a 'disease' and as such it was sufficient in itself to provide a defence in law. Griffiths LJ, Pain J and Beldam J decided that PMT was not acceptable as a defence to any crime, Griffiths LJ adding that Mr Keith Evans 'invites this court to make a leap in the dark and make a special defence to someone suffering from PMT (*Guardian* 28 April 1982). PMT has also been applied somewhat more widely. An industrial tribunal ruled it unfair to dismiss a woman who had a 'pre-menstrual tantrum'. And in 1982 at Burnham Magistrates' Court a twenty-two-year-old woman avoided a possible driving ban after claiming that PMT caused her to crash.[20]

Feminists the world over are objecting strenuously to the use of PMT as a mitigatory or contributory factor. Their resistance is to the promotion of the view of 'biology as destiny'. Juliet Mitchell had some time earlier astutely remarked, 'Female biology and nature have increasingly been devalued in our culture but women have not yet been freed from being defined in biological terms.'[21] Indeed, it is only a recent development that women have succeeded in demolishing the age-old argument that they are controlled by their biology, and thereby eroded another bastion of justification for their unequal treatment. And thus the reinvocation of this pathological argument is vehemently challenged and contested.

The consequences of the invocation of the 'biology as destiny' argument go far beyond the confines of criminal law and the criminal justice system, extending also into the political arena. For instance Hubert Humphrey's doctor, Edgar Berman, in 1970 announced that the menstrual cycle subjected women to 'raging hormonal influences'. And he went on to add that women 'weren't fit to be presidents of banks because they could hardly be trusted to handle making a loan at "that particular period" ' (Bullough 1976: 148). More recently at a meeting of the United Nations Security Council, 22 May 1982, Mr Illuwca, Panama's Foreign Minister, remarking on Mrs Thatcher's intransigence over the Falklands implied that she sometimes lost control of what she was saying because she was a woman subject to the menstrual cycle (Edwards 1983b). It may be well for us to remember that the exclusion of women from education and the professions was based on just this ground (Sayers 1982: 120–4).

And positivistic research has compounded the belief that menstruation is debilitating in asserting that hormonal changes lead to impaired judgment, accidents and unpredictable behaviour. Dalton's research is full of anecdotes from women whom Dalton considers to be genuine victims of an hormonal imbalance. One chiropodist is quoted as saying 'If ever I do cut a patient you can be sure it will be during those pre-menstrual days.' Dalton also selects remarks of this kind from a library assistant to advance her case: 'You don't stay away from work merely because of your bad temper, instead you soldier on and cause chaos by misfiling, and you get yourself a bad name.' Or as one teacher wrote, 'Every month there are one or two days when I am simply not worth the salary my employers pay me.'[22] These are comments engineered to advance her case and certainly not the case of equality between the sexes. In conclusion we may do well to consider the wisdom of these remarks:

Menstrual politics has dominated social and economic relations between the sexes since the beginning of time. In all their struggles for equality – the suffrage movement, the labour movement, the struggle for ERA – women have been obliged to fight against the enemy who will not contend with them in the halls of Congress or the courts of law. The enemy is within every woman, but it is not her menstruation. Rather, it is the habit of mind regarding menstruation into which she has been led by centuries of male domination. She has been taught that menstruation is disabling and so she has been disabled.[23]

Puerperal psychosis in law

Whilst PMT as a physiological condition has increasingly been considered as a contributory factor in female crime, puerperal psychosis as a physiological condition following childbirth is now widely questioned, social factors being considered of greater import as extenuating factors. Difficulties encountered by the mother at this time are considered the result of social stresses, the 'biology as destiny' argument now widely contested.

However, from the middle of the nineteenth century, puerperal psychosis or puerperal insanity as a physiological condition arising following childbirth was accepted both as a defence to child murder, and also as an extenuating factor in other crimes. And by 1922 the possibility that following childbirth a mother might kill her newborn was provided for in statute, the culmination of pressure for legislative reform since 1860. Prior to 1843 in those cases where puerperal insanity was considered in evidence a defence of temporary insanity was put forward. But following the McNaughten rules on insanity pleas, an insanity defence was hard to prove, replacing the verdict of 'not guilty on the grounds of insanity' with the illogical verdict of 'guilty but insane'. Many women were nevertheless acquitted of child killing because of a temporary insanity. But as C. Damme (1978) points out, 'Yet these legally untenable insanity pleas were accepted, even solicited, in the case of infanticide by juries and courts and this stands as further proof of the special status afforded one accused of infanticide.'[24]

In case law puerperal psychosis following childbirth was frequently introduced as an extenuating factor. In the case of *R* v *Ryder* in 1856, a trial for murder, where a mother had killed her child by drowning it in a pan of water, Erle J in summing up remarked that the insanity was due to the effect of childbirth. In the later case of *Vyse* (1862) 176 ER 111, the defendant had poisoned two of her children. Her counsel raised the defence of insanity and introduced evidence which related to the effect of undue lactation. In mitigation her counsel introduced the hereditary evidence of insanity and the question of the defendant's health after excessive lactation. 'Whilst she was suckling her last child her health became very much deteriorated.' By 1862, a precedent had already been established in this respect. And in the case of *Law* (1862) 175 ER 1309, where the defendant had curiously killed both her husband and her child, it was held: 'A married woman having killed her husband immediately after an apparent recovery from a *disease (the result of childbirth)* which caused a great loss of blood and exhausted the vessels of the brain . . . was not in a state of mind to know' what she was doing (my emphasis).

Since the turn of the nineteenth century an alternative charge was made available to certain women who had killed their children. The Ellenborough Act of 1803 provided that women acquitted of murder could be charged with a lesser offence, though interestingly it was a provision which applied only to mothers of illegitimate children – interesting insofar as it suggests that the courts and Parliament were prepared to accede that child killing may also be precipitated by social and economic stresses.

Later in 1874, the Committee in discussing the Bill made similar submissions. Mr Chorley, QC, in giving evidence to Mr Stephen, QC on the question of the reduction of a murder to a manslaughter charge, remarked,

> If the person whose death is caused is the child of the person who caused it, and if the act by which death is caused is done while such last person, though not entitled to be acquitted on the ground of insanity, is deprived of the power of self control by any disease or state of mind or body produced by bearing the child whose death it had caused'.[25]

Sentencing policy throughout the nineteenth century was similarly shaped by the view that in many cases of maternal filicide mothers were indeed suffering from some illness. Whilst judges were reluctant to impose a sentence of death on any woman they were particularly averse when the indictment was one of child murder. Paris and Fonblanque noted this tendency as early as 1823 and called it 'judicial evasion'.[26]

Whilst no statutory provision was made for infanticide until the twentieth century, efforts to reform the law in this direction were strenuously canvassed. And by 1872 the Homicide Law Amendment Bill recognised the contributory role played by puerperal insanity in child murder. Clause 22 read, 'When any woman murders her own child at or soon after its birth, and whilst deprived of her ordinary power of self control by the physical effects of its birth, she may upon concretion thereof, be sentenced, if the judge in his discretion thinks fit, to penal sentence for life, or for any term not less than five years.' By the turn of the twentieth century the campaign for legislative change was stepped up considerably, in part as a response to the Louise Masset case where a mother was hanged in 1899 for the murder of her illegitimate son. This was followed by another *cause célèbre* in the history of infanticide reform.[27]

And by 1908 when the Children Bill was being discussed in the House of Lords, Lord Loreburn, the Lord Chancellor, with the concurrence of the Home Secretary proposed to insert a new clause providing,

> Where a woman is convicted of the murder of her infant, and that child was under the age of one year, the Court may, in lieu of passing a sentence of death, sentence her to penal servitude for life or any less punishment.

This was followed by the Infanticide Bill and the Child Murder Trial Bill, preludes to the 1922 Infanticide Act, which read, 'An Act to provide that a woman who wilfully causes the death of her newly born child may, under certain conditions, be convicted of infanticide.' And so the possibility that the puerperal state may contribute to this crime was enshrined in statute.

However, restricting the definition of newly born to an infant of twenty-eight days implied that maternal filicide on an infant of twenty-nine days was in fact murder. The case of Mary O'Donoghue in 1927 where the child was thirty-five days old when killed demonstrated the absurdity of imposing such a rigid time limit to the condition, with the result that the defendant was not entitled to a conviction on a charge of infanticide and was tried for murder, convicted and sentenced to death, though the judge accepted evidence of insanity due to the effects of childbirth and lactation. The defendant appealed against conviction and sentence on the ground that puerperal derangement could last from two to six weeks following childbirth. It was decided that she was suffering from post-puerperal psychosis and the death sentence was commuted to one of penal servitude for life. As she said in a signed confession, she had killed her child because 'I had nobody to mind him and no money'.

The case of O'Donoghue together with the case of Hale in 1936 called for a reconsideration of the provisions in the Act, and growing pressure from the medical and legal professions resulted in the introduction of a Bill by Lord Dawson into the House of Lords which not only allowed for an extension of the time limit of puerperal insanity but also took into account the effect of lactation on the mother's state. In the case of Hale, the defendant in a state of severe depression cut the throat of her child and then attempted suicide. Humphreys J said in summing up that he was bound by the decision in O'Donoghue, 20 CAR

> I venture to express a hope that Parliament may, in the near future, be disposed to insert a short section into the Act of Parliament saying what is the definition of a newly born child.

The revised Act provided:

> Where a woman by any wilful act or omission causes the death of her child (under the age of twelve months), but at the time of the act or omission the balance of her mind was disturbed by reasons of her not having fully recovered from the effect of giving birth to the child or by reasons of the effect of lactation consequent upon the birth of the child, then, notwithstanding that the circumstances were such that but for this Act the offence would have amounted to murder, she shall be guilty of the offence of manslaughter of the child.

With the introduction of the Homicide Act 1957 there has been increasing pressure to abolish the infanticide statute since the Act provided for the first time for a verdict of diminished responsibility. Glanville Williams, for instance, advocated that if a defendant was suffering from puerperal mania, if she was insane, then the verdict should be one of insanity, the defendant should be charged with manslaughter and puerperal mania be dealt with along with other factors, especially since section 2 acknowledged the causative effect of an abnormality, thus accommodating the possibility of infanticide.

Indeed, the recommendations of the Butler Committee of 1974–5[28] proposed firstly that infanticide need no longer be distinguished from diminished responsibility. Secondly, they maintained that the medical principles on which the Act is based may no longer be relevant, puerperal psychoses being regarded as no different from others, childbirth being only a precipitating factor. Smith and Hogan (1978) similarly argue 'It appears that the principle on which the Act is based may no longer be relevant and that mental illness is not now a significant cause of infanticide.' This was a view expressed sometime earlier and already even with the introduction of the 1938 Act members of the medical profession were of the opinion that the illness following childbirth belonged more appropriately to the exhaustion psychosis group.

This was a view shared and expressed in the fourteenth report of the Criminal Law Revision Committee who were not satisfied that 'every disturbance of mind which now leads to an infanticide verdict would in all cases be regarded as mental disorder'. As Nigel Walker (1981) points out,

> The fact is that psychiatrists have moved far away from the original conception of infanticide as a crime committed in a state of mind attributable to physical processes which are peculiar to women – that is to parturition or lactation – and use it to cover 'stresses' which are due to a miscellany of social difficulties.[29]

Moreover, the Butler Committee in their report quoted at length evidence submitted from the Governor and staff at Holloway Prison which stated:

A combination of environmental stress and personality disorder with low frustration tolerance are the usual aetiological factors in such cases, and the relationship to 'incomplete recovery from the effects of childbirth or lactation' specified in the Infanticide Act is often somewhat remote'.

Whilst on the medical and sociological front it is being increasingly contended that 'there are no specific mental illnesses related solely to pregnancy, childbirth and the puerperium', it is increasingly argued that depression following childbirth is very common.[30] Indeed the research studies conducted by Ann Oakley reveal the nature and experience of postpuerperal blues or depression amongst women.[31] It is widely conceded in the medical and legal field that social and economic facts are as relevant as physiological ones. It has also been said that there is a case to be made for the possibility of paternal filicide (Smart 1976: 190). Thus it is equally important to consider other stresses. D.J. West found that the operative factors in child killing were related to stress of child care and as such also extended to the father or surrogate mother and were not necessarily restricted to a twelve-month period following the birth.[32]

Given the existing Infanticide Act and the legal requirement of evidence of mental illness, i.e. puerperal psychosis, the medical profession understandably continue to use the dead-letter concept. Consider for instance the following tragic case. In an infanticide case heard before Manchester Crown Court in 1981 the defendant had drowned her three-month-old child and at the same time attempted to kill herself by electrocution. Medical evidence adduced on her behalf revealed that she was severely and critically depressed following the birth of her child and rendered even more unable to cope following the death of her mother. Both medical reports tendered for the defence and for the Crown concluded that this was a case where puerperal psychosis was present and thus a conviction under the Infanticide Act was possible, perhaps more favourable than a manslaughter conviction under the 1957 Homicide Act. This is clear for two reasons outlined in the Butler Report. First, it allows the prosecution to charge infanticide rather than to proceed with a charge of murder and then wait for the accused to set up diminished responsibility as a defence. And second, by charging infanticide the prosecution concedes the mental disturbance without requiring proof of the fact. As the law stands at present a certain amount of collusion is in evidence, where the legal alternative if no puerperal psychosis were indicated would be the reduction of a murder charge to manslaughter due to diminished responsibility.

The law as it relates to infanticide and the presumptions upon which it is based, demonstrate considerable confusion and ambiguity regarding precisely what circumstances are relevant in defence mitigation, and what factors exactly ought to be relevant. The gross limitation of existing law is that it permits post-natal difficulties to be adduced in defence only in those cases where a mother successfully kills her newborn. Post-natal problems do not constitute a defence if the child survives, if the child injured or killed is over this arbitrary twelve-month limit (even though the mother may be suffering from post-natal difficulties in respect of another child born yesterday!), or if these difficulties contribute to other kinds of criminal conduct. It is because of these absurd limiting conditions that this law can be described as at best an act of misguided toleration, at worst retrogressive and inconsistent. In addition, surrogate 'mothers', be they men or other women, receive very little legal understanding either. In 1981, a young nanny was convicted in just such circumstances of the manslaughter of an infant in her care. Her counsel explained, 'the nearest explanation that anybody can give is that she became overtired'. In addition, the press repeatedly reported that there might have been some pre-menstrual tension and a belated effect from her grandmother's death (*Guardian, The Times,* November 1980).

Men, too, are subject to the social stresses of rearing children, particularly if unsupported by women. Donald Boswell was sentenced to thirty months' imprisonment for the rough handling of his five-week-old daughter, which resulted in her death (JP 146, 51/52, p.793). And in a pathetic case heard before Manchester Crown Court in 1981, both wife and husband were so incompetent that they neglected the child to the point that, suffering from lack of warmth and nourishment, it went to sleep and died. Both parents were sentenced to four years for (as the law would have it) *wilful* neglect. It did seem palpably obvious that neither could do anything wilfully. In the midst of this young couple's misery (they were both under twenty years of age and had three children and another on the way at the time of the first committal which was later adjourned) social workers present in the courtroom were very much more concerned about whether their lack of judgment and integrity might be called into question whilst at this moment two inadequate people are serving prison sentences. (see *Sheppard and Sheppard* (1980) 70 CAR 210 for a similar case and the legal meaning of 'wilful neglect'.)

Far too infrequently are 'supporting' agencies questioned for non-intervention. Instead the many victims of enforced isolation and round-the-clock motherhood become twice victimised. In the Sokell case, as in so many others where, being human, adults have failed in their role, duties or obligations, the judge punitively asserted, 'and you will never look after children again!' So untenable, unthinkable and inappropriate the crime, so much is it at odds with normal motherhood or the feminine predilection for surrogate motherhood that such women can only be immutably unnatural. Their crimes are considered innate and pathological, thus the possibility of recidivism is considered an ever recurrent one. Women are punished for society's failure, a reality which becomes translated into one of a pathological dimension. It is still the case that post-natal difficulties are regarded as invariably medical rather than social matters where symptomatology is more relevant than recognition of social factors or political factors (see Dean and Kendell 1981).[33]

The politics of physiological explanation

The medicalisation of social problems is a well-recognised ploy of social systems in their refusal to recognise or to give credence to competing and sometimes potentially threatening ideologies. Thus medical stigmas, mental illness in particular, have been invoked to explain and thereby control the conduct of dissenters and objectors (Chesler 1972). The imputation of a 'mentally sick' label conveniently defines away contesting argument as having no logical or reasonable basis. Such conscientious objectors become in Szasz's terms 'psychiatric scapegoats'. This strategy has had an impressively successful record throughout history. The suffragettes were so labelled, and more recently student unrest and demonstration were explained in psychiatric terms from a Freudian perspective, as a deeply unconscious desire to be beaten over the head by a police baton.[34] The process of calling the criminal mentally sick 'is to avoid granting the criminal the "legitimacy" of a rational interest contradictory to the requirements of morality and social order'. Mills (1943) similarly recognised the tendency to depoliticise social problems. And latterly we find perhaps only too often that social workers are moving towards a psychiatric treatment model of personal pathology (Hardiker and Webb 1979, Halmos 1978).

In this exploration of the varying degrees of assimilation of assumptions of 'physiological' crises in women at various levels of criminal jurisdiction, certain analytical questions remain unanswered. First, one would wish to know why in the last few years we have witnessed a revival of the presumption that the behaviour of women is in response to an inner physiology. Second, one would also wish to discover why such an explanatory model of PMT in relation to crime is only successfully invoked and credited in cases where the crime committed is of a particularly violent nature and the mode of violence out of character or untypical of appropriate female behaviour.

The individualisation of the processing and particularly the sentencing of defendants in the criminal justice system was regarded as a most innovatory step forward in the handling of the offender. The tariff system of sentencing, whilst it could maintain a level of consistency of sentencing, was unable to meet the needs of treatment and rehabilitation of the individual. Thus the process of sentencing the offender to the most appropriate sentence rather than making a sentence fit the offence was a development much welcomed by liberals and humanitarians.

But whilst the philosophy of 'individualised justice' was progressive enough, the very medical model which was adopted to facilitate treatment and rehabilitation was not. This shift unwittingly contributed to the general revival of theories on the pathology of offences. The political ramifications of control in the individualisation of treatment of offenders was largely obscured by the considered liberal façade of attempts to rehabilitate rather than to punish. For in the very process of the endeavour was a strong element of state control, as social practitioners as well as medical professionals intervened and the social inquiry report became of increasing necessity (see Cohen 1979).

The more recent application of PMT in the courtroom as part of the defence case reflects the predilection to regard untypical female crime as the product of a sick body reinforcing the view that normal women after all do not really commit crime. The tendency to medicalise deviant behaviour is an approach particularly characteristic of interpretations of female crime and is reflected both in the readiness with which medical and social inquiry reports are requested and also in their content. The tendency to request a medical report is where an untypical violent crime is committed (see Chapter 8).

But there is yet another reality behind this tendency, particularly well recognised by feminists who refuse to be part of the conspiratorial view that women's conduct is in response to physiological processes. Such arguments act as a prop to the ideology of the primacy of gender divisions predicated on sex difference.

The ideology of normal motherhood both guides and informs society's intolerance and rejection of women child abusers. The underlying assumption is that every normal woman wants children and a family life, and in this framework work and a career become construed as a sublimation of this desire. Thus it is normal for a woman to want to put her baby first (an orientation dominating Penelope Leach's writing). Penny and Andrew Stanway maintain (in Oakley 1981) 'Mothers who take to mothering naturally don't want to leave their babies – they'll go through all sorts of hardships to stay at home.'[35] This enforced childcare is supported by the kind of ideologies advanced amongst others by the late Mia Kellmer Pringle, who asserted recently, 'in western societies, no wholly adequate substitute has been found for the one-to-one, close, continuing, loving and mutually enjoyable relationship which is the hall-mark of maternal care' (*The Times*, 14 January 1976). Yet as feminists have argued, enforced childcare is more like a hall-mark of women's oppression (Firestone 1972, Friedan 1965, Scutt 1981: 9). With the consequence that any expression of manifestation of difficulty in caring adequately for the child following its birth is translated into being a matter of hormones. The explanation 'it's the hormones' is invoked to render intelligible a multitude of difficulties. This interpretation is similarly adopted by mothers; one woman explained the experience in this way: 'I would like to go back to work . . . it has been so intense with her, because it has been every minute of the day thinking baby things, which I haven't particularly liked.'[36] In addition, most women are alienated from one another by their feeling of failure in their inability to cope, and in their desire to appear capable, hide their feelings from others and often from themselves. Moreover, the few social agencies now prepared to recognise this dilemma encourage mothers to disclose innermost fears of child abuse, and then set in motion control surveillance which only induces further feelings of inadequacy (see Christine Bohanna's experience, Chapter 7).

Given this conspiracy of silence and motives for concealment, it is little wonder that, frustrated and feeling inadequate, mothers blow up and strike their children. Thus an understanding of the relationship between women and certain criminal behaviour must be examined in the context of the position and role of women in the family (Klein and Kress 1981: 158). It must take into account the social constraints placed on women, their duties and the obligations they are expected to fulfil, rather than giving a blanket analysis of women *per se*.

The criminal law in its response adds to this injustice and, without recognising that anyone responsible for a child twenty-four hours per day is in an invidious position, prefers to gloss over this hard fact and talk instead in terms of inadequacy and physiological malfunction. As Scutt (1981: 7) explains,

> The law of infanticide illustrates clearly the stand and attitude of the criminal law towards socio-political problems created by role stereotypes. It illustrates too well the refusal of society to recognise the sexism inherent in our culture and endemic in the family unit as it exists under patriarchy.

Surely the blame should rest with a society which completely washes its hands of providing any support, provisions or facilities for the family, whilst hypocritically bleating about the need to strengthen the family – the Conservative Party campaigns being particularly guilty of this ingenuity – and then when something goes wrong quickly reaches for the 'sick' label. During the past few years, and especially under the present Conservative Government, there has been an increasing reluctance to accept responsibility for social ills. Rising unemployment, rising crime, inadequacies in housing and service facilities and urban unrest were all problems which were the result of individual traits and not ministerial policy. Yet by 1980 the few nursery facilities, such as they were, were being closed down at an alarming rate.[37] In 1983 the concept of nursery provision is redundant. This deliberate shift or unloading of responsibility from the political to the personal (Halmos 1978), the growth of the professionals in the state sphere of social work has characterised this individualised justice.

What we have in part then in these essentially hormonal theories of crime is an understanding of deviance which deflects attention from social and political ills to concentrate on problems of individual pathology. As Rafter and Natalizia (1981: 87) write, 'the research questions should be highly particular, aimed at detailed analyses of the relationship between women's socio-economic position and the crimes committed by them in specific social contexts, both past and present'. And it is to these questions we should be turning in any analysis of 'women only' crimes and 'women only' extenuations.

4 · Female sexuality – Changing conceptions in the criminal law

> ... through centuries of suckling men emotionally at our breasts we
> have also been told that we were polluted, devouring, domineering,
> masochistic harpies, bitches, dykes and whores.
>
> Adrienne Rich, *Of Woman Born,* 1976.

Introduction

One of the central concerns of my earlier work *Female Sexuality and the Law,*
1981, was to assess the influence and impact of contradictory images of women's
active and passive sexuality as they informed the various levels of criminal
jurisdiction, in case law, statute and the administration of criminal justice. Whilst
acknowledging that such ideas were assimilated inconsistently and to varying
degrees, a consideration of those divers occasions where notions of sexual
passivity and precipitation had been informative in a consistent manner were
chiefly explored, although it was also conceded that 'the wide diversity of statutes
governing sexual expression thwarts any provision of a general theory on the
nature of the specific relationship of sex legislation to social or economic faces',
and 'The range of sexual behaviour being regulated has resulted in a series of sex
laws that are often contradictory and anomalous' (p. 17). The exploration of
statutory provisions that followed revealed Parliament's adamant refusal to
recognise that women, prostitutes excepting, were capable either physically or
mentally of committing a sexual offence, whilst in the case law relating to offences
of a sexual nature where women were the victims the reverse was true and, the
rules of evidence governing the trial process together with counsel's interpretation
of those rules revealed the presumption of sexual precipitation on the part of the
complainant.

This present discussion draws upon just some of the themes presented in this
earlier work. Whilst the earlier work focused on victims of sexual assault, this present exploration examines the social and legal constructions of the female sex
offender, about whom very little is written, with the notable exception of Mackesy
(1956). Focusing on the female sex offender is not to detract from the realisation
that women are more sinned against than sinning, nor is it to place such a discussion in any position of priority.

Politically, a consideration of the victimisation of women is of course more important, as it is a lived experience, arising from power inequality, spanning in-

stitutions of marriage, occupation, education and medicine and entrenched in ideologies which inform them. Victimology has now been granted the status of a subject in its own right, although the only victim given legitimate recognition is the victim of a defendant within a legal framework, with the consequence that victim-support schemes were principally to assist the victim of a perceived physical injury or property loss or damage. Victimology as understood by conferees at the Second International Institute of Victimology held in Italy in 1982 insisted that a more radical view of the victim should be adopted, so that victimology should include institutionalised victimisation of groups within the wider socio-political context.

The victimisation of women in medicine is and has been particularly obnoxious, particularly since medical intervention, surgical, psychological or psychiatric, is always 'for her own good' or in 'her best interests'; this professional lie is well recognised in the work of Ehrenreich and English (1979) and Daly (1978). Studies of the history of the use of clitoridectomy have observed that it is not a survival of a relic relating to tradition and customs but was used in Britain and elsewhere in the nineteenth century as a surgical technique in the control of female sexuality (Edwards 1981a). Women are also the victims of present-day medical technology and particularly in obstetric practice where only the medical man is 'wiseman' and episiotomies are routine practices (Edwards, 1982i) always in her best interests.

Nevertheless, conceptually there is a need to understand what notions of femininity are mobilised when women take the initiative in sexual encounters, and whether this construct is paralleled in an understanding of female sex crime. Within the criminal law women have traditionally been excluded from certain crimes on the basis that they could not commit them. Over recent years it would seem that legal practice has given way to a new notion of female sexuality in one area of its jurisdication. This changing conceptualisation in itself demands some comment in the context of the changing construction of sex roles. Consider for instance that in 1981 in the Manchester City Magistrates' Court twelve women were prosecuted for indecent assault on females, eighteen for indecent assault on males and six for gross indecency with children, whilst in the Crown Court two women were prosecuted for indecently assaulting females, six for indecently assaulting males and two for offences of gross indency with children. How the courts viewed them and how they dealt with them is not known, although it is a matter addressed in the latter part of this chapter.

First, in looking to those offences regarded as sex crimes the activities are diverse. A recent article by James, Davis and Vitaliano (1982) entitled 'Female sexual deviance' examined prostitution only. For this reason some preliminary clarification is required, since offences recognised as sexual crimes may include conduct as disparate as managing a brothel and rape. Glanville Williams, in *Text-*

book of Criminal Law, 1978, sets the scene for the analysis of sex crimes under two separate headings, 'Sexual offences may be broadly grouped into two types of sexual aggression and breaches of sexual taboo' (p. 186), a distinction Brazier (1975) made sometime earlier though preferring to exclude offences such as abduction, prostitution, indecent exposure, conspiracy to corrupt public morals and to outrage public decency, where he proposed an innovatory formulation of two new crimes based on the presence or absence of individual consent, and crimes where there is no 'consent-in-law'.[1] Williams's taxonomisation is similarly based on the consent standard, maintaining that 'Those in the first group consist of injuries and affronts to a non-consenting victim, while in the second group the conduct is illegal, whether or not the victim consents' (p. 186), with the proviso that the distinction is not a precise one because of the ambiguity of the word 'consent'. He adds that the matter may be further complicated if sexual motivation is to be taken as the primary feature in the definition of sexual offences since almost any crime from murder to necrophilia may have a hidden or overt sexual motive. If sexual offences are so prescribed by the presence of a sexual component which may or may not constitute the motive or the gratification then the analysis of sex crimes becomes profoundly complicated and any attempt at theorising requires a further breakdown and separation of the conduct into sub-categories.

The implacable treatment of subjects, objects and ideas in other areas has revealed the problems arising from the too ready application of the inductive method, where generalisations are too readily derived from particulars. Revolutionary or radical ideologies and reactionary ideologies seem to be in their enthusiasm for their commitment equally culpable of such an error. Susan Brownmiller, in a general treatment of all kinds of rape in all kinds of society both in peace and in war, leaves us with the message that it is an expression of extreme domination. 'All rape is an exercise in power', she says,[2] a proposition which may hold true for the victim but not for the offender. Such theoretical universalities lead similarly to erroneous generalities in the sentencing and treatment programmes of convicted rapists. In this respect there is nothing like one lenient or inappropriate sentence to generate a level of public interest whose indignation is such that one sentence for all offenders regardless of individual circumstance is demanded.

The recent public demand for a mandatory sentence for all offenders convicted of rape followed the almost immediate release from detention of one convicted for the rape of a six-year-old girl.[3] The public shock, outrage and indignation which followed is understandable, but is it not curious that a mandatory sentence was preferred, rather than an immediate review of the sentencing system which gives judges so much discretion, allowing appeals to be lodged by the defence only? However, it was suggested by some legal practitioners and commentators that such cases should be triable only before judges of the High Court, an alternative in the attempt to reduce the possibility of erroneous sentences preferable to the imposition of Hobson's choice in the proposal for mandatory sentence! A similar call for a mandatory sentence for rapists followed the case of *Allen* in 1982, where the defendant was fined £2000 for rape. In the wake of this case, both the Prime Minister and the Home Secretary were unanimous in their call for the introduction of mandatory prison sentences thereby approving the assertion of the Lord Chief Justice, Lord Lane: 'Rape is always a serious crime. Other than in wholly exceptional circumstances, it calls for an immediate custodial sentence' (CAR 16 January, 1982). In this direction too, Mr Robin Maxwell-Hyslop has introduced a Private Member's Bill in which he proposed a minimum of two years' imprisonment for convicted rapists.[4] At the Court of Appeal the presiding judges gave five reasons in support of the necessity for custodial sentence: first, to mark the gravity of the offence; second, to emphasise public disapproval; third, to serve as a warning to others; fourth, to punish the offender, and fifth to protect women. The Lord Chief Justice went on to enumerate the reasons for this necessity and instanced eleven features which might aggravate the crime:

(1) Where a gun, knife or some other weapon had been used.
(2) Where serious injury, mental or physical, had been sustained.
(3) Where violence over and above the violence necessarily involved in the act itself had been used.
(4) Where there were threats of a brutal kind.
(5) Where the victim had been subjected to further sexual indignities or perversions.
(6) Where the victim was very young or elderly.
(7) Where the offender was in a position of trust.
(8) Where the offender had intruded into the victim's home.
(9) Where the victim had been deprived of her liberty for a time.
(10) Where the rape or succession of rapes had been carried out by a group of men.
(11) Where the offender had committed a series of rapes on different women or, indeed, the same woman.

Whilst such a clarification of law is indeed welcomed some assurance is also needed to impress that where such features are not always apparent these victims will be given the protection of the law, since this statement of features said to aggravate the crime may unwittingly have the effect of reinforcing the view that rape is a crime perpetrated by force and fear which must be seen to be against the will of the victim rather than without her consent. Whilst there is certainly a need for an immediate revision of the range of sentences for rapists in order to achieve a greater measure of consistency, a mandatory sentence should not be introduced since a flexible sentencing structure is important to allow for the accomodation of the particulars of each individual case. The Report of the Advisory Council on the Penal System (Sentences of Imprisonment, 1978) has made some moves in the direction of such a revision, although it seems unlikely as far as rape sentences are concerned that the proposals will be welcomed. The Advisory Council proposed a new maximum (for ordinary cases) based on prison sentences imposed at Crown Court trials during the period 1974–76. At present the life sentence is the maximum for rape whilst the proposed new maximum (not applicable for exceptional cases) was set at seven years (p. 81).

The sentencing structure for rape offenders should continue to be optional for two very important reasons. First, since the Sexual Offences (Amendment) Act 1976, we have, in theory at least, a law which defines the act of rape as non-consensual sexual intercourse. A man commits rape if 'he has unlawful sexual intercourse with a woman who at the time of the intercourse does not consent to it, and at that time he knows that she does not consent to the intercourse or he is reckless as to whether she consents to it' (section 1(1)(a) and (b)). Embodied in the spirit of the statute at least is the presumption that consent does not have to be proven to be vitiated by force, fraud or fear. This was affirmed in *R* v *Olugboja* [1981] 3 WLR 585 (CA), where there was no struggle, no resistance and no screaming. It was held on appeal that submission in the absence of force, fraud or fear did not imply consent. As W.T. West points out (JP 146, 1: 8–11, 1982), the conviction of Olugboja and the sentence of two and a half years imprisonment which was imposed, will cause disquiet in the minds of many. But if rape is really about non-consensual intercourse, the interpretation of the Act in *Olugboja* was not only right but should be followed, and a sentencing structure should indeed be sufficiently accommodating to provide for such cases.

Secondly, it is well recognised that jurors tend to acquit in contested rape cases. Tony Clifton's figures for 1974 reveal a 65 per cent conviction rate for rape, compared with 74 per cent, 77 per cent and 79 per cent for murder, indecent assault and malicious wounding respectively.[5] The most reliable figures we have are provided in research by Adler, in which she systematically monitored the interpretation and implementation of the Sexual Offences (Amendment) Act in some fifty contested cases. In perhaps the most excellent research on the workings of the criminal justice sustem and trial process for this offence the acquittals and convictions shown in Table 4:1 were observed in trials at the Central Criminal Court.[6]

Since jurors are more likely to convict in rapes where there is violence, if in addition mandatory sentences are implemented, the real meaning and intention of the 1976 Act will never be realised and jurors will not convict in cases of non-aggravated rape such as the *Olugboja* case if a prison sentence follows as a matter of course upon conviction. If the law is to be implemented and interpreted according to the intention of Parliament non-consensual intercourse commissioned in the absence of force, fraud or fear must also be provided for and its eventuality accommodated in sentencing. Mandatory prison sentences can only have the unwitting consequence of turning back the clock on reform of the law as it relates to rape, since it will have the practical effect of legally realising only those rapes accompanied by brute force and physical violence as 'true' rape.

Table 4:1   Outcome of contested trials

Outcome of trial	No. of defendants		%
Convicted as charged	34		42.4
Convicted of lesser offence	7		8.7
Total convicted		41	51.2
Acquitted by jury	24		30.0
Acquitted by judge's discretion	5		
Acquitted because Crown offered no evidence	8		
Total acquitted		37	46.3
Retrial ordered		2	2.5
Total		80	100.0

In this respect it is also noted with considerable consternation that some of the views expressed in the Criminal Law Revision Committee's Working Paper on Sexual Offences 1980 will have a retrogressive effect if heeded since the working paper proposes that absence of consent should receive a more limited interpretation. It is apparent that its authors wish to retain the more traditional view of forcible rape – of the type expressed in *R v Camplin* (1845) 1 Cox CC at 220, embodied too in the spirit of the Criminal Law Amendment Act 1885 (section 4). In addition, it is also proposed that sexual intercourse by fraudulent means should not in fact be rape and the example is provided of a male housing officer who may offer alternative accommodation to a woman in return for intercourse, but who in fact has no authority to offer alternate accommodation. This view is enshrined also in the Criminal Law Amendment Act 1885 which deems such instances of fraudulent means to obtain intercourse to be misdemeanours, whilst in *R v O'Shay* (1898) 19 Cox CC at 76 such instances of fraud were to be considered as indecent assault. So in much the same way as it is erroneous to understand all rape as purely a matter of male domination and to sentence all convicted rapists to a specified term of imprisonment, it is also absurd to treat all legally defined sexual crimes as either similar or as sharing a family resemblance. It is for this reason that I propose a classification of sex crime which is firstly based on the presence or absence of economic or sexual motives and gratification, and secondly based according to Brazier's distinction on the consent standard.

Whilst of course men commit far more sex crimes than do women, women's only involvement in these offences is either for gain, or in crimes of sexual aggression as an accomplice. The law traditionally excludes her from crimes involving aggression of a sexual nature principally on the grounds that she is physiologically and morally incapable. This total exclusion of the 'subject' female and inclusion of the 'subject' male is predicated on essentialist grounds. For this reason I take issue with the notion that all men are potential rapists and the notion that women *per se* are incapable of committing a sex crime.

The sex crimes women commit

Many sex offenders, so called, are motivated by a desire for monetary rather than for sexual gratification; defined collectively under the auspices of the Sexual Offences Act 1956, sexual offenders are guilty of a wide and disparate range of offences. The economic crimes includes those of procuration, brothel-keeping and exercising control over a prostitute. But unlike other offences the law or the law enforcers have never been over-zealous to bring to task those who profit from prostitution. The Criminal Law Amendment Act 1885 represents the last major review of legislation relating to brothel-keeping where the penalty following a first conviction was a £20 fine or three months' imprisonment. Nothing seems to have changed much since then. Whilst the exploitation of women was a problem widely recognised – Flexner writing in 1919 (in James 1951: 9) that 'Prostitution is an industry deliberately cultivated by third parties for their own profit and the instinct readily lends itself to artificial exploitation' – it is baffling that the law has not afforded prostitutes any greater protection from exploiting profiteers. Indeed, one of the principal objections to existing legislation is its impotence in bringing to trial those who manage brothels and exercise control over prostitutes in the confines of the 'new brothels' – the massage parlours and saunas. Typical of the new brothel is the recent case involving Cynthia Payne, who was convicted on several counts of exercising control over a prostitute and one of keeping a disorderly house. The particulars of the brothel and its clientele paralleled the Cleveland Street scandal of a century earlier.[7] That too implicated male clients who occupied powerful social and political positions. The prosecution of Cynthia Payne was met with an overwhelming sentiment of righteous indignation, and support for her grew as she was depicted as a victim of a hypocritical morality whose laws condemned her whilst reserving their comment on the clergy, parliamentarians and respected citizens who frequented this house of ill repute.

She was initially sentenced to eighteen months' imprisonment, but the sentence was reduced to six months on appeal. Payne, the 'Madam', had, like any true professional to this calling and like her nineteenth-century predecessors, Mary Wilson and Marie Aubrey,[8] provided for all sexual tastes and had been punished accordingly, whilst the secret predilections and reputations of the 'gentlemen' who frequented the address in question remained of course *in camera* and intact.

> The disorderly house was a brothel organised in a suburban house, which contained all the equipment necessary for running a brothel and catering for different sexual tastes, pornographic films were shown and demonstrations of sexual intercourse took place. [1980] (2 CAR (S) 161)

This was her fifth conviction for this offence. In this case the appellant was not charged under section 33 of the Sexual Offences Act 1956, but at common law, thereby allowing the court to impose whatever penalty it thought fit. The number of cases of brothel-keeping which are proceeded with each year are few and the activity goes on relatively unabated. One of the principle objections to existing legislation is its inability effectively to regulate nascent sexual activity in massage parlours, clubs and saunas which are frequently 'fronts' for prostitution.

One such case of brothel-keeping and exercising control was the substance of a successful prosecution at Manchester Crown Court in 1981, where a husband and wife were both convicted, the husband of living on prostitution and the wife of exercising control. The particulars of the case involved the management of bogus saunas in both Blackpool and Manchester where sexual favours were provided, for a fee. The girls allegedly 'employed' never received any payment from the owners, instead they paid the owners £2 per day for powder and oils. As the evidence unfolded the girls, one by one, testified to the fact that they received no payment, provided extra services, worked both in Manchester and Blackpool and pocketed the proceeds. Clients too were called to give a graphic account of the transactions which occurred. The defendants had both pleaded not guilty from the onset until the prosecution offered its two most damaging witnesses. The first, a client who visited the sauna out of curiosity, paid for no more than heavy petting and felt deeply ashamed of his measure of infidelity. He confessed what little there was to tell to his wife who sat supportively in the court. The other prosecution witness was a brash, coarse young woman who exclaimed in reply during examination-in-chief, 'Nothing was said about pay, I knew what I was going to do' – earning, as she said, £102 on the first day.

Following the prosecution's production of these two 'ace' cards the defendants, sensing which way the wind was about to blow, changed their plea. The judge responded with leniency imposing a fine on the female defendant whilst sentencing her husband to a three-month term of imprisonment. The disparity in sentences was a matter of some concern as it was considered that both defendants were equally culpable. The judge later reconsidered and the husband was also fined, though required to pay more than his wife – a judgment presumably based on an assumption that wives are under the coercion of husbands (a preferential treatment abolished under the auspices of section 47 of the Criminal Justice Act 1925). But it is a belief which even to this day can be detected in disparities in sentences when both partners are equally culpable (see *Police Journal* 1946–7: 8; *R v Williams* (1953) 37 CAR 71, Walker 1965: 298, Pearson 1976: 267).

Clearly the motive for such conduct is economic and whilst the management of a brothel frequently involves no action since the prostitute wishes to do business and the client is desirous for sex it is also the case that girls being 'managed' are grossly exploited. It is this probability of exploitation that the criminal law was devised to contain, but since the 1959 Act it has been rendered increasingly ineffective in the face of widespread sexual activity in saunas and massage parlours.

Women's visibility in exercising control over prostitutes, though considered immoral, is nevertheless not considered untypical. The female 'madame' and procuress has had a place in history, particularly well recognised since W. Stead's exposure of the traffic in women and girls in the nineteenth century, a revelation which paved the way for the passing of the Criminal Law Amendment Act 1885.

The involvement of women in the sale and distribution of pornographic material is on the contrary regarded as 'untypical' and an involvement the courts have some difficulty in explaining. In such a case, heard before the Crown Court in Manchester, the female defendant was charged with thirteen men on charges of conspiracy to publish obscene material contrary to section 2 of the Obscene Publications Act 1959. Prosecuting counsel asserted that such behaviour was 'considered characteristic of men and unscrupulous young women'. The marginality of women's involvement in such offences is revealed in the rarity of their appearances on such charges. A total of three such cases against women were proceeded with during a twelve month period, only one resulting in a fine whilst the judge required the other cases to 'lie on the file'.

Sexual motives

Where activity or conduct referred to similarly as a sex crime is instead motivated by the desire for sexual gratification women are by definition excluded. Whether the conduct involves persons who participate freely or else persons subjected against their will or without their consent, only men have been regarded as the initiator or aggressor, women more typically are regarded as the participator or victim. This presumption is founded on the belief in the passivity of women especially in matters sexual, and has contributed to their almost total exclusion from the interpretation and meaning of sexual offences statutes. Conversely, in those few instances where statute has provided for the possibility that women may commit sexual assault on men, such transgressions are not likely to be reported since men are thought unlikely to bear any grievance. Moreover whether the police proceed with such matters is another important area where discretion may be exercised.

On the other hand women have been frequently described as seductresses and controls outside the criminal law have circumvented both their social and sexual activity. Within the legal definition and rules of evidence this construction has been acknowledged and women remonstrated with in various ways for precipitating male loss of sexual control. It has not only been the complainant of sexual assault whose behaviour and conduct, past and present, has been monitored for its possible seductive content. For instance Cecil Bishop, writing in 1931, refers to an ancient law which prohibited women from walking alone between certain hours,[9] a salutary fact of which women who have walked in Reclaiming the Night marches may not be aware. The Reclaiming the Night walk of 31 October 1978 involved a peaceful demonstration of feminists who were attempting to draw attention to the exploitation and degradation of women in pornography, and to assert their equal right along with men to walk through the streets at night unmolested and unharmed. The final outcome of the peaceful gathering was bitterly ironic. A confrontation outside the Swedish Cinema Club in Soho led to the arrival of the police who, instead of coming to their aid, 'began striking out with their truncheons, viciously hitting women on all parts of their bodies'.[10] The women claimed that sixty of their gathering were injured; by contrast, police reports claimed that about thirty had sustained mild bruising to the head. The outcome was that sixteen women were officially charged and sent for trial on charges ranging from obstructing the highway, assault on the police and threatening behaviour (*Time Out*, 10-16 November; *Guardian,* 1 November 1978; *London Evening News,* 17 January 1979). There was no investigation into the use of police violence. Curfews still operate in India, as in other parts of the world (*India Today,* 15 April 1983). In another context altogether, Eva Hunter makes reference to the earlier prohibition under Scottish law of the use of false bosoms, bums and make-up.[11] Though, interestingly, the cod-piece was never subject to such scrutiny or restriction.

The desire to protect men from such alluring women is manifestly overt or else discernible in its covert form in several statutory regulations. For instance, throughout the nineteenth century and possibly long before, wherever and whenever women have been subordinated to men in their capacity as guardians, employers and teachers, sexual intimidation and harassment have flourished unparalleled. Women and young girls have too frequently been confronted with the all too familiar *quid pro quo* – silent submission or the 'sack'. The Criminal Law Amendment Act of 1885 purported to provide for the protection of young women from just this kind of blackmail but its double intent was made evident in its handling of such assaults as 'misdemeanours only' if committed by employers, guardians or masters. Otherwise known as 'An Act to make further provision for the protection of Women and Girls, the Suppression of brothels and other purposes', it provided also for the reduction of a rape charge (Edwards a 1981: 138) to that of misdemeanour and thereby exemplifies the early forerunner of plea bargaining in such cases.

During recent years elements of the feminist movement have turned their attention to the exposure of sexual intimidation both in the workplace and in higher education. A. Sedley and M. Benn (1982) in their study 'Sexual harassment at work' reveal the extent of this both in its overt and covert expressions in the everyday life of skilled, unskilled and professional women.[12] However, the recent acquittal of Inspector David Henry charged with slapping the bare bottom of a woman police constable may deter others of similar subordinate status from reporting similar instances of harassment. The complainant alleged that she had been presented with the ultimatum, 'bend over or resign' (*Guardian,* 8 September 1981). Again, as in rape cases women feel that the court is monitoring their past moral conduct, contributory fault, or 'seductiveness', rather than assessing the facts of the case. These contributory fault components were also influential in an indecent exposure case heard before an Inner London Magistrates' Court. The complainant alleged that the taxi driver had exposed his penis as she went to pay him after her journey. The defence made the imputation that as a divorcee she was a woman of some sexual experience, whom men found attractive. The defence successfully transformed the complainant, who was of a pleasing appearance, into a tigress. All of this very deliberately led up to the finale of the contest, that even if unwittingly she had by her appearance invited the driver's abandonment.[13] Yet, women's almost total exclusion from statutory law represents the view of their fundamental passivity. Perhaps in following the legal definition, criminological, sociological and medical studies have similarly ignored the possibility that women may *commit* indecent assault, indecent exposure or incest. The offence of indecent assault has traditionally been considered a male crime, although during the last few years police have preferred a number of prosecutions against women which have forced the judiciary amongst others to reassess the parliamentary wisdom of statute and the heritage of case law, and insofar as women are concerned have elected for treatment rather than punishment as the most appropriate way of dealing with such sexual miscreancy.

Parliament then has only provided for the legislation of criminal or harmful behaviour – presumably then until recent times the absence of female homosexuality and indecent assault from the statute book suggests that no moral harm is done. However, whilst the law as an arm of the state has not been seen to prohibit, other 'arms' have exercised this social control, as in the cohabitation ruling in welfare provisions, and lesbianism and child custody.

Interestingly sexual offences, involving sexual gratification, have been regarded as 'typical' male offences. From the socially tolerable to the bizarre and often pathological sex crime, men have been prosecuted as sex offenders. Parliament has only provided for the socially unacceptable and pathological manifestations. In this sense other forms of behaviour considered offensive to women and its victims have been normalised within a patriarchal sexist social structure. Sexual harassment at the workplace has never been a matter for legislation. And when women have challenged this male prerogative through the legal machinery their agitation has been met with fierce resistance.

Indecent assault – are women capable?

Although traditionally excluded from sexual offences statutes, over recent years crimes of indecent assault have been recognised as committed by men and women equally. A recent decision of Lord Lane CJ, Boreham and Drake JJ at an appeal hearing in the Divisional Court in April 1981 established an important precedent as far as the law relating to indecent assault committed by women is concerned. The hearing in question was the case of *Faulkner* v *Talbot* [1981] 3 WLR 1523, 1981 CLR 705, CL December 1981 at para. 39, and (1982) 74 CAR 1, where sexual intercourse had occurred between a female over the age of sixteen and a boy under the age of sixteen. The boy in question had consented to the sexual intimacy which took place. In law, what had occurred did not because of the presence of consent automatically legitimate their behaviour. Indeed, it was decided in this case that the female defendant had committed an offence, namely that of indecent assault. First, since he was below the statutory age of consent set at sixteen years, the boy was rendered incapable of giving consent to sexual intimacy which would provide a defence. Second, because he was under sixteen the defendant had, according to case law, committed a criminal offence even though she may well have been a passive party (*R* v *Hare* [1934] 1 KB 354, 98 JP 49). Third, by the fact of her role in foreplay which preceded intercourse she was declared guilty of indecent assault, although the decision to disallow her appeal was unanimously held, the law relating to indecent assault committed by women on young boys has been far from clear, its history protracted and confusing. Case law reveals a wide inconsistency in the interpretation and application of the law. Judges in similar cases, preceding the decision in *Faulkner*, have often declared that there is no case to answer of *Mason* (1968) 53 CAR 12, *Upward, Guardian*, 8 October 1976, unreported, whilst statute for its part has never regarded such behaviour as criminal.

Turning first to the 'age of consent', this statutory limit has been established primarily to protect young girls from the welcome and unwelcome advances of older men who may because of age, status or authority exploit this trust. When the protection of young boys is at issue the 'age of consent' has been largely concerned with protecting them from the advances of older men and the moral danger of homosexuality. By contract, there has been no consideration whatsoever of the need to protect young boys from the sexual advances of older women. In this respect discussion has focused on young girls only. Since 1885 sixteen has been the statutory age of consent, and nearly one hundred years later the recommendation of the Policy Advisory Committee on Sexual Offences, Report on the Age of Consent in Relation to Sexual Offences (April 1981, Cmnd. 8216, para. 19) has been to retain sixteen as the statutory limit. Furthermore, a recent Home Office research study 'Sexual offences, consent and sentencing'[14] in its data bias unwittingly reflects an almost exclusive concern with the female 'victim' of heterosexual assault and the male 'victim' of homosexual assault. The authors, Roy Walmsley and Karen White, gave little credence to the possibility of indecent assault on a male by a female, as their data and analysis indicates. Indeed there was no discussion in their entire study of this possibility although they discovered that out of 802 persons convicted of indecent assault on a male, 8 of the offenders were in fact female.

Indeed, when the Policy Advisory Committee Report considered the question of the protection of young boys (para. 40) there was no mention of the need to protect them from the advances of older women. Instead, the report was more concerned that adequate protection be provided from the 'possibility of seduction by an older man in a position of authority, responsibility and trust'. Whilst some changes have been made in the direction of extending the legislation to prohibit similar sexual advances by women, this possibility has never been given serious consideration, although the Sexual Offences Act 1956, section 15(1), states, 'It is an offence for a person to make an indecent assault on a man'. This provision was extended, or so it was thought, in the Indecency with Children Act 1960, section 1(1), to cases where children were under fourteen years of age. Section 1 states, 'Any person who commits an act of gross indecency towards a child or who incites a child . . . to such an act . . . ' – thereby allowing for the possibility of assault even where the adult did nothing to the child but invited the child to do something amounting to sexual or indecent conduct to him or her.

However, it still appeared in law at least that until *Faulkner* the possibility of indecent assault arising in a context of consent between a child of fourteen or over with an older woman was not to be taken seriously. Apart from the Sexual Offences Act 1956 which applies to 'a man' (the interpretation to include boy) no statutory provision specifically forbids a woman to have sexual intercourse with a boy under sixteen. Indeed the position remains as in 1948 when Sir William Norwood East wrote, 'It is still not a criminal offence *ipso facto* for a woman to seduce a boy under the age of 16.' 1 *(Journal of Criminal Science* 1948 1, p. 62), although section 15(2) of the Sexual Offences Act provided that 'A boy under the age of sixteen cannot in law give any consent which would prevent an act being an assault for the purposes of this section'. But how far this section has been applied in this connection is a moot point.

Contradictions and inconsistencies at various levels of the jurisdiction and in statutes from criminal to civil and family law are observable. With regard to the 'age of consent' for instance, there is a high degree of ambiguity regarding the sexual capabilities of a boy under sixteen. In this respect one might wish to query why a boy under sixteen but over fourteen cannot in law give his consent to intercourse (since he is not considered of sufficient physical maturity to be capable of achieving intercourse) though he is considered capable of committing rape. And further a boy under fourteen is deemed incapable of committing a rape and unlawful sexual intercourse, a fiction Williams describes as 'silly'. Indeed these and related questions have been considered by the Working Party on Sexual Offences (October 1980, para. 27), where the committee felt that the present law which states that a boy under the age of fourteen be triable only for aiding and abetting a rape is a matter which requires urgent change and for which they could see no justification. In addition, with regard to the civil law, a recent paternity case reflects how the law in this instance acceded that a boy under sixteen was capable of fathering a child. This case reported by Marjorie Jones (JP 145 4:60, 1981) considered the case of a schoolboy then aged fifteen, who had been ordered to pay 5p per week in maintenance to the mother since he had fathered her child. At the time of the conception the father was in fact under fourteen. As *The Times* (1980) pointed out, 'Although in criminal law there was an irrebuttable presumption that a boy under 14 could not commit sexual intercourse, there did not appear to be any similar presumption in civil law.'

In *Faulkner,* by having sexual intercourse with a boy under sixteen the defendant had made it possible for a charge of indecent assault to be brought against her. However, what actually constitutes indecent assault on a young man by a woman is a matter which has never been defined in statute. Whilst sexual intercourse is not of itself an offence between a woman and a boy above the age of fourteen, what transpires before and following intercourse may well be. Accordingly with the decision in *Faulkner* sexual foreplay and sexual conduct following intercourse are to be monitored for the degree to which she initially did something to him, in this respect following *Fairclough* v *Whipp* (1951) 35 CAR 138 where Goddard CJ remarked, 'It seems to me there must be an act done to a person.'

The particulars of the offence by Patricia Faulkner are these. The fourteen-year-old boy was living in the defendant's home, and after watching a horror film on television the boy was frightened. The defendant invited him to sleep with her and later invited him to have sexual intercourse with her. She allegedly pulled the boy on top of her and taking hold of his penis placed it inside her vagina–thus initiating sexual conduct. She was found guilty of indecent assault at the Magistrates' Court from whence she appealed against conviction to the Crown Court, stating as her reason that in touching the boy as a prelude to intercourse she could not be guilty of indecent assault. The judge dissented and dismissed her appeal. This point was then presented for the consideration of the Court of Criminal Appeal where it was unanimously held that touching was an assault and by its nature indecent, and that a boy under the age of sixteen could not give his consent. In giving his decision Lord Lane cited *R v McCormack* [1969] 2 QB 442, where the Court of Appeal heard that an indecent act done to a girl of fifteen with her consent is an indecent assault. In this case the defendant inserted his finger into the vagina of a fifteen-year-old girl. Lord Lane together with Boreham and Drake JJ overruled the decisions in *Mason* and *Upward*, where in *Mason* the judge advised the jury that, 'A woman who passively permits sexual intercourse at the suggestion of a boy of 15 is not assaulting the boy. I have equally no doubt that if the original suggestion came from her, it is still not an assault on the part of a woman' (Veale J). In *Upward,* Wien J declared,

> It has never been an offence for a woman to have sexual intercourse with a boy, perhaps for the simple reason that Parliament has never thought it fit to legislate for it, or alternatively it may be that Parliament, which passes these Acts, takes the view that no great moral harm is done.

The prosecution concurred in admitting that the case 'would have to rely on an indecent assault preparatory to the act or during the act and to my mind that creates an absurdity' (JP p. 564, 1976).

Prior to this decision both Glanville Williams's *Textbook of Criminal Law* (1978: 202) and Smith and Hogan's Criminal Law (1978: 420) came to the view that the decisions in both of these cases were in fact wrong and could not stand with *McCormack*. Lord Lane cited the case of *Hare*, where Avory J having stated the facts of the case asserted that there was no reason to limit indecent assault to its sodomitical character as laid down in section 62 of the 1861 Offences Against the Person Act, asserting 'that there is no reason for saying that the phrase "Whosoever . . . shall be guilty . . . of indecent assault" does not include a woman', thereby deciding that indecent assault had taken place. Boreham J cited the judgment given by Fenton Atkinson LJ in *McCormack*, where it was decided 'it is plain beyond argument that if a man inserts his finger into the vagina of a girl under sixteen that is an indecent assault . . . however willing and co-operative she may in fact be'. By extension Boreham argued that 'Where it is the woman who deliberately gets hold of the penis of a young boy, then she too is equally, and beyond dispute, guilty of indecent assault (and I quote the words again) "however willing and co-operative (the young boy) may be".'

But the decision in *Faulkner* is not the only accedence that women could commit indecent assault on a boy in the annals of law. Although the doctrine of 'passive indecent assault' has guided much of the thinking on this matter at magistrates' courts where the focus has been on the impact occasioned by the victim/complainant, since it was believed that women or young girls could not or were not capable of doing anything to 'him'. In a hearing before Colchester Magistrates' Court in 1938, a girl of seventeen was charged with indecent assault on a boy of 15, though she became pregnant by him, and was found guilty of indecent assault and placed on probation (*Police* v *Marchant*, 2 *Journal of Criminal Law* 324). Similarly, another case in 1979 involved a young woman charged with indecently assaulting a thirteen-year-old boy though he had consented. The defendant in this case was placed on probation with the condition that she received hospital treatment. In a later case in 1979 where a young woman was convicted of indecent assault whereby sexual intercourse had occurred with a juvenile, the court took a rather different view and sentenced the defendant to a term of six months' imprisonment suspended, though in an earlier case in 1977 the jury decided the child had invented the sexual liaison and acquitted the defendant. Nevertheless the *Faulkner* case breaks new territory, and the decisions of Wien and Veale, JJ, in the Crown Court hearings, have been overruled and a precedent has now been established for future cases of a similar nature, although an obvious practical difficulty will arise in such cases in determining just how far she did something to him. The preliminary touching of the penis or some other part of the body by an adult woman may be a clear case of indecent assault, but in matters of a sexual nature during intercourse, in particular, who did what to whom and when, is not an easy matter for the prosecution to establish.

Moreover, in situations such as this – that is in consensual acts of a sexual nature between girls of fourteen and over with older men, and boys of fourteen and over with older women – is the application of indecent assault really appropriate? In the words of the Working Party on Sexual Offences (para. 87) 'We have said that we favour the removal of the fiction of assault.' Indeed, Professor Williams favoured a departure from the term 'indecent' as in 'unlawful sexual intercourse', since 'indecent assault' smacks of nineteenth-century morality, Professor Williams preferring 'sexual misconduct' or 'serious indecency', the latter term to apply only in cases where persons are prosecuted under the Indecency with Children Act 1960. Indeed it is also important to consider just how damaging such a prosecution may be to the 'victim' of the indecent assault whom the law is endeavouring to protect. Just how damaging such criminal prosecutions may be is considered in the work of Garretto based on twenty years' study of the victims of incest.[15]

Whilst in law an assault does not have to be a hostile act, nevertheless the case of indecent assault in *Faulkner* must surely be a fiction. Now that women are to be prosecuted a revision of the criminal law along the lines suggested by the Working Party on Sexual Offences would certainly be a step in the right direction. In this respect we would do well to remember that sexual intercourse of an older woman with a younger boy is not an offence. The Criminal Law Review has expressed it indefensible that lesser sexual contact should be an offence (CLR 1982 706). The only case of indecent assault by a woman on a young boy was not proceeded with during the data collection at the Crown Court.

Untypical crimes – treatment paradigms

In cases where women are seen to initiate sexual advances which become offences in law because of the respective ages of the other involved, or else because it was commissioned against their will, their punishment takes the form of treatment, chiefly because women are not thought to be capable of committing a serious sexual offence or else because sentencing, irrespective of the legal decision in *Faulkner* v *Talbot,* reflects the view that no moral harm is done. Offenders are frequently given probation orders, though offences against children under the age of fourteen are viewed in a very different light altogether. For instance, in a case heard in 1980, Ms Groves pleaded guilty to two counts of indecent assault and one of indecency with a girl of eleven years. The court responded with sentencing her to a term of imprisonment for two years, a sentence with which the Appeal Court agreed (JP 144, 1980, p. 340). The tendency to deal with such women via probation rather than a fine is not merely with a view to treat but to control, as the following disparate treatment of a sexual demeanour reveals.

On 5 July 1980 two teenagers appeared before a magistrates' court on charges of insulting behaviour. The particulars of the offence were that the couple had been making love for all to see in a local discotheque. The couple admitted using insulting behaviour but denied intercourse. The seventeen-year-old boy was fined £15 whilst the sixteen-year-old girl was remanded on bail for reports (*Manchester Evening News*). And in a case heard before a Crown Court in 1981 a young woman who pleaded guilty to a charge under section 1(1) Indecency with Children Act 1960, and to indecent assault on boys under sixteen was placed on probation for two years, though in the first case the particulars of the offence were particularly abhorrent since she had permitted a young boy to enter *per vaginam* her twenty-month-old daughter.

As regards the question of victims and offenders of 'sex crimes,' any interpretation is marred by a belief in the activity of victims and passivity of offenders. Recent deliberations have demonstrated the simplicity of this taxonomy since certain areas of the criminal jurisdiction women are now considered capable of sexual assault. This new construction may well have arisen in conjunction with the charges in attitude to women's sexuality generally, or else the recognition of the necessity to introduce some consistency within case law in accordance with previous decisions.

However since the so-called indecent assaults have taken place with consenting male parties, if there were to be true consistency then the charges of indecent assault would be dropped and unlawful sexual intercourse with a boy under sixteen would be substituted as is the case with men who have intercourse with girls under sixteen. But female defendants cannot be charged with unlawful sexual intercourse since the law does not consider them guilty of this, only of conduct before or after. This too seems absurd – that they can be charged with a prelude to an act which of itself is not unlawful. In the quest for consistency and presumably equality of treatment, the criminal law has created further confusion which it will yet have to consider.

Part Two · Gender considerations in the administration of justice

5 · Indicators of suspicion – Detecting and apprehending suspects

Dinah is shifty
Dinah is a thief
All thieves are shifty

Introduction

Much of the preceding discussion has focused on ideologies of sex and gender implicit in criminal law and the justice process. Such constructs also intervene, inform and influence the legal process at earlier stages in the criminal justice system. And it is apparent that law enforcement agencies in their routine activities of surveillance and apprehension of suspects are indeed guided in decision-making and encounters with private citizens by conceptions of female criminality, typicality and incongruity. Most crimes are brought to the attention of the authorities following complaints or observations made by and/or on behalf of the public. But certain crimes – prostitution and shoplifting provide two examples – depend for their detection on the activities of law-enforcement agencies. The importance of this discussion serves to reveal the nature of those 'indicators' which act as 'preludes' to criminal infraction as constituted by the police and store detective. Already there is a vast and increasing body of literature and research on routine encounters of police and public,[1] although the role of gender sexuality in particular as it mediates that process has not been fully contemplated,[2] notwithstanding the contribution made by Roby (1969) and Cunnington (1980).

Apart from being a matter of purely sociological and criminological interest the way in which law-enforcement agencies 'come to know' that a crime is about to be committed or a law about to be infringed is also a matter of some direct social policy and civil liberty concern, because it is in the very essence of the nature of these methods that partiality thrives unbridled. It is clear that if the police adhere to a certain image of the demeanour, location and behaviour of a streetwalker, only women bearing those particular characteristics will be selected for surveillance and of those women some may as a result be arrested and charged with having committed an offence (see Swigert and Farrell 1977). Others similarly loitering for the purposes of prostitution who work in other non-'red light' areas and do not conform to stereotypes of the prostitute will probably avoid detection and in turn will not constitute part of the population of those proceeded against. As Swigert and Farrell[3] have expressed it, 'Stereotypes not only shape public attitudes and behaviour toward deviants, but guide the very choice of individuals who are to be so defined and processed' (p. 17).

In this context it becomes of paramount importance to identify the nature of the process in which the boundaries of a deviant population become so defined by the routine activities of policing agencies. And although Smith and Visher (1981: 167) are of course quite right when they assert 'police arrest decisions reflect the seriousness of particular violations rather than the situation or characteristics of the violator' it has been found that police decisions are influenced by gender appropriateness. In the case of prostitution and shoplifting offences I shall argue that what passes as suspicious conduct in the minds of social control agencies provides the key to their cautioning and arrest decisions. The difference is located by Sacks (1972: 445–6):

> If one feels that it is strange that the rate of crime vary with suspiciousness of the police, one probably has in mind crimes of violence or robbery as typical crimes. And these might be expected to be reported by the public. However, such matters as gambling, prostitution, dope-selling depend for being listed in statistics on the ability of the police to locate arrestable persons. (c.f. Matza 1969: 181)

Perhaps one of the most visible and recently discussed instances of how the images of deviants subscribed to by law enforcement officers have resulted in the apprehension of those displaying such characteristics, is the law relating to suspected persons, now replaced with the recently questioned impartiality of the Criminal Attempts Act 1981. The major criticism directed against the operation of the 'sus' law was that it worked principally to the disadvantage of black youths, rastafarians in particular, who because of their high visibility were easy targets. Furthermore, because of the obvious cultural conflict between white conservative men and black, dreadlocked youths, the vulnerability and victimisation of particular sections of the black community was increased. Parallels can be identified in the work of Matza (1969: 192) who points out, 'Contrarily, the aspiring juvenile "tough" and more recently the long-haired, unkempt "hippy" exemplify portions of the population who for reasons of gross resemblance are especially noticed and scrutinised by police.'

It is widely assumed that in detecting law-breaking activity both police and store detectives see the infraction and then apprehend and arrest. Thus the patrol officer is thought to have seen a woman get into a man's car or else to be 'servicing a client' prior to his intervention. Similarly the store detective is often considered to have seen the suspect place the stolen goods in her handbag before she intervenes. It is true that that sequence of events occurs occasionally, but if crime detection were to depend on this consecution criminal statistics would be considerably reduced. It is fair to say that officers and detectives do not rely solely on the method of pragmatic deduction. Instead, the police and the store detective in the course of their routine encounters, guided by inductive reasoning, build up a perceptual shorthand of 'preludes' to particular kinds of law-breaking activity.[4] These 'preludes' form the basis of presumptions about the likelihood of a crime being committed. Thus it is the presence or indeed absence of a 'prelude' which lead police or store detectives to conclude *a priori* that there may be adequate grounds for suspicion, or sufficient grounds for letting a setting, situation, or person 'pass'. Consider for instance the grounds for Sherlock Holmes's suspicion following a report of an intruder:

> 'Is there any other point to which you would wish to draw my attention?'
> 'To the curious incident of the dog in the night-time.'
> 'The dog did nothing in the night-time.'
> 'That was the curious incident', remarked Sherlock Holmes.[5]

Out of place and incongruous

The offences to be investigated in the study are loitering for the purposes of prostitution and theft from shops and departmental stores. The corresponding law-enforcement agencies implicated in the respective detection of these infractions are patrol officers and store detectives or else persons delegated to act as security officers. As I have indicated, it is the way in which the 'apparatus of control' functions which influences the images of deviants held. And as Lemert (1951) has so adequately indicated, secondary deviation results in adaptations by deviants to that control. 'Having discovered the prosaic nature of much of his life under a new status, the deviant, like other people, usually tries to make out as best he can.'[6] There is then a continual interplay between law-enforcement agencies and the deviant, which I will refer to from now on as a 'circular feedback loop', where the strategies, ploys, and activities of the law-breaker often represent survival strategies characterised by evasion tactics, disguise, decoy and avoidance.

Central to the police officers' endeavour is the necessity to evolve what has loosely been described elsewhere as a 'lay sociology of crime'. But in their rather unique role as law-enforcement officers the 'lay sociology' to which they subscribe is somewhat more specific to the police as a group. As Young explains this is principally because the police have, 'by the very nature of their role, a high degree of face-to-face contact with deviants'.[7] In the process of building up and constructing this lay knowledge officers evoke a 'perceptual shorthand' (Skolnick 1966: 45) which guides and directs them in assessing persons and situations. This knowledge is founded on a series of background assumptions concerning what is expected or typical of a setting, locality or person and what is untypical or out of place, what particular features of persons or places indicate suspicion, and finally, if and when a crime has been committed, what features indicate 'normal crime' in the sense that explanations and motivations for crime methods and locations take on common characteristics.

The first aim of policing agents, then, would be to acquire a 'particularisation of knowledge of people and places'. In a study of peace-keeping Bittner (1967)[8] points out how as a general rule the skid-row patrol man knows about the residents in his area, likely activities, social scenes and networks. This leads him on to develop a knowledge of people who are, as Piliavin and Werthman described, 'out of place',[9] or as Adams says, 'people who do not "belong"'.[10] The police in routine encounters with neighbourhoods soon become aware of persons who are 'out of place', the well-dressed woman in a slum neighbourhood for instance. In this context Adams (1963), in an article which discusses subjects for field interrogation, advised officers to be suspicious and look for the unusual. Of the list of likely persons subject to field interrogations he included (1) suspicious persons known to the officer; (9) unescorted women or young girls in public places, particularly at night in such places as cafés, bars, bus and train depots and street corners; (17) persons wearing a coat on a hot day. The nature of police discretion is yet another important consideration in the final selection of 'out of place' suspects. Similarly, David Powis (1977) in a British police training manual describes in elaborate detail the kind of person who is a possible prostitute or thief. The classical conduct of a prostitute is described in these terms:

> Evidence of her entering motor cars frequently, with the driver, who is almost invariably the sole occupant, and then to return half an hour or so later, to the same place, by the same car, is the classical conduct. So is her friendly acceptance by smiles, greetings and gossip with other women acting in a similar fashion nearby.

Whilst the classical conduct of the thief is described thus: 'A woman dressed in a feminine fashion without a handbag . . . The tip is only really significant with a woman who looks out of place without a handbag,' always identifiable by 'the direct and incursively searching glance'.[11] Piliavin and Briar (1964) reveal the way the police, for instance, have the discretion to bring certain juveniles to trial whilst ignoring the identical infractions of others.

The sequential process of identifying 'preludes'
In routine encounters with certain deviants it has been suggested elsewhere that the police develop a perceptual shorthand in order that they may identify certain

people as 'symbolic assailants', that is, people 'who use gesture, language and attire that the policeman has come to recognise as a prelude to violence' (Skolnick, 1966, p. 45). Consider for instance Jock Young's conclusion, that being West Indian, wearing dark glasses, being 'cool', were considered by police in the late sixties and early seventies as indicators of drug use. Cicourel (1968) similarly found that police develop 'theories about individuals and groups, morality and immorality, good and bad people, institutions, practices and typifications of community settings, and such theories or conceptions are employed in routine way'. Thus the officer's preconstituted typifications and stock of knowledge of particular ecological settings, of persons with known styles of dress and physical appearance, provide him with quick inferences about 'what is going on'. These assumptions of activities, characteristics of persons which act as pointers or 'preludes' go hand-in-hand with particular offences, so that there is a given image or set of typifications that go together to construct the police stereotype of the homosexual, the prostitute or the shoplifter. The image may bear little relation to the reality but it may have some considerable influence in affecting those deviants apprehended. Indeed, 'These types are assigned names and roles, are attributed a *modus operandi* and are known by their dress, posture.'

Neither the police nor the store detective proceed in a classic manner, though in describing their activities they may claim in their respective ways to do policing according to a precise method of deduction.[12] The store detective is perhaps particularly guilty of this occupational role presentation. When questioned about the main things to look for, a detective typically recalls as if by rote of order of events necessary to a successful prosecution, known somewhat affectionately to those in the business as 'the three Cs' – (1) see the item taken; (2) continue to see; (3) see failure to pay – thereby imbuing the detection process with a prescribed order, of surveillance to fit prosecution sequencing.

On the contrary, detection, as I have stated earlier, depends on a method of pragmatic induction. Thus other characteristics of persons and places are important in indicating suspiciousness. As Werthman and Piliavin (1967: 75) observes, 'Policemen develop indicators of suspicion by a method of pragmatic induction,' and the apparent success of employing such a method depends very much on 'inferring the probability of criminality from the appearances persons present in public places'. (Sacks 1972: 282) But as Skolnick critically points out, 'In order to locate "suspicious persons" police must use indicators, each with a specific but by no means perfect probability of leading them either to the discovery or prevention of a crime' (Werthman and Piliavin 1967: 75). Thus 'their task is to locate suspicious people on sight, and this must be done by inferring moral character from appearances' (Werthman and Piliavin 1967: 75).

Suspicious appearances

In drawing on the work of Goffman (1963: 83) and others, suspicious behaviour is indicated by persons being out of place or 'inappropriate in the situation'. In turning specifically to the question of appearances and inferences which the police draw from such appearances, indicators of suspiciousness can be seen very much as the consequence of the way in which the observed and observer are so tightly bound. However the method of inferring suspicion itself is criticised by, amongst others, both Matza and Cicourel for being taken for granted. Amongst these operational routines is the practice of always surveying those persons known to the police, whose moral character has already been established. As Cicourel (1968) indicates, certain males are always watched at football games and questioned in connection with certain offences[13] (cf. Matza 1969: 194). But what is the method routinely used to infer moral character of suspicious persons unknown to the police? Sacks (1972) in 'Notes on police assessment of moral character' provides the most illuminating description of a practice used by the specialist in recognising 'suspicious persons'. He describes the method as an 'incongruity procedure'. In this procedure the learned normal appearances are to constitute the background expectations so that any slight variation may present itself as a matter for investigation. Provided with the notion of normal appearances Sacks goes on to argue that a notion of 'normal crime' may be constructed. Using the term 'normal crimes' in a slightly different sense to Sudnow, he writes: 'it may be defined as that crime that is so managed within an area that those so engaged appear while so engaged as features of its normal appearance' (288). With regard to the visual encounters, 'the police soon learn to rely on hostile looks and furtive glances as signs of possible guilt'.[14]

Police encounters with prostitutes in Moss Side

As I have indicated earlier images of deviants are frequently synonymous with sex, class and gender such that the image of the murderer is invariably male, the shoplifter invariably female and the drug pusher black and male, and so on. The images may seen unwarrantable and unconvincing when reality is examined. The streetwalker is inevitably regarded as female as defined in statute. But in reality characteristics of persons relating to class, appearance, socio-economic position, etc., are by no means as legally determined. The images of the streetwalker subscribed to by the law-enforcement agencies is crucial in the surveillance, apprehension and arrest of particular women. And it is important to discover the particular typifications of streetwalkers, indicators of suspicion, and the mental check-list patrol officers adopt, in establishing the routine grounds for the basis of their 'suspicion'.

The researcher and her assistant were granted the opportunity of working with one divisional area police force in the Greater Manchester area, and observing the routine activities of patrolmen performing their duties of the cautioning and arresting of prostitutes. Part of this exercise necessitated discussions and interviews with police patrol officers. As Skolnick discovered in his study of the organisation and functions of the Westville vice control squad composed of a lieutenant, three sergeants and sixteen patrolmen,

> By describing the behaviour patterns of the prostitutes in the context of police administration, her symbolic criminality, her ability to frustrate conviction, and her role in the operation of the vice control squad, it should be possible to demonstrate further how interactional patterns between police and suspect affect the police conception of a criminal case and its outcome. (1966: 96)

Adopting a sequential model, the police in their routine encounters with prostitutes build on an already held stock of knowledge of their activities, behaviour and demeanour. In their response to constant surveillance prostitutes in order to evade detection evolve a series of 'making out' or adaption strategies which are specifically intended to immunise them from preliminary or further detection. Police in turn soon come to identify these strategies of evasion and thus the prostitute is forced to be constantly alerted to evolving new ways of becoming invisible and avoiding police detection, with the consequence that an escalating spiral of evasion and counter-evasion strategies develop.

The procedure

The activities of patrol officers in various regions are shaped by the criminal law, the prosecution process and by regional policies as much as by individual discretion, which lead to inter-urban variations in the use and application of the cautioning system. A system introduced following the 1959 Act it was intended to allow for arrest and charge only of those women observed loitering for the purposes of prostitution on the third occasion. The precise interpretation with regard to the implementation of the cautioning system is provided for in a number of Home Office Circulars, 108, 109 and 112, 1959.

Paragraph 5 of Circular 108/1959 states:

> The procedure which will be adopted in the Metropolitan Police District is as follows:
> On the first occasion when a woman who has not previously been convicted of loitering or soliciting for the purpose of prostitution is seen loitering or soliciting in a street or public place for that purpose the officer seeing her will obtain the assistance of a second officer as a witness, and when both officers, after having kept the woman under observation, are satisfied by her demeanour

and conduct that she is in fact loitering or soliciting for the purpose of prostitution they will tell her what they have seen and caution her. Details of the caution will subsequently be recorded at the police station and in a central register for the Metropolitan Police District. The two officers, after administering the caution, will ask the woman if she is willing to be put in touch with a moral welfare organisation or a probation officer and invite her to call at the police station at a convenient time to see a woman police officer for these arrangements to be made, unless she prefers her name and address to be given to a welfare organisation or probation officer without going to the station. If the woman continues to loiter or solicit for the purpose of prostitution, a second formal caution will be given in the street and recorded, and a second offer will be made to put her in touch with a welfare organisation or probation officer. She will not be arrested until she is seen loitering or soliciting on the third occasion.

This procedure was introduced in other areas in accordance with Paragraph 7 of a later Circular 112/1959.

The purpose of the cautioning system is to avoid the possible wrongful prosecution of women who are not prostitutes and to enable officers to put women in contact with the probation service (see Chapter 2). But since cautions are not a formal prerequisite of conviction the system has generated much criticism, as it is open to wide interpretation and discretion. It has been recognised by many and acceded more recently by some members of the Criminal Law Revision Committee 1982 that 'cautioning facilitates the conviction of the guilty' (3.15) but the fact that a woman has been cautioned repeatedly is not conclusive of her being a prostitute.

The system also contributes to the peripatetic existence characteristic of many prostitutes and exposes them to continual harassment. As the Criminal Law Revision Committee again have stated:

A system which leaves the police with considerable discretion is bound to expose them to this kind of criticism, especially from interested parties. It tends to make adversaries of prostitutes and police officers.

The method

The entire divisional team of officers responsible for cautioning, apprehending and arresting prostitutes was questioned, including the ranks of inspector and sergeant. Informal discussion schedules were devised and in a confidential setting each officer was provided with the opportunity of responding to a series of questions put to him/her. Information was collected on all aspects of police work including attitudes to the present law, cautioning system, prosecution process, and sentencing of prostitutes. In contrast to the popular belief that police merely uphold the law, responses to certain questions revealed a deep dissatisfaction with the law and a commitment to the need for reform of the law relating to prostitution, although it seemed clear that collectively officers were not always inclined to present this image in public places and particularly in the presence of other male officers.

Indicators of suspicion

One of the main objects of such interviews was to discover the methods used for inferring moral character from appearances. The following question was asked: 'In your routine encounter with the prostitutes in the street, what features of their behaviour/demeanour indicate to you that they are "loitering for the purposes of prostitution"?' The problem of verbalising hunches, feelings and subsequent actions which are conveyed in signs, gestures or glances as adequate grounds for arousing officers' suspicion was a difficulty expressed by most interviewees. This led to establishing their belief in adequate grounds for suspicion though the cues could not be verbalised:

'You know what you've seen but you can't describe it.'

'About three or four of the older girls really look the part.'

'There's something about a girl when she's actually doing it that's different, you can pick her out even if you don't know her.'

'Sort of feeling you get . . . I couldn't describe it, but if you see one walking down the street you could point her out and you would be right.'

Despite the certainty of this last statement officers are not always accurate. One officer related the occasion when he erroneously apprehended a woman leaving a church, and another, perhaps in eagerness to demonstrate his surveillance skills as we drove slowly behind a pedestrian exclaimed 'She's one'. Upon driving past 'she' came into full view — complete with moustache and beard; patrolmen's guides for suspicion are not always adequate!

But in doing police work in most cases locating a prostitute depends on the psychological 'figure all effect' and is largely implicit. Attempts to establish the method of inferring 'she's one' from appearances was revealed, if ever so slightly, by further questioning. Officers particularly noted and associated purposeless behaviour as indicative of suspicious. Cues or preludes to prostitution were to be inferred from 'non-purposeful behaviour', Officers made repeated reference to 'walking slowly, walking aimlessly', 'standing on a corner'. Such conduct was responded to by an increase in surveillance in order that the basis of their assumptions may be tested. Prostitution activities were even more strongly indicated by women who were seen to be looking at drivers and particularly at lone drivers in passing cars, whilst 'bending and peering into cars' was taken as hard evidence, not merely one among other indicators, that such activity was indeed going on.

Roughs and respectables

Cues relating to dress and physical appearance provided adequate grounds for excluding certain women or alternatively inferring a commitment to prostitution. In this context patrol officers subscribe to an image of 'roughs' and 'respectables'. Thus a woman with an aura of respectability would be beyond their suspicion. As one officer explained, 'It goes back to the class system of this country, I would think twice about a respectable-looking woman even if I may see her.' Whilst another officer, again using lack of respectability as a central defining feature asserted, 'It's not really the clothing, they've got no self-respect.' From this basic division of women as a class, officers explained that the prostitute was easily detected because of the image she portrayed: wearing tight skirts, low-cut blouses, short dresses and thigh boots, uplifting bras and suspender belts. Types of attire or their absence were read as a means of facilitating business and since the wearing of tights posed a particular time-consuming hazard, women without tights were immediately suspected of prostitution.

'Out of place' and innocent

Particular clues and behaviour patterns frequently suggested to an officer that the girl being surveyed might in fact be innocent. 'It may be obvious from what she is wearing or carrying that she is innocent'; the officer goes on to qualify this: 'I have never seen a punk prostitute . . . or a prostitute carrying a bag of shopping.' But it is not always certain that all officers will agree. Conversely another officer stated that carrying a shopping bag, taking kids along, standing outside pubs and shops is also a typical avoidance strategy. Although as some of the more experienced officers pointed out, efforts by prostitutes to throw police off the scent do not always work. One officer asserted, 'You can tell from the way they're walking it's not the way you would walk to a chip shop.'

Apprehending the 'known prostitute'

Most patrol work involves encounters with known prostitutes. One officer explained that, 'In 70 per cent of the cases you know the girl anyway.' And it is here that the use of discretion by officers is the most criticised. As Carol Smart (1976) alleges: 'Once a woman has actually been arrested for soliciting she becomes known as a "common prostitute" and if she is found soliciting again, or merely loitering in a public place, she is subject to further arrests.' It is by no means always the case that apprehension follows the patrol officer investigating a situation where there are 'reasonable grounds for suspicion' for example if girls have been seen to approach a vehicle, talk with the driver, or get into the car. The 'known prostitute' is by her notoriety already a prime target for surveillance and because of her reputation encounters frequent police harassment, based on a presumption of the likelihood of recidivism. In this respect the spirit of the judgment in *McArdle* v *Egan and others* [1933] All ER 611 – 'the fact that a suspect has in the past been convicted of similar offences would not *by itself* afford "reasonable suspicion"' – is not being followed.

Encounters at the station

Contrary to Skolnick's findings, when brought in to be cautioned or charged, prostitutes were on extremely friendly terms with the police, although it was clear that this depended on the reciprocity of sociability. As the sergeant said to the uncooperative prostitutes, 'You be fair with us and we'll be fair with you.' No woman was ever degraded, handcuffed or brought in forcibly, as was reported in Skolnick's study. On the contrary suspects were encouraged to phone friends and more importantly to ensure that children were being properly supervised. They were often provided with cigarettes, tea and sympathy. The postures that Skolnick observed in Westville were not evident in Manchester. Encounters at the station carried an aura about them that the game was over. Indeed encounters at the station, like those on the street, were very much characterised by an 'indulgency pattern', bound by a set of informal rules.

Patrol officers were also asked whether this interpretation of them was a fair one: 'The police are charged with interpretation of the law where, as in offences related to prostitution, a double standard applies; their harassment of prostitutes and reluctance to pursue kerb-crawlers is revealing.'[15] All officers interviewed thought that this was an exceptionally naive assertion since they agreed that if they had a law they would arrest the punters. As one officer remarked, 'We can't decide what is good or bad law'. This suggests that the police have little choice but to implement the law, though the way they enforce it is open to scrutiny. 'Indeed the police are in a sense the fall guys of the legal system, taking the blame for any injustices in the operation of the law, both in theory (in the assumption like Skolnick's that they break the rules) and indeed, in the law.'[16]

Officers agreed that prostitution was only a violation rather than a real breaking of the law. Some officers argued that it should be legalised, whilst others maintained that the apprehension of prostitutes was not proper police work, diverting valuable force strength away from the 'real' police work of protecting the public from mugging and violence. One officer demanded, 'Legalise it and let us get back to proper jobs!'

Prostitutes' encounters with police – the data

Twenty-two women formed the interview sample and were selected as they were detained at the local police station for the purposes of recording and caution or else for the purpose of arrest. Following the initial charge or caution they were approached by the researcher and asked if they would be prepared to give their views on the existing law. Women were interviewed in a special room allocated for the purpose, where all interviews were treated confidentially. All women approached during a two-week period in April 1982 agreed to participate and in fact were more than glad to do so.

Prostitutes as victims

In talking with prostitutes and observing their self-images and definitions a conflict of imagery between police definitions and self-definitions was immediately apparent.[17] Firstly, rather than perceiving themselves as offenders, women frequently regarded themselves as victims (see James 1978b). This feeling arose because of their treatment by the criminal law in general, and because of the non-prosecution of the kerb-crawler or punter. Prostitutes felt victimised by patrol officers and particularly resented surveillance by women patrol officers. A similar conflict of interests was evident between prostitutes and women magistrates, but here the resentment and feeling of victimisation was felt much more strongly: 'you see the way they look at you when in the dock. They're always old bags with sour faces who walk past as if you are a slut.'[18]

This feeling of victimisation extended outside their treatment in the criminal justice system for offences of loitering extending to their realistic assessment that they were denied equal protection under any statute within the criminal law (see Chapter 2). They felt particularly vulnerable due to a lack of protection regarding assault. One woman complained, 'If a prostitute gets raped or battered the police won't do anything about it unless they have got a car number. They just haven't got time to make note of it . . . ridiculous!'

There is of course every justification for this feeling of being a social victim. Since the 1976 Sexual Offences (Amendment) Act, rape trials in particular have been monitored for the degree to which they are conducted in accordance or at variance with section 2(1) of the Act.

> If at a trial any person is for the time being charged with a rape offence to which he pleads not guilty, then, except with the leave of the judge, no cross-examination shall be adduced or asked at the trial, by or on behalf of any defendant at the trial about any sexual experience of the complainant with a person other than the defendant.

Yet if the complainant is a prostitute past moral character is still admissible in accordance with section 2(1) of the Act. Moreover, Adler's research has overwhelmingly revealed that applications by counsel were more readily allowed if the moral character of the complainant was in doubt and particularly if the complainant was a prostitute.[19]

In the event of injury following criminal assault, claims for compensation made by prostitutes may be considerably reduced or indeed rejected altogether simply because of their 'life style'.[20] Consider, for instance, the application made by Marcella Claxton to the Criminal Injuries Compensation Board following injuries received in May 1976 from Peter Sutcliffe. Her original claim for compensation in 1978 was refused on the grounds of her supposed 'way of life', and that she had 'clearly misled the police and provoked the attack' (*Yorkshire Post,* 22 December 1982). After five years the Board acknowledged that there was no question of provocation (and remember we are talking about the Ripper!) following evidence from the police officer who had interviewed Sutcliffe when he pleaded guilty and admitted that he had attempted to murder her. Ms Claxton was finally awarded £17,500.

Within the criminal justice system itself prostitutes continue to feel they have a raw deal, regarding any instances of just treatment as merely one-off occurrences. The details of the case of Alan Allcot found guilty of the rape and buggery of a prostitute in 1978, [1981] 3 CAR (S) 18–20 reveal the not uncommon unsavoury experience of the prostitute. The details in the Allcot case are in fact typical of the experiences of prostitutes and since the general view is that 'she' will do anything or if 'she' is unwilling 'who cares', then the courts and the public are not usually sympathetic. This attitude has changed very little; as George Vivian Poore wrote in 1901 of the victims of Jack the Ripper, 'they were not violated because most of them were prostitutes'.[21] And whilst prostitutes are frequently raped and sodomised, rather than attempt to bring a criminal prosecution they accept such instances of male violence as an inevitable hazard of their trade (McLeod 1982). As Miers (1978) asserts, 'Whether a prostitute can recover damages from a dissatisfied customer who attacks her is not a question which frequently exercises the courts' (c.f. *Hegarty* v *Shine* (1878) 14 Cox CC at 145; *Burns* v *Edman* [1970] 2 QB at 541; *Gray* v *Barr* [1971] 2 QB at 544).[22] Perhaps the case of Mary Bernard, a Wolverhampton prostitute who was not prepared to accept the brutal intimidation of a bullying and violent husband (who had forced her into prostitution) and poured paraffin over him, setting him alight, reflects the occasional sympathy of the law in this respect: she was merely put on probation for three years (*The Times,* 18 June 1982).

Second, and again in contrast to police images of prostitutes, many women also subscribed to an heroic or altruistic view of their work and role in society. They considered themselves as responsible for allowing the moral bedrock of society, in marriage, to perpetuate. Some, in fact 20 per cent, actually saw their role as 'marriage-saving', a theme recurrent in sociological analyses of prostitution. Kate Millett's (1975) case study of four prostitutes provides invaluable insight into the strength of this view among American call girls.[23] Similarly, in this context consider Lecky's assertion that harlotry sustains the family[24] and Engel's comments on prostitution and marriage.[25] Prostitutes, instead, perceived their service to society as one of allowing the free expression and safe channelling of sexual perversion which, if frustrated, would otherwise be expressed in rape, sexual assault, child molestation or murder. In interview women remarked:

'If it wasn't for us there'd be a lot more rapes . . . can't see why they curse people like us, we are doing society a great favour . . . ', 'saves a lot of marriages and rapes', 'saving a lot of rapes and child molesting. A lot of men pull up and say "Can you get me a young girl?"', 'I'm saving peoples lives from being raped and murdered.'

The argument that the free expression of pornography may in fact avert sex crimes was a consideration raised on a more informed level by some members of the Williams Committee (Report of the Committee on Obscenity and Film Censorship).[26] Members of the Committee agreed with Kutchinsky's research in Denmark which revealed that certain categories of sex crimes declined significantly with the free availability of pornography,[27] though that is not a view supported by Gray (1982)[28] who argues that pornography sets the scene for the way in which men habitually view women.

Selling sex – cash or kind

Feelings of victimisation also stemmed from the reaction of society to them. During interview women pointed out that their selling of sexual services for money was no different from a wife's sale of a sexual service to her husband or a woman's sale to a man for 'kind'. Indeed, prostitutes considered their transaction a more honest one.

'It's my body and I can do what I like with it. Everyone is a prostitute in some way If a wife wants a fur coat she will go to bed a bit earlier with her husband.'

'It's better to sell sex than give it to any Tom, Dick or Harry . . . They're tramps those who do it for a bottle of wine or a meal.'

Prostitutes see prostitution very much as the giving and withholding of sexual favours for an ulterior economic purpose, a view Kingsley Davis would challenge.

He identified several crucial differences between prostitution and other institutions involving sex differences resting upon the functional relation between society and sexual institutions. Prostitution he distinguished from other sexual institutions since the arrangement is impersonal, contractual for money and for pleasure – a means to a private end, although Engels maintained that marriages of convenience in particular may be instances of the crassest prostitution, 'more generally on the part of the wife, who differs from the ordinary courtesan only in that she does not hire out her body, like a wage-worker, on piecework, but sells it into slavery once for all.'[29]

How much?

There were certain similarities in the observed street transactions regarding services offered and the price decided, compared with the research findings of Skolnick (1966) Greenwood (1981) and McLeod (1982). The women in the sample all said they offered 'straight' sex though many were reluctant to discuss the breadth of other services rendered. Clearly, a tacit scale of earnings was understood by both punters and prostitutes. The going rate for a 'play-around' was £5, 'straight sex' inside a house or apartment £15 and sex 'in a gam', which (to those unfamiliar with the argot) indicates fellatio with the use of a sheath, £10. The average wage of girls varied considerably (McLeod 1982: 43). One prostitute interviewed who claimed to be quite different from the streetwalker who she regarded as her inferior, said she could earn £600 a week. Most of the women earned considerably less, possibly £100–£200 a week.

Secondary deviation or adaptation and modus vivendi

Lemert suggested that one of the key aspects of the deviants' response to societal reaction expresses itself in adaptation. But just as law-enforcement agencies develop a method of inferring moral character from appearance, deviants or would-be deviants soon learn the 'perceptual shorthand' held by the police and alter their appearances and conduct accordingly, a matter Werthman and Piliavin (1967) were soon to discover. Indeed, prostitutes, shoplifters and other lawbreakers are constantly evolving ways of beating the system and 'making out'. In their study of gang members Werthman and Piliavin found that one of the 'making out' or 'adaptation' strategies was to evolve a socially acceptable reason or justification for being on the street in the first place.

Prostitutes together with the homosexual and drugtaker depend upon their visibility on the street for successful business transactions. They are in the unique position of having to maintain a level of visibility for the purpose of clients, yet invisible for evading police detection (Sacks 1972: 283; Rock 1973: 113; Sudnow 1965: 261). The first strategy is naturally to avoid arousing police suspicion.

Goffman has already talked at length of such strategies and Lemert has similarly asserted, 'There is always some basis for adaptation or a modus vivendi open to the deviant.' In efforts to remain visible yet invisible prostitutes will depend firstly on the props of neutralisation of suspicion and secondly if detected on the provision of acceptable alibis. In her routine business of loitering she will frequently create a degree of uncertainty and ambiguity about her purpose for being on the street. She will frequently be seen carrying either a shopping or washing bag so that her behaviour may be considered beyond suspicion and 'normal' or else if under suspicion soon normalised with the ready provision of an alibi. Children are occasionally strung along to act as decoys or a *modus vivendi* when loitering is done in pairs. In addition, prostitutes are now taking to standing outside pubs or restaurants with the acceptable alibi of 'just waiting for friends'. For the woman living in the area the problems of ordinary mobility are great, placing her under constant suspicion and surveillance. And for the known prostitute who is a resident, life can become intolerable.

Rough justice, or fair cop?

In their encounters with police, prostitutes will work out a communication system and indulgency pattern whereby each can go about their street activities in mutual co-existence and not as adversaries. Prostitutes regarded police as straight and merely doing a job, thus when cautioned or arrested that was viewed as an inevitable occupational consequence, although what was considered a fair apprehension was nevertheless bound by a set of implicit rules. The 'fair cop' was regarded as a charge after patrol officers had seen the suspect soliciting on two occasions, whilst 'rough justice' was being cautioned twice in one week. Rough justice lead to an inevitable breakdown of the indulgency pattern. Two girls cautioned on consecutive nights responded to this 'rough justice' by being uncooperative, causing a considerable disturbance and disruption at the local Station. However, the picture painted by Skolnick of the girls is not true to the Manchester study, where any lack of co-operation took place in the context of response to what the girls considered to be unfair treatment. Some known prostitutes felt that they were particularly in receipt of 'rough justice'. 'Once you're known they pick you up for nothing'; 'One thing I don't like is once they know you and you pass walking down the street the police will pull up in their car and look at you. It's not very nice if I'm with the family.' But some identified the game-like quality of evading the police, 'I'm happy: it's a cat and mouse game'. Implicit rules of the game were shared. Police were nice to the girls and expected co-operation in fingerprinting and statements in return, and the girls in time went along quietly expecting police to turn a blind eye on the next occasion. An 'indulgency pattern'[30] was evident between patrol officers and prostitutes, where the police were lenient and a flexible application of the rules of cautioning and prosecution was regarded as necessary to achieving a mutual co-existence on the streets.

Store detectives and suspicious shoppers

Again as with the police study a sample of twelve store detectives were selected from a number attending a Group 4 Training programme in Worcestershire (which the author attended), and from those working in department stores in the Manchester area the aim being to discover whether store detectives operated with prescribed images of typical or likely shoplifters such that surveillance, apprehension and prosecution practices were affected. Once again, the focal question considered the extent to which particular images of female shoplifters in influencing perceptual constructs held by the store detective may have the impact of sifting out as suspects only those persons conforming to the stereotype. Suppose, for example, that the majority of convicted shoplifters at any one time had only one hand and were short in height. The consequence of this image for the detection process would have the impact of ensuring that store detectives would survey only those persons bearing these characteristics.

Store detectives' demeanour – to catch a thief

In order to catch a thief, unlike the police in relation to street crime, the store detective must go unnoticed. It was not altogether surprising that the author found only one male security officer amongst two groups of women participating in a Group 4 Training programme. The sex-relatedness of the store detective is significant since it is women who figure most visibly as household consumers and purchasers. As one senior security officer explained, 'Women blend more into the background as there are more women shoppers.' Indeed, the degree to which store detectives looked invisible also indicated the likelihood of their success, and depended on (amongst other things) clothing, demeanour and facial expression. The first requirement was expressed by the need to go unnoticed in the particular store in which they were working. Two detectives from Cumbria talked of the need to vary costume in order that they may not appear out of place or obvious. One talked of wearing tweeds and jodhpurs, whilst another detective working in the London area talked of wearing a headscarf and glasses,' dirty shoes, old clothes and a mac' in the anticipation that she might 'pass' as a typical shopper.

Detectives talked also of the facial appearances it was necessary to maintain in order that they might 'pass'. The need to look absent and vacant, and not alert and inquisitive was stressed most forcibly. It was not surprising therefore to find that a naturally extremely glum and expressionless member of the Group 4 course team had a most impressive record of arrests. Similarly the need to merge successfully with shoppers in a particular shopping precinct in Manchester has resulted in one city store recently employing two black male store detectives to deal with young blacks found pilfering.

Subjective indicators of suspicion

In conversation, store detectives revealed that they operated with a blueprint for locating suspicious persons. From the overall manner of suspects, to more particular features of demeanour, detectives agreed on some of the more salient features. Persons looking around, standing with an article in their hand, eyes wandering slowly looking for shop staff or the store detective, were persons whose behaviour constituted reasonable grounds for suspicion.

Particular emphasis was placed on the significance of eye contact. Drawing on the work of Goffman (1963: 93) on 'face engagements', eye contact can be an important indicator of conduct. One detective explained, 'You can judge a person with shifty eyes', whilst another emphasised, 'the facial expressions are always a give-away. They are looking for assistants not assistance and their eyes are moving from side to side.' Detectives talked too of the carbon-copy shoplifter. Such observations were in line with research conducted by Bennett (1968), who found that security officers maintained that they could recognise a shoplifter as soon as he entered the shop. Store detectives also shared knowledge not only about the demeanour of a suspect shoplifter but her/his likely location in the store, since 'doing pilfering' is less readily detected in a secluded area.

Unfortunately information was not available on the number of occasions so-called suspicious-looking persons were surveyed and yet suspicions falsely held, though as a recent *Guardian* article (19 January 1983) reveals there are many innocent victims. For instance certain behaviour such as glancing around after an item has been concealed, and no attempt to pay has been made, may reasonably be interpreted as looking for assistants. In the event of no item being taken similar gestures are normalised as looking for assistance, goods, husbands or fellow shoppers.

Objective indicators of suspicion

Certain manoeuvres, gestures and attire of shoppers were frequently considered to be pointers to particular methods of shoplifting. Knowledge of the 'Booster's box' and peacher's apron alert them to certain garments. Other methods were to conceal goods in a smock or in a sleeve, or to conceal items in a hat, gloves or scarf. Attention was also alerted to the 'wear away' situation where shoplifters enter a store without a coat and leave wearing one. Another ploy is to enter a store and then to leave looking eight months pregnant. In all sixteen of the accounts analysed and in a further nine of cases observed store detectives noticed one or more of the following: unzipped shoulder bag, bag with one handle on the wrist and the other hanging thus leaving the bag open, carrying hat, gloves, scarf, newspaper in hand, and carrying some of the aforesaid items in a shopping bag. Most indicators related to women and their conduct. Indeed, literature on shop theft observes principally women (see Bennett (1968) and Merricks (1970), whilst Gibbens, Palmer and Prince in a ten-year follow up study of 886 shoplifts in 1971 found significant differences between men and women, where Gibbens presented a clinical picture of a woman with mixed physical and mental symptoms. Detectives also look for people who are out of place, children of school age in the store during school time, individuals in the wrong areas of the store, e.g. men in the cosmetic department.

Retrospective interpretations and reconstructing suspicion – evidence in court

When called upon to give evidence in court the store detectives' observation of the sequence of events is presented in a chronological order. The ordering of events proceeds from noticing the accused prior to the theft itself. This reconstruction suggests to the audience that there was already something unusual about the behaviour and manoeuvres of the accused. In fact suspicion is not aroused in any logical sequence at all. Once a suspicious sequence has been observed all previous activity is reinterpreted in the context of that one event (see Kitsuse 1964: 96).

In order that we may examine in greater detail the circumstances surrounding suspicion and the manner in which the story is related to the court in a trial, the trials of twenty defendants were analysed and the statements of sixteen store detectives scrutinised. The attention of store detectives is often drawn depending on the objective and subjective method of the shoplifter adopted. Consider the following statements.

Statement One

I was on duty when my attention was drawn to the accused. She was in possession of a wire basket, provided by the store, which contained a Debenham's carrier bag. The basket was in her left hand together with her own handbag. I saw Smith select a tray of steak which she placed into her wire basket face down on top of the carrier bag, and then folded the bag over the steak, partially concealing the tray pack. She selected further goods as she walked round the store, . . . I followed her and saw her looking about continually.

Statement Two

I was on duty in my employer's store in Huddersfield Road, Oldham, when my attention was drawn to a woman I now know as Green. She was pushing one of the store's wire trolleys and I noted she had a navy canvas shopping bag hung on the end of the trolley, one handle on the hook and the other handle on the thumb of her right hand so that the neck of the bag was open. I noted she had several items in the base of the trolley and on the ledge of the trolley she had two 'Lyons' spice cartons and a packet of nuts. She appeared to be looking about her in a nervous manner and when she was in the gardening aisle and no one was near her, I saw her take one of the 'Lyons' spice cartons off the ledge of the trolley and she put it in her own bag.

Statement Three

On duty in Tesco I saw the three accused standing near the display of ladies' clothing. They had a wire trolley which was empty. Mary was carrying a black shoulder bag which I saw her put on the shelf of the trolley. Jane unzipped the bag which I could see was empty. She picked up a jumper folded it over and then it disappeared. I could see she had not replaced it on the display or put it in the trolley. The same thing was done again with another jumper. I moved my position slightly where I was able to see Claire zipping up the bag, which was bulging; she passed the bag to Mary who left the store without attempting to pay. Claire was also carrying a similar bag. This too she put on the shelf of the trolley. Both were talking and looking around in a furtive manner.

What is quintessentially important about the sequential order of the statements of events is the discrepancy between the order of conceptual and perceptual events as they really happened and as they are recorded and presented for the prosecution case.

There are certain similarities between the sequential reconstruction of K's behaviour as described by Dorothy Smith following a medical diagnosis of mental illness, and the behaviour of the criminal accused following a charge of shoplifting. This shift in the sequencing of events is undertaken by the store detectives in their role as 'translators of reality'. What the court process demands in evidence is the structuring of events which point to guilt. Dorothy Smith explains this sequencing of events in connection with mental illness:

It is not just a record of events as they happened, but of events as they were seen as relevant to reaching a decision about the character of those events. But this method of inferring illness, guilt or whatever, by retrospective reconstruction is also a consequence of institutional demands and procedures for the correct assembling of relevant information. (p. 24).

As Smith says:

The various agencies of social control have institutionalised procedures for assembly . . . information about the behaviour of individuals so that it can be matched against the paradigms which provide the working criteria of class-membership. . . . .' (p. 24).

Like mental illness, the contruction of guilt involves a sequencing of events, judgments and preconceptions, not as they actually happened but in accordance 'with the "instructions" the concept provides'. Thus in court the store detective is prompted by the sequential order of counsel's questioning to give a particular retrospective interpretation and ordering of events. For instance, if the store detective were to provide an account of what happened in the following manner, it would soon be rejected as inadmissible though it might very well provide a more accurate account of what had occurred.

I was on duty in my employer's store in Huddersfield Road, Oldham when I saw the accused. I don't know exactly what it was about her but I just knew she was up to no good. I had this feeling she was going to lift something. I watched her carefully, and when she took one of the 'Lyons' spice cartons off the shelf I just knew she was going to steal it, and then well it just disappeared and I knew then for sure that she had taken it. Besides, the way she was carrying her shopping bag, one arm hung over the end of her trolley so that it was gaping open. She kept looking round to see if she could see a store detective, with a nervous look upon her face.

Doreen McBarnet (1976: 178) discusses the way in which the subjective decision to plead guilty 'is directly related to the legally defined situation in which it is taken; that the tendency to conviction is not arbitrary but built into the pattern of rights, limitations and powers established in pre-trial procedures to the benefit of the prosecution'. This tendency is particularly apparent in the legal processing of certain crimes, theft and loitering for the purposes of prostitution in particular. However in a trial, although the defendant is provided with the opportunity of stating what happened, certain versions are 'authorised as *that* version which can be treated by others as *what has happened*'.

And of course in the case of shoplifting many defendants, though seen to leave a store with item(s) unpaid for, do not necessarily intend the conduct, though some of them plead guilty.

Preconceptions and negotiated reality

Policemen and store detectives, like laymen and women, subscribe to relatively fixed characterisations of the typical offender and hold stereotypes of sub-categories of offenders such as prostitutes and shoplifters. Whilst in most situations stereotypes are thought to develop in the absence of first-hand information, both police and store detectives have first-hand knowledge which one would think enables them to reject the characterisation in preference for the real face-to-face encounter. But as I have indicated, the position of the police and store detective 'make for a reinforcement rather than a elimination of mass-media stereotypes'.[31] What happens in fact is that reality is negotiated to fit the preconceptions already held by the policing agencies. In consequence in the very process of apprehending a suspect, policing agencies unwittingly amplify the probability of detecting those persons whose mannerisms and demeanour are in accordance with the familiar stereotype (see Swigert and Farrell 1977). In turn the prosecution and conviction of such persons tends to confirm the image of the deviant initially held. The chicken first, egg last, it makes no difference, the concept of the offender so held dictates who is apprehended and in turn those apprehended define the nature of the deviant, so that what we have is a prophecy fulfilled and once again the principles for a future fulfilment. Such negotiations are informed by gender assumptions relating to demeanour and appearance. As one notorious female offender, Zoe Progyl, once wrote, 'Maybe it was the hat – I don't know – but it was surprising how many shop assistants accepted my phoney cheques when I dressed like this.'[32]

6 · Sentencing negotiations – Excuses and justifications

> We only ask about a man's motives when we wish in some way to hold his conduct up for assessment.
>
> Peters, *The Concept of Motivation* (1958: 29)

Introduction

Ordinary everyday conduct such as walking to the newsagents, taking the baby to the child-minder, catching a train to the city, clocking on before starting work, constitute part of our framework of unquestioned constructs. Such activity is part of what everyone knows and takes for granted. Such instances of behaviour are treated as non-problematic, bound by tacit rules and conventions which are never called into question even less acknowledged. However, when behaviour departs from these shared rules its 'out of place' or unconventional character is scrutinised and explanations warranted in order to redress the equilibrium. Garfinkel (1967) in his celebrated seminal paper 'Studies of the routine grounds of everyday activities'[1] makes out a case for the study of commonsense activities as topics of inquiry in their own right. Drawing heavily on work of Schutz, he sets out to examine the unnoticed background expectancies or 'attitude of daily life', in order to make known the underlying rules which bind everyday conduct.

The problematic or non-problematic nature of conduct as he and others observe is not determined by factors inherent in its nature alone but relies on the relation of conduct to role, culture and history.

Take, for instance, a person riding a bike – conduct not of itself problematic. The conduct of a man in riding a bike with a crossbar is behaviour which passes unquestioned. Conversely the conduct of a woman in riding a bike with a crossbar would not only be registered but immediately called into question. The observers would then wish for a satisfactory explanation of how this incongruity occurred, whether there is a shortage of bikes without crossbars, whether the procedure is safe. Such conduct where the woman is heavily pregnant would be met with even greater disbelief, amusement and perhaps alarm. As well as rule following or conforming behaviour the unusual or untypical is similarly circumscribed by a set of tacit rules and conventions which demand conformity within the prevailing paradigm, being designated as typed according to the social setting.[2] Consider the nature of the rules in these following situations, the first being bound by legal rules the second by social conventions. The murderous conduct of Peter Sutcliffe was met with the unanimous response 'He must be mad' (though for reasons relating to legal technicality and the promise of punishment jurors were not prepared to sanction such a definition). His murderous conduct defied all possible explanation, breaking all rules even within the boundaries of untypical behaviour.[3]

Law-breaking and deviant behaviour is similarly bound by tacit rules and conventions which render criminal conduct more or less understandable, such that under certain conditions it is considered justifiable – such as self-defence, or a legitimate response to extreme provocation, or the result of a rational decision because of dire economic need in petty pilfering. Particular forms of law-breaking conduct are typically accompanied by specific patterns of justifications and excuses. In the event of law-breaking conduct where there is an admission of guilt certain socially prescribed and acceptable verbalisations are invoked which have a special relevance to observers. Whilst most explanations for conduct in everyday life involve an element of 'remedial work', in the situation of the legal defendant in the criminal justice system this remedial aspect assumes a far greater importance as it may effectively result in a reduction of sentence. At appeal hearings judges are frequently observed varying appeals not on the ground that the magistrates' were too severe, but on the grounds that appellants have suffered enough. This is particularly the case if the appellant has tried to make amends, or shown guilt or remorse for her actions.

But the process from offering explanations for crime to remedial work is not necessarily logically causal, since as particular modes of conduct become identified with particular explanations modes of conduct actually evolve simultaneously with a corresponding explanation. We would not expect a sex offender to offer the verbalisation that he was short of money in explanation. Nor would we expect an offence of violence to be explained because of a desire to pay the gas bill. Indeed, explanations that are considered incongruous with the offence often serve as a pointer to uncooperative behaviour or mental illness. It is frequently the case that certain explanations come to characterise certain types of conduct. Deviant conduct is therefore typically characterised by a predefined possibility of explanations such that a deviant identity involves the verbalisation of a particular account. In another setting this identification of typical features of crime has been referred to as 'normal crime' where certain criminal conduct is characterised by a well-defined series of explanations.

At various stages within the criminal justice process following an admission or finding of guilt the defendant is provided with the opportunity of explaining her crime. This remedial procedure of stating why the rule was broken or law infringed is a significant feature of the role of mitigation by counsel and its possibility is also provided for in probation officer's social inquiry reports to the court. A significant feature of the social inquiry report, whose object amongst others is to provide the court with information which may 'serve as a pointer to delinquency', is provided by the accounts rendered by the client in explanation of the crime. Defendants' explanations and excuses are important for the impact they have on negotiating sentence, thereby representing an actor's practical method of bargaining for individualised justice.

Although there may be many explanations which characterise a particular activity, the remedial work done must be legally effective rather than merely socially exculpatory, so only those explanations which are likely to have an impact on sentencing are invoked. In this respect, and for this reason, accounts rendered by defendants are more likely to represent their anticipation and understanding of 'observers' rules' of relevance, rather than private motivational states, and especially in the case of a second or subsequent offender, are likely to be tailored to conceptions of magistrates' and judges' rules of behaviour rather than to the 'generalised other'.[4] Thus the extent to which such motivatory accounts are honoured or rejected depends very much on the defendant's correct anticipation of 'observers' rules'. Whilst much of the research on sentencing has monitored the possible impact officers recommendations have on final sentencing outcome the practical effect of the defendant's mitigation on sentencing has been considered of tangential importance. In the scarcity of research in this direction we can first of all draw on knowledge of the practical impact of explanations and apologies in remedying the situation in everyday life. A child, following an admission of guilt, is told, 'Now say you're sorry.'

The legal situation is similarly bound by admissions, apologies and admonitions. A judge in sentencing in the event of a guilty plea typically says, 'I accept your plea of guilt and make allowances for this in sentencing. However, that is not to say that what you did was not a very evil thing. Nevertheless I take into account that you have shown remorse for your actions . . .' Judge John Sirica in his handling of the Watergate trials explained his sentencing of defendants in terms of whether they expressed sorrow, regret, remorse and contrition. Those defendants who did not were given harsher sentences.[5] (See Thomas 1979: 217.)

An examination of accounts also provides an occasion in which an understanding of female motivation emerges in relation to specific patterns of conduct, and may be instrumental in inducing sentencing discounts. This discussion then proceeds with a more specific consideration of the function of motive in conduct and considers the impact of remedial work and the forms and patterns it takes in the offences of shoplifting and prostitution.

The sociology of explanations

Sociological theory from Max Weber onwards has indicated that motivation arises socially in a process of interaction and not psychically, psychologically or as a result of physiological impulses. Such exegeses have also demonstrated that motivation arises in the very process of action itself and not purely as some antecedent function – that is, as variable precipitative action or a *de novo* rationalisation after the event. An example of this approach is found in Becker's work on marijuana use (1963) where he proceeds from the position that deviant motives actually develop in the course of experience with the deviant activity. 'To put a complex argument in a few words: instead of deviant motives leading to the deviant behaviour, it is the other way round; the deviant behaviour in time produces the deviant motivation.'[6] In stressing *process* Becker perhaps overstates his case, replacing one determinism with another. Within these various seminal papers there is considerable dissension regarding the function of motive in conduct, the status of motive and exactly whose rules motives are.

In *The Theory of Social and Economic Organisation* (1964), Max Weber advanced the view that motive is a complex of subjective meaning which seems to the actor himself or to the observer as an adequate ground for the conduct in question.[7] Unwittingly his ambiguous position fuelled a debate which has continued up to the present, resulting in a division between those who favour a definition of motive as the actors' subjective meaning and those who prefer a definition of motive as observer's method. Before turning to a discussion of these competing perspectives a preliminary clarification of Weber's position is required. First, an immediate problem of uncertainty arises regarding whether motive belongs to the actor or else to the observer, which has implications for the function of motive in a social situations. Alfred Schutz (1972) in his critique maintains that Weber is incorrect in his conflation of the two quite different aspects. This is how Schutz distinguishes between them:

(*a*) that context of meaning which the *actor subjectively feels is the ground* of his behaviour and (*b*) that context of meaning which the observer supposes is the ground of the actor's behaviour.[8]

The first problem concerns 'whose rules' or methods motivatory accounts are based upon. In dealing with this problem Schutz addresses his argument first to the actor himself and second to motive as the meaningful ground of his behaviour. In pointing to the status and function of motive he identifies two specifically different modes, 'in-order-to' of the action and the 'because' of the action. These criticisms and diversions will be taken up again later in the rather more structured argument that follows. And so within the sociology of motivation four major problems arise which require some preliminary consideration. The first problem considers the function of 'motive' in conduct, whilst the second considers 'motive' – whose method? We examine thirdly normal crimes and observer's rules and finally the role of negotiation as a function of accounting.

The function of 'motive' in conduct

In a most lucid exposition on the subject of motivation H. Gerth and C. W. Mills (1970) are especially eager to observe the function of motive imputation and avowal in certain types of social situations, and at particular moments of accounting to others. In looking at the process of accounting both to oneself and to a variety of significant others they suggest that a man may begin an act for one motive but in the course of his action may afterwards adopt an auxiliary one. The authors explain that the use of an auxiliary motive is often an appeal to an acceptable vocabulary of motives, 'associated with expectations with which the members of the situation are in agreement'.[9] They suggest that different vocabularies of motive are used by an actor when alone, amongst family members or when with co-workers[10] or as in the empirical case which follows with probation officers. If this is the case, the function of motive in conduct must be discerned in the context in which accounting is done; to whom and when must also be observed. Mills (1940) in his writings had already allowed for the importance of the situational context in observing vocabularies in certain 'historical epochs and specified situations'.[11] In looking more closely at this he examines vocabularies in capitalism and argues that certain vocabularies might characterise class and status groups. Schutz in addition contrasts the two types of motive according to its function in conduct by identifying, 'in-order-to' and 'because' of statements. In explaining the difference he writes:

> Suppose I say a murderer perpetrated his crime for money. This is an in-order-to statement. But suppose I say the man became a murderer because of the influence of bad companions .. the in-order-to motive explains the act in terms of the project while the genuine because-motive explains the project in terms of the actor's past experience.[12]

Put in another way he proposes that this illustrates the double relational sense of action since 'the "in-order-to" statement pictures the goal as future while the pseudo 'because' statement pictures it as a project which occurred in the past'.[13]

Sociological theory in the work of Mills (1940), Sykes and Matza (1957), Matza (1964), Sudnow (1965), Scott and Lyman on motivation (1968), Cressey (1962) on differential association and compulsive crimes, and more recently Hardiker and Webb (1979), and Rothman and Gandossy (1981) on accounts given to probation officers; have built upon these ideas and have been rather more concerned to locate the secondary verbalisations. Mills captured the very types of motive Weber and Schutz tried so hard to distinguish, Proposing that 'vocabularies of motive' functioned as justifications; 'motives are accepted justifications for present, future, or past programs of actors!'[14]

Sykes and Matza (1957) located a number of secondary verbalisations which served to neutralise behaviour in functioning as antecedent rationalisations. The authors contend that there are five major techniques available to the delinquent with which to neutralise official norms. They are not just rationalisations after the event in order to deflect punishment but serve as justifications before the event. First the offender may deny responsibility for his actions, either his behaviour was an accident or else blame is placed on a 'bad' environment. Second, the offender may deny injury, claiming that no harm was done, Third, the offender denies the rights of the victim arguing that 'he deserved it'. Fourth, the offender condemns the condemners. Finally he appeals to higher loyalties; although the act is recognised as wrong it was nevertheless engaged in because of higher loyalties to friends and to principles.

Scott and Lyman's (1968) work much later returned to an examination of the function of primary verbalisations and in returning to an earlier bifurcation in Weber and Schutz identified two types of accounting, justifications already identified by Mills and Sykes and Matza and excuses. Briefly, justificatory accounts are those wherein the person accepts responsibility for the conduct in question, but denies the pejorative quality. A good example of this is provided in accounts of motivation of women charged with loitering for the purpose of prostitution where whilst they accept that they have broken a law deny any pejorative quality by arguing that the activity should be decriminalised. Justificatory accounts might also be used where women accept responsibility for their conduct but also argue that as in fraudulent DHSS claims they were trying to redress the system which anyway in the first place gave them insufficient benefit.

Excuses, on the other hand, are accounts which frequently accompany admissions of guilt, but wherein full responsibility is denied. Excuses then function as socially approved vocabularies for the mitigation of conduct. Scott and Lyman identify four model forms: (*a*) appeal to accident, (*b*) appeal to defensibility, (*c*) appeal to biological drives, (*d*) appeal to scapegoats. The appeal to biological drives is a model which above all others mentioned by the author has some relation to sex roles and by definition to sex-specific crimes such as rape. Crimes such as grievous bodily harm and shoplifting are thought more likely to be committed by a particular sex, in this case by men and women respectively. The appeal to biological drives is invoked particularly in crimes of rape and violence where the notion that 'a man's health requires sex'[15] may function to excuse sexual assault, and the male aggression theory may excuse violence. Biological 'drive theory' is also frequently invoked in crimes of shoplifting (a 'typical' crime within the female role) yet also in untypical female crimes such as arson and murder. This merely reflects the view that female physiology is regarded as both normal and pathological. Scott and Lyman also argue that the individual actor will change his account for different role others.[16] In this event then motives have a function of reducing responsibility, blameworthiness and guilt as an end product whereby the deployment of certain excuses function to bring about this end. Later work has further attempted to examine the function of motive in conduct. Explanations for conduct according to Hardiker and Webb (1979) take on character of 'action' or 'infraction' depending on whether the actor accepts or denies responsibility.[17]

'Motive' – whose method?

Motives given in explanation for conduct vary enormously, even with the same actor, and depend as much on the audience as anything else. Motive is not merely the actor's subjective expression of his knowledge of the reasons for conduct available to him, but is rather a social representation of observers' methods as constituted and understood by individual actors. At least this is the contention of Blum and McHugh (1971) when they write, 'motive is a member's method for deciding what other owns'.[18] The extent to which this is so depends too, on the time, place and function of accounting. That is not to replace individual self-determination with an equally determinist societal reaction, but to regard actors' conduct and method of accounting as part of a continual interaction process. The authors offer the most original exposé of the part played by 'observer's method' in constituting motive, which functions as or in so far as they acquire analytic force as observer's rules for depicting grounds of conduct. Over the question of whose method, they extend the discussion addressed in the first instance by Mills, who maintained that motives 'stand for anticipated situational consequences of questioned conduct'.[19] In extending and building on the importance of this debate they take issue with Weber's definition of motive first in its conflation of actors' and observers' methods and like Schutz examine closely the role of the observer. In developing this theory they emphasise that motive is a public method and therefore is an observers' rule of relevance.

Blum and McHugh extend this to examine the way motives also formulate actor's methods:

> To formulate a type of person is to formulate a course of action on the grounds that no matter what one predicates substantively of persons to make their biographies relevant to the event, such relevance is only assigned on the assumption that the predicates depict a typical, possible course of action. Person, then, depicts a typical possible actor.

They continue:

> To say his motive in murdering his wife was his jealousy is to explicate the cir-

cumstances which make him the type of jealous person who would (could) murder his wife — that murdering his wife is one possible method available to him for doing jealousy. In this way, the event is formulated as the agent's possible method for doing whatever the formulation of the motive requires as a course of action.[20]

So indeed in Schutz, Blum and McHugh we have a clear demonstration that the analytic force of motive is derived from observers' rules and not as reasons, justifications, intentions or accounts. Whilst Blum and McHugh rightly argue that motives are observers' methods, their reflection on motive solely as reasons, justifications or excuses presents a major limitation on their work.

'Normal crimes' and observers' rules

In emphasising that motives are situationally defined, it is necessary to examine the characteristics of certain situations and individuals and the vocabularies that are correspondingly generated. Certain patterns of conduct become recognised as characteristically part of a wider process of action, motivation and explanation. In some instances this interactional process is suggested in and by the very language we use. Kleptomania and pyromania provide two such instances (see Cressey 1962). Sex offenders provide further support to this view; Taylor in his work on the subject writes, 'Different vocabularies of motive are tied to different roles and social institutions.'[21] In taking up Taylor's assertion it is important to realise that actors acting in roles, prostitute or shoplifter for instance, will account for shoplifting or prostitution conduct in a typical way. Vocabularies of motives are, as Scott and Lyman recognise, likely to be exclusive to the circle in which they are employed. They assert that 'the drug addict may be able to justify his conduct to the subcultural world, but not to the courts'. Thus certain motives of conduct are seen to characterise specific contexts. Sudnow invokes the concept of 'normal crimes' to denote that criminal conduct which has a characteristic pattern of accomplishment from motivatory accounts rendered to social and personal characteristics of the offender. His emphasis is on the process by which observers, in this case the public defender, evolve 'background expectancies' of crime.

In the course of routinely encountering persons charged with 'petty theft', 'burglary', 'assault with a deadly weapon', 'rape', 'possession of marijuana', etc., the P.D. gains knowledge of the typical manner in which offences of given classes are committed, the social characteristics of the persons who regularly commit them, the features of the settings in which they occur, the types of victims often involved, and the like.

Sudnow goes on to define 'normal crimes': 'I shall call *normal crimes* those occurrences whose typical features e.g., the ways they usually occur and the characteristics of persons who commit them (as well as the typical victims and typical scenes), are known and attended to by the P.D.'[22] Scott and Lyman in adopting this concept of 'normal crimes' elaborate further the features which identify them. They point to the way in which language plays a vital role in indicating crime and motivation and hence certain matters are settled in advance. Howard Becker following Sudnow's formulation invokes the term 'conventional crime'. He argues that crimes take on the conventional character by 'the character of rationalisation used to justify the "criminal" act, and the perceived or actual likelihood of punishment'. As Blum and McHugh point out, 'motives formulate a type of person, such that experience can be allocated to the agent of the act experienced and the related character of the event'.[23] Similarly Blumstein (1974) maintains that in accounting for conduct the observer expects particular accounts to have an internal consistency, a congruence with the facts of past conduct – as Foote (1951) points out, in *de novo* situations persons are more likely to provide rationalisations 'whereby one relates his acts to previous experience and to the values of the groups which he feels he must justify his behaviour'.[24]

Vocabularies of motive tell us about how a deviant views his infraction, how society views it, and how it is regarded by specific significant others. Vocabularies of motive as reported to the sub-culture, the prison, or borstal population, or to friends, may be slightly different from those offered to conventional moralists. For instance, a fellow student once explained the theft of books by a justification offering a political account for consideration (particularly fashionable in the early 1970s), by stating that in fact he was diverting money from the capitalist classes (booksellers) and assisting a more equitable distribution of resources to students. He was not apprehended as far as I know. If he was, it seems unlikely that this account would be proffered to a bench of magistrates. And so it seems reasonable to conclude that vocabularies of motive are situational depending upon the particular observer, and are considered according to their congruency with prior antecedent history, and role expectation. In examining vocabularies of motive in this specific situation we are observing how female crime is explained by defendants and honoured by observers.

Negotiation as a function of accounting
Strictly within the legal context Walker (1978) in identifying the various functions of explanation argues that they can offer help in predicting or manipulating the future and can exert an influence on an individual's culpability. Explanations in the context of this present discussion are viewed to the extent to which they are manipulating or negotiating future decisions. It has been already suggested that

motive has a specific function in conduct deriving an analytic status as observers' rules of relevance. Within the sociology of deviance and within the precise context of delinquent accounts, motives provided to significant others – magistrates, judges, social workers and so on – may be seen as having a negotiatory function.

In considering the responses of others to particular accounts and the possible final sentencing outcome defendants manage their own remedial work. That is, they are responsible for 'changing the meaning that otherwise might be given to an act, transforming what could be seen as offensive into what can be seen as acceptable' (Goffman 1971: 109). This interchange is triggered off by an offence, and closed with a gesture of honouring on the part of the offended person. But not all accounts are honoured by significant others. As Blumstein *et al.* point out, the observer(s) will only honour accounts meeting certain normative specifications.[25] For instance it is reasonable that accounts rendered by a repeated violator of social norms would not be likely to be honoured especially if the violator was invoking accident as an excuse. In the light of this possibility it might be necessary to examine the previous criminal record of those providing the explanation. The process of accounting to others in the legal situation is almost always manipulated by defendants seeking sympathy, understanding and in turn a lighter sentence. And some explanations are more likely to be effective than others. For instance the defendant who said to a judge recently, 'I hope you die, you bastard, screaming of cancer', was not uttering a verbalisation likely to invoke the sympathy of the court. However 'accounts claiming such forms of reduced responsibility as external culprits or forces, uncontrollable urges and impulses, unforeseeability of the consequences of the deed, lack of intention for such consequences, etc. manipulate this process'. The extent to which an account is honoured will however depend ultimately on the background expectancies of criminal conduct of the interactants. When accounts are not honoured they are seen as illegitimate or unreasonable. In general those who persist in giving unreasonable accounts are likely to be labelled as mentally ill.

Perhaps the classic statement of accounts as they function in negotiation in deviant 'action' or infraction' is provided by G. Sykes and D. Matza in their work on 'techniques of neutralisation' (1957). They examine reasons given by males to neutralise male deviant conduct thus rendering a wholly male-specific view of this process. The authors point out that techniques of neutralisation are not just rationalisations constructed *after* the event in order to mitigate conduct and deflect punishment but serve as justifications *before* the event.

Thus accounts of conduct may be negotiatory, but in a situation where a lighter sentence is to be negotiated techniques of neutralisation are not merely *de novo* rationalisations but emerge in the course of conduct.

Accounts and legal constraints

In the precise context of the criminal law and the courtroom scenario, accounts rendered by defendants are not merely as Henry (1976) asserts, self-defensive rationalisations, nor as Matza originally proposed 'techniques of neutralisation', but 'Instead the structure of the criminal law paradoxically invites the individual to neutralise his normative attachment to it' (Matza 1964: 61). And so quite apart from the defendant's perception of attitudes of significant others in the presentation of explanation she is also required to consider the particular legal constraints, such that within the criminal law certain defences to crime provide the opportunity for a given explanation, a possibility noted by Cressey (1962: 44). And as Scott and Lyman (1968), Taylor (1972) and Ditton (1978) pointed to justifications and excuses as competing explanations, these may be given a particular legal credence as a defence to certain crimes. Fletcher in *Rethinking Criminal Law* (1978) distinguishes between the two as wrongdoing and culpability, both being exculpatory. Non-exculpatory defences are those tendered in cases of previous conviction or as Williams points out 'the objection that the information for a summary offence was out of time'.[26] The parallels between everyday and legal methods of accounting are obvious, so too the reasons for rejecting accounts.

The criminal law itself has also to some extent given credence to the distinction between justification and excuse. In the case of *Cogan and Leak* [1976] QB 217, which concerned the rape of a wife as part of a husband's revenge, this distinction was followed. In the crime of shoplifting, the law provides the opportunity for the defence of mistake, accident, otherwise known as lack of *mens rea,* and the defence of irresistible impulse. Such defences are excuses in the strict legal sense. Justifications, on the other hand, for the purpose of the criminal law are invoked whenever the objective wrongness of an act is denied.[27]

The distinction between excuse and justification and its application and acceptance in crimes of prostitution and theft are strengthened within the criminal justice process, not merely by everyday methods of apology and mitigation, but also by the provision for such explanations within the legal framework of defence. And although defences within the criminal law are costive those already existent lend support to the credence of everyday notions.

A total of 150 social inquiry reports for offences of loitering for the purpose of prostitution and a total of 78 for offences of shoplifting prepared on defendants who entered pleas of guilt were examined, with a view to discerning the reason(s) for offending as provided by the defendant. The accounts rendered were analysed first for their function in conduct – that is, whether they were intended to justify or rationalise behaviour. They were analysed, secondly, for their congruity with the offence indicated, and, finally for their impact on sentencing outcome. From the onset two key methodological problems were encountered. First, a major problem was presented regarding the reliability of defendants' statements since verbal accounts provided by clients to probation officers are liable to a certain amount of distortion by the report writer, the particular problem encountered by Hardiker and Webb (1979) who observed that the officer 'may be granted the legitimacy to admit or exclude certain vocabularies of motive'.[28] Defendants' accounts, the authors noted, may be translated or accepted. The translation problem was one frequently encountered in this study particularly where no explanation was rendered by the accused for the offence. Consider the following examples: one client was described as 'a pathetic personality damaged by an early history of inadequate personality and impulsiveness – prostitution is her response to stress', and in another 'Apart from limited finances, Mary's explanation for her recent offence revolves around her mood swings. These moods seem to be related to Mary's menstruation cycle.' In another report, rather than giving a diagnostic account and identifying biological or psychological factors the officer excuses the client in this way; 'in common with other young women in inner cities she has resorted to prostitution to supplement a low level of income.' The only reports included for analysis are those where the officer writes: 'She says . . . '.

A second difficulty which is perhaps conceptual rather than methodological arises from the use of the inconsistent plea, (see Chapter 2), since within the legal situation a guilty plea is not always accompanied by an admission of guilt, the plea being a mere technicality. This eventuality poses a problem for interpreting remedial work in this setting. Moreover, certain offence categories by their nature result in a greater frequency of disparity between plea and admission.

The analysis

The various accounts invoked by the defendants were variously grouped according to whether they accepted responsibility for the offence – justifications (voluntarism) or denied responsibility – excuses (involuntarism). Where responsibility was accepted justifications tended to follow in subsequence, where responsibility was denied excuses were invoked, usually of a pathological nature. The intermediate category was invoked in cases where no explanation was given or else in instances where no offence was intended and no subsequent excuse or justifications proffered.

This particular division of categories is derived from earlier work on accounts of sex offenders by Taylor (1972), a distinction which works equally well in the case of shoplifting offences but which is not appropriate in cases of prostitution because of the often inconsistent plea and the belief that prostitution should be decriminalised. The main categories of explanation serve as a general indicator of the function of motive in conduct, whilst the sub-categories provide more specific verbalisations.

Shoplifters' excusatory tales

A total of seventy-eight accounts of conduct for petty theft from shops was recorded. The distribution of explanations of conduct in these categories took the form, firstly, of *voluntaristic accounts (justifications)*. In approximately twenty-two accounts (28 per cent) of the sample, defendants explained their conduct as arising for economic and financial reasons. This form of explanation locates persons as responsible for their action and therefore culpable. However, such factors when presented together in efforts to explain conduct do not always function as motivation but as background information which renders accounts congruous with background factors.

The various functions which financial reasons may perform in explaining or providing a social context to petty theft are explored. In thirteen accounts (16 per cent) of total sample (59 per cent in this category) conduct was explained as the result of 'because of' statements. In these instances petty theft was justified via the retrospective necessity to solve a difficulty in past experience. At the same time 'because of' statements also can be seen to diminish the actor's responsibility such that the actor is caught up in a chain of reactions where he can do no other but act. Whilst the 'because of' statement does not function so as to make the actor's role in conduct an involuntary one, it functions in conduct as exculpatory and to diminish moral responsibility. A typical explanation is provided in one report. The officer writes, 'she tells me that she stole *because* she couldn't afford to pay for it'.

In nine accounts (11.5 per cent) of the sample (41 per cent in this category) defendants explained behaviour via 'in order to' motives. There, the function of motive in conduct seeks to orientate action with regard to a prospective goal. The goal is an anticipation of a future state, where petty theft provides the means to that end. In this situation 'in order to' motives do not usually diminish responsibility. One officer wrote 'as far as the offences are concerned she tells me that she had to sell the goods she stole in order to pay the bills'. A further example is provided in this: 'she stole in order to pay for rent arrears and intended to sell the clothes in order to provide the money'.

Within this particular category another level is evident, that of situational context, whereby a distinction is evident between those who locate their action in the context of providing extra resources, supplementing a low income, or else dire hardship.

The use of disposal amongst these twenty-two cases were recorded as follows: Four women were fined (three being in receipt of supplementary benefit), eleven women (six of whom officers considered had extreme difficulties in coping with life) were given probation orders, six were conditionally discharged, one was given a deferred sentence.

Within the second sub-category, three cases (4 per cent of the sample) were instances of attention-seeking conduct whose petty theft and subsequent apprehension provided an occasion of seeking attention. In these instances the func-motive is not always clear because of the difficulty of conflation of psyche/motivation. Accounts given to officers were of this kind; 'she tells me that she felt the offence of theft was a cry for help', and, 'she said she wanted to be caught'. The cases were disposed of in this manner: one probation order; one fined (accompanying medical report indicated depressive illness) for theft of seven dolls; one woman was sentenced to three months' imprisonment.

The third sub-category included two accounts, 2.5 per cent of the sample, where one defendant explained, 'it was there and I took it'. One defendant received a supervision order, the other a suspended prison sentence.

Within the *intermediate* category somewhere between voluntaristic and involuntaristic conduct, five defendants (6 per cent of the sample) explained their conduct as an accident or mistake. One defendant invoked an auxiliary excuse — she had been drinking before the offence. This defendant was disposed of by means of a suspended prison sentence. One defendant explained that she was forgetful and was similarly dealt with. Two defendants explained that the accidental conduct had occurred whilst their mind was distracted by the activities of their children. In both these instances the women concerned received probation orders. One defendant, a first offender, who was dealt with as if her mistake was genuine (she invoked no auxiliary excuse or motive) was given an absolute discharge. In five cases (6 per cent of the sample), defendants gave totally unacceptable accounts, accounts which in no way excused or justified their conduct. Furthermore such accounts were not honoured by probation officers. In such cases unrealistic accounts may serve as an indication of mental illness (see Scott and Lyman 1968, Scheff 1966). Instances of unrealistic accounts range from lying to the bizarre: 'she said she was in a hurry as she had to attend a wedding and felt unable to wait to be served', 'she said she stole . . . as visitors were proving difficult to get rid of'.

Explanations of conduct took the form, secondly, of *involuntaristic accounts (excuses)*. Most accounts for petty theft from shops fell into the third major category. In 42 per cent of the total sample women had involuntarily committed the offence. Within the first sub-category, in nine accounts (11 per cent of the total sample), women accounted for their behaviour by explaining that they were tempted (prospective) or that it was an impulse which propelled them to act. In this category most accounts were accompanied by a rational auxiliary motive. In its purest form one report read, 'she doubts her ability to withstand further temptation'. Of the incontrollable impulse accounts one report read, 'she tells me she couldn't stop herself', and another, 'as she said herself, "I don't know what came over me"'.

Those accounts accompanied by an auxiliary reason involved a blend of financial motives. For instance one report read, 'she finds it difficult to explain her recent behaviour and can only say that she acted on impulse at a time of financial worry'. Another spoke of 'limited finances and a sudden compulsion to steal'. One account located the function of conduct in this way: 'she tells me that she gave into this temptation as she was expecting an electricity bill' and also 'hoped to buy some presents in advance for her daughter's birthday'. This final account demonstrates the way in which temptation is normalised and given into when other pressing circumstances are evident. In this category five received probation orders (three were tempted, two compelled to steal), four received community service orders and four 'spoke of incontrollable impulses'.

In the second sub-category fifteen cases (19 per cent) could offer no explanation for their conduct but provided auxiliary excuses and verbalisations. In seven cases defendants were puzzled by their action and said they were deeply ashamed, sorry, or felt foolish. Four were dealt with via probation orders, one by suspended prison sentence, two were fined. In the remaining eight cases the defendants were puzzled and could not remember the incident. Auxiliary verbalisations ranging from depressive states to taking tranquillisers were mentioned. Of these, one received a conditional discharge, three received probation orders, one a term of imprisonment and three not known.

In the third sub-category four instances (5 per cent of the total sample) explained petty theft as an involuntary response to other influences. They were dealt with in this way: two received probation orders, one a sentence of imprisonment (although a psychiatric report was rendered to the court), and one received a suspended prison sentence.

Table 6:1   *The function of motive in conduct: shoplifting*

Voluntarism	%	Intermediate	%	Involuntarism	%
(1) Financial	28.0			(6) Temptation/ compulsion	11.5
(2) Attention-seeking	4.0	(4) Mistake	6.0	(7) No explanation	
				Can't remember	19.0
				Sorry	
(3) Opportunism	2.5	(5) Unresponsible		(8) Drugs/ alcohol	5.0
		Illegitimate			
		Accounting	6.0	(9) Physiological episodes	2.5
Accept responsibility	2.5			Emotional	4.0
	37.0		12.0		42.0
			Non-recordable		8.0
			Not-guilty pleas not known		
			Total		100

In the fourth sub-category three accounts linked their infraction to emotional problems. Two accounts linked their infraction to physiological crises. In the former case two were disposed of via a probation order and one by a period of community service. In the latter case the defendants received probation orders. For instance in the latter case one report read: 'She gave a coherent account of how she stole the dress and was able to explain only that it was committed within a relatively short time of the birth of her child.' The other account suggested that conduct was related to the menopause.

Justifications for prostitution

Out of a total of 150 accounts provided by women on one or more charges of loitering for the purpose of prostitution, explanations or 'vocabularies of motive' rendered were present in eight of the nine categories invoked in shoplifting offences, with a significantly different pattern of distribution. Social inquiry reports were collected on defendants appearing before the courts in the areas of Manchester, Birmingham, Inner London, Sheffield and Liverpool. Comprehensive reports were available in three of the five areas. The importance of considering the issues of these methods raised in the earlier part of this chapter becomes clear. Prostitutes unlike any other law-breakers, with the possible exception of some motoring offenders, the National Front and political offenders, do not accept that their behaviour is 'criminal'. Prostitutes are in most if not all cases responsible for their activities, and justifications and not excuses are consequently provided.

A further sub-sample of forty accounts was examined in relation to the final sentence outcome. This sample represents forty out of ninety-six social inquiry reports prepared in Manchester during the first few months of data collection (see Table 6:2).

Table 6:2 *The function of motive in conduct: prostitution*

Voluntarism	No.	%	Intermediate	No.	%	Involuntarism	No.	%
Not a crime, a way of life	4	10	No explanation	7	17.5	Temptation	2	5
Financial	20	50				Alcohol/drugs	4	10
Appeal to higher loyalties	1	2.5				Threats from men	2	5
Total	25			7			8	
						Grand total	40	

Within the first category of voluntaristic accounts explanations ranged from the need to decriminalise prostitutes to the need to supplement finances. 10 per cent of the sample maintained that prostitution was an acceptable way of making a living. One defendant said that she felt soliciting should not be an offence and spoke of it as a business venture, whilst another maintained it offered independence from men and a reliable source of income. The offenders were dealt with by means of a fine, a probation order, conditional discharge and community service order. In the second sub-category twenty defendants (50 per cent of the total sample) argued that prostitution was engaged in to provide certain necessary funds. Necessary finances ranged from money required to pay off existing debts and money needed to meet a future goal, the saving of a deposit on a flat.

In most cases women identified some particular situation or need with which they tried to explained their conduct of occasional prostitution. Mr Clive Soley, MP, in a recent Parliamentary debate on prostitution echoed the sentiment that prostitutioñ stemmed from short-term economic gain 'to pay the rent or avoid having the electricity cut off'.

In three cases defendants asserted that prostitution was a means of supplementing a low income. In one account it was revealed that prostitution provided lucrative extras. Two defendants said that finances were provided just for occasions, whilst five saw prostitution as a positive alternative to supplementary benefit. Two defendants whilst offering no explanation provided rituals of contrition verbalising their remorse. The defendants in this category were disposed of in the following way: two received community service orders, eleven probation orders, two received fines, two suspended prison sentences and three cases were dealt with by means of a conditional discharge.

In the two major categories in seven cases (17.5 per cent of the total sample), no explanation for prostitution was volunteered. The defendants were disposed of by means of a conditional discharge, three suspended prison sentences, two probation orders and one term of imprisonment.

In the third major category 20 per cent of the sample expressed motives which reduced their responsibility for their conduct, 10 per cent said that drinks and drugs removed their responsibility for prostitution, but also created a need for extra funds. 5 per cent said that they were threatened by men and forced to prostitute themselves against their wishes. 5 per cent said that income from prostitution was a temptation, or a trap into which one defendant at least claimed she had fallen.

In situations where the criminal law is at complete variance with the moral consciousness of those who infringe it little remedial work is done. As such few prostitutes apologise to the courts though apologies may function in reduction of sentence. In this sense the prostitute has much in common with the political criminal at variance with a regime or with the coteries of law-making.

Accounts and their consequences

Whether explanations for criminal conduct are effective depends on the degree to which they are honoured. For instance, probation officers' reinterpretation or translation of accounts reflects the degree to which they find them acceptable. Officers who regard accounts as reasonable and acceptable frequently excuse their client; where accounts are absent or unacceptable a diagnostic interpretation is evident. And whilst minor infractions are more easily understood, in rather more serious crime diagnostic judgments are made. Thus crimes of violence are less readily explained by mistake or accident and more readily explained by reasons of pathology. And as 'certain characteristics of the offender and certain extenuating circumstances of his situation constitute grounds for withdrawing or attenuating legal sanctions, e.g. insanity, mental defect, mental disease, extreme youth, self-defence, coercion, etc.', it seems important to examine accounting in its legal context. It is not surprising to find that the shoplifter, whilst pleading guilty, claims that she was not responsible, whilst the prostitute claims full responsibility but refuses to accept the criminalisation of her profession. These diverse characterisations come to influence the specific pattern of accounting rendered in the particular criminal categories studied.

7 · Crimes unnatural – Some criminological, social and legal questions

A woman's 'highest duty is so often to suffer and be still'.

Mrs Sarah Stickney Ellis (1845)

Introduction

Conceptions of social conduct in everyday life are formulated synonymously with corresponding identikits of appropriate social actors. Of course this is not true of behavioural conduct which everyone does, such as walking and talking, but holds true for activities of housework, mining and statesmanship since the very invoking of the term conveys not only particular action but also a particular actor. Quite apart from being sex- or gender-specific, conduct may be associated with race, age and social class. Consider for instance how drug use in the early 1970s was immediately associated with black youths. But whether an actor's conduct is offensive or virtuous, it is bound by rules and requirements anticipating certain action of particular actors. When and insofar as a particular role is performed by another actor, these rules are considered broken and the relation of actor to action may no longer be deemed appropriate but 'incongruous'. The social and gender role adopted by the male transsexual provides an instance of such incongruity, a conundrum so much 'at odds' with expectations of others that transsexuals frequently feel compelled to seek sexual reassignment through surgical means. Transsexuals thus aspire to sex-change operations in order to go along with convention.[1] In observing the basis of patterns of congruity through the character of Agnes, a transvestite, Garfinkel explored those 'background relevances that are easily overlooked or difficult to grasp because of their routinized character'.[2]

The compexity of this relationship of conduct to actor has been considered in its factual uniformity by Weber, but it is in a later work of Alfred Schutz (1970) that this particular exegesis flourishes, particularly with regard to the way associations are conveyed to us in and by language. And in another context Dale Spender has explored how language conveys both actor role and conduct.[3]

It is not the morality or immorality inherent in the act which is of concern but instead the degree to which patterns of conduct may be deemed inappropriate if performed by particular actors. One would not for instance expect the village idiot to sing an aria from Tosca, though we might expect him to fall backwards off the church wall. Similarly, we would not expect illiteracy of the local squire. Such instances are occasions where as in Mead's terms the rules of congruity as subscribed to by the 'generalised other' have been broken. Indeed, anyone whose behaviour steps out of line with appropriate sex, gender, class and occupational roles is thereby deemed 'out of place' and abruptly brought back into the consensual fold by a series of stigmatisation-degradatory ceremonies or punishment procedures. Only those whose conduct is motivated by higher ideals of justice, peace and freedom, such as the women of Greenham Common, find societal reaction possible to sustain. The recent campaigning and resistance of women to the Cruise missile, their commitment to 'higher loyalties' (Sykes and Matza 1957) or higher ideals of peace has led to a number of mild skirmishes with the law. Infringing the law by obstructing the highways is a typical peaceful means of voicing resistance. One woman charged with breach of the peace said,·

> I challenge you now to show me this peace that you talk about. How can you say such peace exists, when people are dying all over the world? If you ask me now to keep the peace, I shall say you are either blind or a fool. (*Daily Mail,* 17 February 1983)

In some contexts behaviour that is incongruous or out of place is frequently considered symptomatic of mental illness, though certain persons are more likely than others to validate or invalidate such an imputation. For example, feminists during the nineteenth century found that their role incongruity frequently invoked the label. From George Sand and Elizabeth Barrett to Virginia Woolf, such women were considered either sick or mad.[4]

When we look to the arena of deviant conduct certain patterns of offending are considered more typical of one group than of another. Offences of a violent or sexual nature are considered the likely conduct of men though unlikely of women, and thereby deemed incongruous. Sudnow (1965) following Mead (1934)[5] and Cressey (1951)[6] observes that certain crimes share common characteristics, relating to 'the characteristics of persons who commit them', amongst others, and explores what Garfinkel identifies as 'background expectancies' in the context of criminal conduct. Activities are classified as typical or untypical, congruous or incongruous of persons as a result of the reification of sex roles within a given culture, such that crimes of violence, robbery and burglary, be they pathological exaggerations of the masculine ethic, are nevertheless regarded as typical of men. In much the same way mental illness is considered merely an extension of the natural instability of women. Schutz, (1970) explains the process by which reification occurs: 'If we see a dog, that is, if we recognize an object being an animal and more precisely as a dog we anticipate a certain behaviour on the part of this dog, a typical (not individual) way of eating, of running, of playing, of jumping, and so on.' (p. 116)

The typicality or non-typicality of the crime which a particular offender commits has very profound implications for the manner in which the various levels of jurisdiction respond to the offender. Typical crimes, with which the police, courts and sentencers are familiar, are met with by typical responses since the procedural rules for dealing with such crimes are already agreed upon and well established. Whilst the untypical, incongruous or abnormal crime engenders responses as diverse as they are conflicting.

In the entire criminal calendar the most unlikely female crimes are those of violence, burglary and robbery, and though this conception is undergoing some modification they still remain untypical or incongruous. Sentencers are at a loss to decide on what sentence is appropriate, variations in sentencing, in mitigation, in self-explanation and in societal reaction are particularly evident.

When judges pass sentences on young women convicted of burglary, robbery and crimes of violence they are presented with a considerable difficulty in assessing the most suitable and appropriate form of treatment. Any apparent leniency is frequently interpreted as arising from the fact that the defendants are women, and leniency is too often interpreted as being a non-custodial sentence. These are two fallacies this chapter wishes to dispel. First, as Ann Smith pointed out some while ago, 'Any special consideration given to a woman is given not because she is a woman but because she is a mother, wife or maintaining an elderly relative' (1965). Indeed, in the light of recent disclosures of Conservative intentions, the proposed gradual demolition of the Welfare State (*Guardian,* 17 February 1983) the familial role of women is being contrived by massive cuts to services making Smith's assertion ever more a reality. Secondly, it has been assumed that the most severe sentences are custodial ones, while non-custodial sanctions are indeed lenient. In this context it is to be noted that non-custodial supervision may be just as intrusive (see Cohen 1979, Conrad 1980) and perhaps more so, as even social aspect of lifestyle and conduct is perpetually monitored not merely for its potentiality for offending but for its unsociability or pathology.

How then does the criminal justice system respond to abnormal crimes? Are women in fact treated more leniently in accordance with their sex or gender role? Drawing on the positive feedback loop initially proposed by Kitsuse (1964), the response to the female offender of untypical crime is proposed in this way:

(*a*) The more incongruous the conduct in its relation to the social actor the less tolerant and more variable the societal and legal reaction.

(*b*) The less precisely defined the societal and legal reaction and the ideology of motivation the greater the disparaties in decision making at each successive stage from formal caution to sentence.

The growth in crimes unnatural

During the last decade the storm and shock which followed the realisation that women too were committing violent crime was met with the need to identify the extent of the problem. Wilkins (1965) was perhaps the first to examine the problems inherent in an over-reliance on statistics purporting to indicate the extent of crime. In his 'decision stage' model he identifies the possible routes which may be taken from crime commission to sentence, described elsewhere by Stephen Box as 'a corridor of connected rooms' (1971: 167). But it was the school of radical criminology following the work of the labelling theorists, especially Becker (1963), and the radical critique of criminology presented by Taylor, Walton and Young (1973) which addressed the political considerations upon which such decisions were founded. For instance, the purported increase in the number of women found guilty of certain crimes (see Table 7:1) has been taken by some as a reflection of a real increase in violent crime, instead of being viewed in its real relation to changes in organisational procedures and the proportion of those pleading guilty.[7]

Table 7:1 Showing increase in number of women defendants found guilty of 'abnormal' crimes: 1969–78 *

	1969	1970	1971	1972	1973	1974	1975	1976	1977	1978
Violence against the person	1120	1305	1521	1790	2165	2337	2748	3042	3277	3267
Burglary	1797	1906	1827	1731	1732	2027	2473	2501	2363	2599
Robbery	138	108	95	147	184	147	204	206	220	196

(*) Information extrapolated from *Criminal Statistics,* 1978, Cmnd. 7670, tables 5:1 and 5:2

The first stage in this enumeration process includes those persons suspected of involvement in criminal activity, since statistical information can only ever be a record of known crimes. Recorded in *Criminal Statistics* as 'crimes recorded by the police' this proportion is derived from the volume of crimes reported by victims and observers, or otherwise detected by the police. What has been variously described as the 'dark figure' or in another not altogether unrelated context as 'secret deviance'[8] is crime which is not and cannot be quantified or verified. This proportion depends also upon a variety of organisational factors.

Certain crimes are particularly difficult to measure since because of their nature they have a low self-report rate. Knowledge of sexual offences perpetrated against women depend essentially on the victim reporting the crime. Complainants fearing retribution, police interrogation and the court inquisitional are not unnaturally deterred from making a complaint. The relatively static level of the reporting rate for the crime of rape suggests that the Sexual Offences (Amendment) Act (1976), in part designed with the intention of encouraging more victims to come forward by disallowing detail related to past moral character, has had only a limited impact. Adler is even less optimistic, stating that it has made no difference at all.[9]

Similarly, the robbing of a punter by a prostitute known otherwise in criminal argot as 'rolling' is rarely reported by the client. Even though robbed sometimes of hundreds of pounds clients are reluctant to come forward because of the inevitable disclosure of their sexual predilections (*Manchester Evening News*, 25 June 1982).[10] In certain crimes then, 'motives for silence' may be more compelling than in others – a further indication of the problems of placing too much reliance on interpreting statistical information as a measure of all crime.

But perhaps the most under-surveyed, under-detected and under-reported crime is that of poncing, the 'dark figure' arising from similar motives for silence that undeniably deter battered women from reporting the incident. And whilst not all men who live with prostitutes are ponces or pimps some most certainly are (see Chapters 1 and 5). Even when crimes are either reported by victims or observers and detected by police in their routine encounters, there is still yet another 'escape route', since crimes reported may not always be recorded. This decision is often left to the satisfaction of the recording or charge office (remember Thames Valley Constabulary on rape, January 1982)! Thus, the police are frequently the ultimate arbiters of whether a complaint may be regarded as false or unfounded, recorded or unrecorded.

In addition, certain offences may be more subject than others to variable police deployment, which may also be influenced by regional decisions or competing demands on police time. The deployment of a police force in crime detection may depend on a variety of pressures exerted more or less forcibly at certain times. Home Office guidelines present a static requirement, but Chief Constables' directives, competing urban crime, public opinion and complaints from local residents are all pressures which are more fluid and variable. During the Moss Side riots in Manchester in July of 1981 the total number of cautions given for loitering for the purpose of prostitution and arrests were recorded at four and eleven respectively. Compare those figures with cautions and arrests for the preceding months and the months that followed. Criminal statistics are formulated as a result of both official and legal activity; as Rock (1973: 173) observes, they are 'indices of official activity', and as Marx succinctly argues, 'law itself may not only punish crime, but also improvise it'.[11]

As a result of the decision to follow up an incident which may amount to a criminal offence, 'Essentially the choice lies between no proceedings, a caution or prosecution' (see Table 7:3). The decision to prosecute as laid down in the Report of the Royal Commission on Criminal Procedures 1981, arising from Lord Denning's pronouncement in *R* v *Metropolitan Police Commissioner*, ex parte

Blackburn [1968] 2 QB at 118, lies with the police.

Table 7:2 *Showing monthly variations in figures for cautioning and arrests depending on competing criminal activity and police deployment, Manchester 1981**

	Cautions	Arrests	Total
January	12	48	60
February	23	33	56
March	20	31	51
April	29	46	75
May	29	61	90
June	32	52	84
July	11	4	15
August	29	31	60
September	42	41	83
October	22	56	78
November	38	36	74
December	25	26	51
Annual total	312	465	777

(*) Figures abstracted from one divisional police area.

Apart from the organisational activity of the criminal justice system, the methods and procedures of recording also go to colour perceptions of crime. First, conviction and acquittal rates are often taken as indices of the predilection of jurors rather than a proportion of those who plead not guilty. There is then the problem of the arbitrary and ever changing nature of legal categories. For instance the Street Offences Act 1959 resulted in a very significant increase in those imprisoned, and similarly the Criminal Justice Act 1982 has resulted in a significant reduction in sentences of imprisonment due to the effect of section 71 (abolition of imprisonment for prostitutes), though in the long term this will be no more than cosmetic since imprisonment is to be retained as a sanction for fine defaulters on this charge, as Mr Kilroy-Silk indicated in its Bill Stage[12] (see Chapter 8).

Table 7:3 *Showing increase in number of women defendants cautioned for 'abnormal' crime 1969–78*

	1969	1970	1971	1972	1973	1974	1975	1976	1977	1978
Violence against the person	225	256	420	555	671	687	796	916	843	873
Burglary	541	610	906	868	904	1165	1101	835	978	865
Robbery	5	9	28	25	29	9	29	13	14	15

(*)Information extrapolated from *Criminal Statistics,* 1978, Cmnd. 7670, tables 5:1 and 5:2

And finally there is the ever changing nature of the classification categories used by recorders. For instance, comparing statistics for 1961, 1971 and 1981 we immediately run into several problems of changes in these categories (see critical commentaries by Walker 1981 and Vennard 1981)[13].

Also of significance is how crime statistics are interpreted by 'significant others'. The key interpreters of statistics and therefore translators of reality are the police, security agencies, politicians, legal personnel, and the judiciary in particular. The main vehicle in the facilitation of this so-called reality is the media. It is at this point that statistical information becomes translated into social facts with social and political consequences. Wiles maintains that 'they themselves become social facts irrespective of their accuracy and validity, in as much as they form the basis for political decision-making debate'.[14] Consider that, in the light of this observation, in 1972 P. Hamilton, author on violence and security, in addressing the Council of International Investigators said that we could no longer assume that women were the gentler sex; 'they were as ruthless as men in violent crime' (*The Times,* 24 August 1972; and see JP, 2 September 1972, p. 573, the journal for practitioners in the Magistrates' Court and Crown Courts, where Hamilton's comments were given wider coverage; 'Even in the realms of violence, women were becoming increasingly prominent, be it in violence for political ends, violence for gain, or senseless and motiveless violence such as football hooliganism'). And already by 1972 some concern was also being expressed in Parliament over the increasing number of women remanded in custody for these offences.

As is the case with most 'moral panics', what begins as an isolated newspaper heading becomes orchestrated by the media and the public into a matter of urgent public concern. Perhaps the most disturbing feature of this apparent concern over the increase in violence by women was that it was interpreted as a direct consequence of the liberation of women from traditional social roles and norms of behaviour. The consequences of such a line of thinking – if taken at all seriously – could have the most devastating effect on their social and political status. And it is significant that in 1978 so real was the disapprobation of the dissolution of traditional roles and so determined was the endeavour in certain quarters to preserve traditional roles that the government held particular discussions in Parliament on 'the family'[15] and its future as if it were a company under threat of closure.

The criminogenic nature of female emancipation

The view that the recent emancipation of women is a significant contributory factor in the relatively increasing participation of women in crime, violent offences in particular, is one shared by a number of criminologists and by the media.[16] The original criminological proponents of this thesis, at least in its contemporary guise, have however never systematically evaluated the relationship they claim, with the consequence that the effect and interconnection of other factors, unemployment on crime for example, have been erroneously excluded from their analyses. Thus in the work of Adler (1975), Simon (1975) and Ward, Jackson and Ward (1980) is found an extremely simplistic and crude treatment of these two factors. Since the appearance of these studies there has been a steady flow of articles and discussions testing, criticising and re-examining the initial hypotheses of this theory – Smart (1979), Kruttschnitt (1982) and Austin (1982), culminating in a recent critique by Box and Hale (1983) which outdoes them all. In criticising the critics the authors establish their warrantability for yet a further discussion on this topic.

Adler, perhaps the most vociferous proponent of this 'theory', suggested that the nascent economic independence of women was contributing to a new and serious form of criminality, a view which received some considerable support by Ward, Jackson and Ward amongst others, who explained:

Women's participation in selective crimes will increase both as their employment opportunities expand and as their interests, desires and definitions of self shift from a more traditional to a more liberated view . . . the trend in violence by women is upward, and the rate may be accelerated as women became emancipated from traditional female role requirements.[17]

The general emancipation–crime thesis has been widely criticised for the reliance its supporters have placed on statistics (the work of both Adler and Simon was based on a very scant statistical observation), and for blatant neglect of any analysis of female emancipation,[18] which has simply been assumed – an omission conceded by Austin. It was taken for granted and moreover the rise in crime was taken uncritically as a real increase rather than as the result of changes in police prosecution and cautioning procedures, an equally visible explanation.

Raya Levin (1979)[19] turning this formula on its head suggests that women's emancipation, if it is at all successful, is much more likely to contribute to a reduction of crime and violence by men, whilst J. Weis (1976) concludes that arrest statistics show that the new female criminal is more a social invention than an empirical reality.

The recent study of female criminality by Box and Hale criticises the recent studies in this field for, amongst other things, their crude manipulation of official arrest and caution data and their failure to control the changing population base of females available to commit female crimes, the changing rate of male crime, the failure to examine different types of crime and for their failure to apply statistical tests. The authors hit the nail on the head when they assert that 'the arguments of those who were tempted to prove a causal connection between emancipation and female crime by merely documenting the historical overlap between these two social phenomena seem to be fatally flawed' (1983: 36). They single cut only the studies of Steffensmeier (1978, 1980), which came close to meeting the above criteria. These studies do not support Adler's view that women will become more violent, or Simon's view that women will become less violent, since they found that female crimes of violence increased absolutely and not relatively, whereas female property offences increased faster than the male rate. Contrary to these analyses, Box and Hale examine the relation of the additional variables of unemployment and economic marginalisation, rather than concentrating on the allegedly criminogenic nature of female emancipation – a necessary consideration already suggested by Klein and Kress (1981: 167), particularly as prostitution and welfare frauds are effected.

And so has transpired in the field of criminology, if perhaps unwittingly, the revival of the second positivist fallacy relating to the explanation for female crime. The revival of the first positivist fallacy centring on individual pathology has already been discussed in some detail in Chapter 3 and will be considered again later insofar as its implications for the disposal and treatment of defendants are concerned. For the present I am concerned to explore the theory that the criminal behaviour of women is determined by their social role and social opportunity, and to examine the implications this has both politically and socially.

Explanations for women's marginal role in crime

Within this particular debate individualist social pathology criticised by Wright Mills in the 1940s has reared its head once more, where explanations are to be located not only in individual but social pathology. In describing this tendency Mills was particularly critical of the way in which social problems were frequently explained either in terms of biological impulses which break through 'societal restrictions' or by social pathologists who 'slip past structure to focus on isolated situations, and the tendency for problems to be considered as problems of individuals'.[20] Social role theory or sex role theory has for a long time been the dominant paradigm in the explanation of human behaviour. Within sociology and deviancy theory it became the key device for explaining differential rates of suicide,[21] mental illness,[22] and, more latterly, crime. And from within the tradition of criminological theory commentators[23] have identified four principal factors which have been variously considered in explaining women's marginal role in crime.

Differences in opportunity and access have been suggested by some to explain the different participation of the sexes in certain criminal activity and thus their absence or else low appearance in that category. Drawing on Cloward and Ohlin's thesis presented in *Delinquency and Opportunity* (1960)[24] writers have maintained that women's opportunities for certain crimes are limited. This 'opportunity thesis' was being discussed much earlier by Gross on the continent, who wrote, 'when the educated woman does nothing more than to steal a pencil from her husband and to cheat at whist, her sole fortune is that she does not get opportunities or needs for more serious mistakes' (1911: 326). But as Shaw and McKay stated in 1942, environment limits or opens access to illegal means and since the socialisation of girls has provided a more rigid control over their lives and activities their environment has limited this opportunity. The close supervision of girls was a factor taken up by Hoffman-Bustamante (1973) and D'Orban (1971), whilst the idea that women were less criminal because their role was in the home was a view advocated by, amongst others, W. Reckless in *The Female Offender* (1957). Interestingly, R. Mawby in 1980 has suggested that women are less criminal because of a more conservative attitude to law and order. Lombroso writing in 1895 had similarly declared that women were more conservative, and indeed opposition to female enfranchisement contained the fear of a conservative gain.

The differential opportunity thesis as an explanation of women's marginal role in crime may embody a modicum of truth. Consider that an infrequent but (typical) nineteenth-century female crime was murder by poisoning. O'Donnell[25] argues that poison was a woman's murder weapon since they are, he writes, physically and mentally ill-equipped for murder by violence. Female poisoners like Mary Blandy and Mary Anne Burdock[26] are well known. But as Ann Jones (1980) points out, women acting in their traditional roles of household managers would have legitimate access to the purchase of poisons for domestic reasons, thus giving some credence to the theory of differential access. Certainly the increasing involvement of women in fraud (obtaining money by deception) and falsifying records for accounts, particularly from banks and limited companies, is due to their increasing yet limited participation in these professions (see Klein and Kress 1981: 167). And a study of their relationship to the market should be rigorously explored in order that this might be tested.

Women however have always had the opportunity for domestic violence and the law as it relates to infanticide during the nineteenth century reflects this recognition. The differential-opportunity thesis thus has only a very limited applicability.

Theoretically what does seem to be of particular interest in the development of criminological theory related to women is that, whereas positivism has been rejected in explaining male deviancy with the possible exception of sex offenders, it is a theory which lingers on when women are considered. In one guise or another the umbilical attachment to positivist tenets remains. The formula is simple — women are either determined by their biology or else by their social role. In both instances reification of behaviour is inevitable whilst causality is reduced to a monocausal fact. The consequences of positivism for the individual are politically disastrous. If such a paradigm is adopted in the explanation of already oppressed groups — blacks, gays and women — the consequence is the marginalisation of women as a group because of their inability to act independent of their social role.

Women, in consequence, have never been acknowledged as authors of their own acts. To follow Matza's distinction, women within this paradigmatic construction have never been guilty of infraction, but only of action. Bertrand takes this total abrogation of feminine free will to its conclusion: 'Women in all male-dominated societies were subjected to a pattern of instrumentality . . . [which] deprived them of their capacity to perceive themselves as 'agents' and made of them ideal "objects" and "victims"' (1969: 27). And it is this deep-seated attitude concerning female nature which sets the stage for the way women are understood when they commit crimes of violence.

Political expediency and the criminogenic nature of emancipation

Of considerable importance to an understanding of the debate condeming the hypothesis that female emancipation is a central factor in increasing violent crime by women is how and why this particular equation, whether fact or fiction, became translated into a reality — reality in this conext being defined as a social reality in the words of Thomas's famous dictum, 'If you define a situation as real it's real in its consequences.' How this reality transpired is a matter which perhaps can be explained by drawing on the sociology of moral panics. In order to understand this process it is necessary to identify the political forces within society and to isolate those groups who may have had reason to oppose the achievements of the women's movement and therefore in so doing sought a variety of means to discredit the changes that had occurred. The suggestion that female emancipation might be a contributory factor accounting for the increase in female crime is by no means new (see Lombroso 1895, Thomas 1923, Bishop 1931) although it perhaps has never been so blatantly asserted. W. Bonger writing in 1916 argued that the highest figures for female criminality are furnished by the great cities and the most economically developed countries,[28] using Morrison's statistics which suggested that, of misdemeanours in London, 25 per cent were committed by women, 33 per cent by Mancunian women, 10 per cent by women in Surrey and 14 per cent by women in Lancashire, he concluded, 'The highest percentages come then in the places where the social position of women is most nearly equal to that of men.'[29]

Since the nineteenth century there have been several orchestrations of this theory, and at certain politically opportune moments this equation has been advanced deliberately to obstruct women's political, economic and social advancement. Throughout the nineteenth century justificatory rationales of the sort which claim that female emancipation would lead to the breakup of the family or to the instability of a nation were promulgated by right-wing public and political opinion in an attempt to preserve the existing division of society along sex and gender lines. Challenges to this oppressive division were fiercely opposed and those women who individually or collectively attempted to break out of traditional roles were publicly discredited, their actions marginalised, slurs cast upon their morality, denounced as sick or as mentally ill. The counter-agitation reached its zenith over the issue of enfranchisement. Women were indeed as Duffin had stated, 'Prisoners of Progress'.[30] Feminism and the cause for the advancement of the social status of women was depicted as a dangerous agitation which would lead to the disintegration of the family and undermine the institution of marriage. Consider the reasons given for opposing earlier attempts for economic independence. Opponents of the Married Women's Property Bill feared that, as one objector expressed it, 'mischiefs would follow from the assertion of this vicious principle'.[31] Financial independence, it was suggested, would result in women investing large sums of money in worthless railway shares, getting into debt or being bailed out of prison. But it wasn't just the odd occasion of debt that was feared. Karslake expressed a sentiment held by many when he said that such independence would effect an entire revolution in the social status of husband and wife.[32]

It was not surprising at all that the qualification of women faced an ever fiercer opposition. Sir A.E. Wright (MD, FRCS) argued that 'the woman's suffrage which leads up to feminism would be a social disaster'. And in his anti-suffragette campaign he tried to discredit the movement by suggesting that it was composed of an 'inbalanced lot'. He enumerated five types, 'those who resorted to physical violence, those women who were sexually embittered, those who had lost touch with fellow man, those poisoned by self-esteem and those who had been educated by suffragettes'. Wright's attitude to women is perfectly illustrated in a story told by Dr E. Carly to the biographer Leonard Colebrook. Invited to Wright's lecture at St Mary's *she,* looking forward to the event, was about to leave the house when a telegram arrived. It was from Wright: 'Have just heard you are a woman. Invitation cancelled!'[33] Later in 1921 the *New York World* (3 February) placed the responsibility of social ills on the Women's Movement,

the modern age of girls and young men is intensely immoral, and immoral seemingly without the pressure of circumstances. At whose door we may lay the fault we cannot tell. Is it the result of what we call "the emancipation of women", with its concomitant freedom from chaperonage, increased intimacy between the sexes in adolescence, and a more tolerant viewpoint towards all things unclean in life.[34]

The belief in the criminogenic nature of female emancipation owes much to the role of the media in the manufacture of this particularly imagery. The idea of women becoming increasingly violent certainly captured the imagination of the public since it existed in stark contrast to the traditional belief that women are passive and gentle. Thus the conflict of images presented a good sell. Chibnall[35] expressed the fascination in this way; 'readers appear to be particularly interested in women who commit violent acts. The reasons for this interest are arguable but they are probably informed by sexual roles which portray women as naturally passive and submissive, the aggressive woman appearing exciting, wicked and unnatural by contrast'. The media has exaggerated the reality of the increase in violence, frequently linking it to women's liberation, whilst the women's movement has been charged with breaking up the family unit. The media in echoing these sentiments reflect the attitude of a society based on a particular conception of the family unit and traditional sex roles. Both the right-wing and middle-of-the-road press echoed the hypothesis that there was a significant increase in crimes of violence by women, the undeniable result of female emancipation. The blame was laid squarely at the feet of a movement which wanted only equality. Support for this theory is found in the work of T.C.N. Gibbens who stated that the 'general emancipation of women is one factor in their increasing criminality'. Whilst Dr P.T. D'Orban (consultant psychiatrist at Holloway) pointed out that the last increase in female crime was during the war years because of increasing emancipation. A recent newspaper article in contribution to the panic gave an 11.8 per cent increase of crimes of violence amongst boys and a 16.6 per cent increase in crimes of violence for girls. In an article in 1973, reported in the *Daily Mail* (23 July) and headed 'When girls put the boot in', it was cited that there was a 60 per cent rise in crimes of violence committed by girls aged 14–17 compared with a 27 per cent increase in similar crimes committed by boys. It stated that, 'Psychiatrists, social workers and prison officers are agreed that the movement towards sexual equality has been taken at its face value by young girls'. Dr Catherine Storr was reported as saying, 'A girl reckons that if she can train to be an engineer like a boy she can go out and beat someone up like a boy.' The headlines of one story in the *Sun* (1 September 1975) read, 'Crime Wave of Lib Girls'. Later in 1976 *The Times* reported that more women were involved in offences and drew attention to these statistics for crimes of wounding: twenty-two girls under 14 were charged in 1974, compared with ninety-nine in 1975. And in 1977 provocatively headlined 'Sugar, spice and bloody knuckles', a *Sunday Times* feature (1 May 1977) took up the issue. The images of passive sweet girl and the new violent offender were counter-juxtaposed at the head of the article. For the first time the press presented an account of women as likely to turn to violence as boys if they have a violent upbringing. Also in the *Daily Mail* (12 April 1978):

A tough new breed of criminal is emerging. Young women whose behaviour is increasingly masculine. Girls are filling the roles of gang leaders, even taking part in hold-ups and seizing hostages. And they are prepared to kill to steal. The disclosure was made last night by Professor Solange Traisier to top police officers from all over Europe.

Every expression of emancipation amongst women in social or legal terms, real or imaginary, has produced a corresponding expression of publicity regarding family breakdown, divorce statistics, children in care and more latterly female crime. As Stan Cohen (1968) explained, society is subject every now and then to periods of moral panic. The moral panic may be a condition, an episode, a person or a group which emerges to become defined as a threat to societal values and interests: 'its nature is presented in a stylized and stereo-typical fashion by the mass media. The moral barricades are manned by editors, bishops, politicians and other right-thinking people.'[36] There is just this kind of 'moral panic' about the increasing violence of women. But it requires some explanation why this 'new strain of crime' and 'new breed of criminal' was identified and demarcated, how and why the equation became mobilised and the political forces in society resisting change largely assisted its mobilisation for their own ulterior ends. But as Steffensmeier[37] and others argue, the crimes of women in modern society continue to mirror their traditional role; it is only the 'image' or stereotype which is changing:

Our interpretation of the forces shaping female crime runs contrary to most popular and sociological writing on the subject . . . female experiences are not moving beyond traditional roles, either legitimate or illegitimate . . . The movement appears to have had a greater impact in changing the *image* of the female offender than the level or types of criminal offence that she is likely to commit.

Whilst women's liberation extended and developed, and crimes amongst women increased, the state deliberately intervened to shore up marriage and the family. The Women's Movement was not only put on trial for the increasing crime rate but for the increasing divorce rate. In the light of this concern it is perhaps not surprising that the institution of the family became cause for concern in Parliament On 17 March 1978 Mr Peter Bottomly moved: 'That this House recognising that meeting the needs of families will require more public education, political discussion and improved representation, calls on the Government to respond to the creation of a family movement and to consider publishing an annual family policy review'. He maintained that in the absence of an efficient family, social services and statutory bodies were called upon. Mr Stoddart said that 'In any debate of this sort mention must be made of the increasing number of married women with children who now go out to work and the effect which this has on family life.'[38] The 1979 General Election campaign had both main parties claiming to be the party of the family, and yet recent disclosures betray these claims as the Welfare State is under threat of collapse.

Violence – untypical of women

What seems to be abundantly clear as far as the courts and the public are concerned is that violence will not be tolerated and violence perpetrated by women whatever the circumstances will not be condoned. The immediate question which arises is whether the use of violence by women in self-defence or provocation is ever regarded as legitimate. And to examine how far legitimacy for action depends not merely on a means-to-an-end basis of justification, but on the gender expectation for role behaviour of the social actor in question. A different set of rules apply when the violent actor is female. The only acceptable demonstration of female physical violence is mild assault, typically scratching, pulling hair and kicking. A bottle to the face following provocation, a sheath knife to the neck in self-defence is not acceptable. The kernel of this whole debate is summed up in an article by Bel Mooney where she asks, 'Has a woman the right to fight back?' (*The Times,* 21 July 1981). This feature raises the much wider question of under what conditions a woman's violence is legitimate? The author relates the circumstances of the case of *R* v *Maguire* heard before Judge Stanley Price at York Crown Court, 17 July 1981.

On the night in question the victim started to walk home after securing her pony and missing the last bus. The accused, aged twenty-four, was being driven home when he saw her walking along a lane. After being dropped off at home, he ran back over one mile and confronted the girl, pretending to be a policeman. He dragged her into a field and told her he was going to kill her. The 'victim', although clearly terrified, managed to pull out a small sheath knife which she used to cut open bales of hay and 'stuck it into the defendant's neck'. The jury found him guilty of threatening to kill her. The judge, who felt that the defendant had already been punished enough, in passing a twelve-month suspended prison sentence remarked: 'This young lady inflicted a very considerable punishment on you.' As Bel Mooney only too correctly noted, a judge allowed a man guilty of an appalling attack – of attempted murder – to go free because his victim protected herself. But there are numerous other instances wherein women have been severely punished for behaviour amounting to self defence.

Later that year on 5 October, Iqbal Begum pleaded guilty to murder. She battered her husband over the head with a five-foot metal bar. She told the police, 'I didn't know what I was doing, but he wanted two of the children to be killed and I said, "Don't let the children get killed"' (*Guardian,* 6 October 1981). It is unlikely that her claim, real or imaginary, had any mitigating effect whatsoever as she was given a life sentence.

In 1974 two women in California were indicted for killing the men whom they alleged raped them. Inez Garcia was found guilty of second-degree murder and sentenced to at least five years' imprisonment, whilst Deborah Kantaen was indicted for first-degree murder. In both cases there was a time-lag between the alleged rape and the shootings, approximately seventeen minutes in the Garcia case, and one day in the case of Kantaen. In the Garcia case, Charles Garry, her counsel, tried unsuccessfully to establish that a woman has an equal right with a man to resort to violence in order that her honour might be protected. But Ms Garcia not only used violence, her whole manner in court showed no contrition. 'I killed that motherfucker, so why don't you just find me guilty and put me in jail, you lousy pig' (*Guardian*, 15 January 1975).

Similarly, in North Carolina in 1975, Joan Little went on trial accused of killing a white guard whom she alleged was trying to rape her. The principle at issue in Little's case is whether courts will continue to deny women the right to defend themselves from sexual assault. On 15 August Little was acquitted, much to the relief of the various groups involved in promoting her cause (*Detroit News*, 16 February 1975).

The issue of whether women can legitimately defend themselves is central in each of these cases. A recent study of women homicide offenders (who kill their husbands or boyfriends) by Bacon and Lansdowne[39] is an attempt to examine these alternative realities. Their research examines the discrepancies in the legal presentation of the case, and as presented by the defendants themselves, concluding that in all cases defendants are victims of violence perpetrated by husbands or boyfriends and are driven to kill in self-defence, provocation, or in order to escape from a life of brutalisation. The authors may unwittingly be setting up another equally problematic positivist tenet, i.e. that women who kill are merely responding with compunction to a violent situation. Nevertheless if some women do respond in this manner it is an interpretation which should not be too readily dismissed. The authors examined seventeen cases of women who had killed boyfriends or husbands and were convicted, and in fourteen out of sixteen cases found that the women had been physically assaulted, and subjected to repeated violence. The images these defendants had of themselves were as women totally dominated, socially, emotionally and sexually, remaining with the men because of fear of isolation. In all but three of the cases according to accounts provided by women themselves they were motivated to kill their husbands to protect themselves from physical harm, so that homicide became a means of self-preservation. Yet in contradiction, the image of these women depicted in court was frequently one of cold-blooded and premeditated action. As the researchers wrote, 'In most of these cases, even the woman's own lawyers could not or at least did not seem to understand her act from a woman's perspective,'[40] concluding that,

> The images of women as victims, neurotics and provocateurs, and the ideology of privacy which surrounds the institutions of sexuality and the family, play a role in perpetuating the domination and violence experienced by these women. The same ideologies and myths pervade the criminal justice system and prevented the actual circumstances of these homicides emerging in the court process which judged and sentenced them.[41]

And again when women's crime seems to be particularly at variance with gender role, motherhood in particular, the courts are more punishing. Lindy Chamberlain, found guilty of murdering her baby daughter, received a life sentence and lost her appeal against conviction (*Standard,* 29 April 1983).

One case involving cruelty to a child clearly reflected the tendency to punish not merely for the crime itself but because it was at variance with appropriate gender role. In a case heard at Manchester Crown Court in 1981 the judge sentenced the defendant to two years' imprisonment, exclaiming that she had been utterly selfish in her own pursuits in studying for a degree and neglecting her child. Her crime was even worse as she apparently opted out of round-the-clock motherhood for something different. The implication was that if she had remained at home this incident would not have happened – her deviation from domesticity had resulted in this offence!

Some violent offenders: legal responses

A total of 63 females appeared before the Crown Court in Manchester on charges of violence against the person (Table 7:4), the charges varying from manslaughter to assault: the victims were men, women and children. Of those particular cases which were observed in court some common features appertaining to processing emerged, in the legal presentation of the case and the way in which the crime was regarded. In all of the cases observed the traditional view of appropriate female behaviour emerged to some degree. Yet in none of the cases was the use of violence considered legitimate. The type of crime committed, depending on the seriousness of the offence, was frequently explained by recourse to individual pathology. In cases where the particulars of the offence, particularly the type of weapon used, were seen as vicious, whatever the outcome the disposal was treatment and punishment. Women were frequently dealt with not merely according to a tariff system but according to the degree to which their behaviour on this occasion had deviated from appropriate female behaviour. In none of the cases was

Table 7:4 Defendants proceeded against for violent crime at the Manchester Crown Court: 1981

(1)Violence	AD	CD 1	CD 2	CD 3	F	SO	HO	CSO	PO 1	PO 1 CT	PO 2	PO 2 CT	PO 3	PO 3 CT	BT	SS	IMP–6mth	IMP–12mth	IMP–2yr	IMP–2yr+	Transferred to Juvenile Court	Found not guilty	PONE	Plea ACC	Found not guilty	Bound over	Lie on file	Not guilty by direction	Total
S.18 wounding	–	–	–	–	–	–	–	–	–	–	–	–	–	–	2	2	1	–	–	–	–	1	–	–	–	–	–	1	9
S.20 wounding	–	1	–	–	–	–	–	–	–	–	1	–	–	–	2	2	1	–	–	–	–	–	–	–	–	2	3	–	6
S.47 assault	–	–	1	–	2	–	–	–	–	1	1	–	–	–	1	2	2	–	–	–	–	4	1	3	–	3	1	–	21
Common assault	–	–	–	1	–	–	–	–	–	–	–	–	–	–	–	–	–	–	–	–	–	–	–	–	–	–	–	–	1
S.18 → s.20	1	–	1	2	–	–	–	–	1	–	1	1	–	2	1	4	1	–	–	–	–	1	–	–	–	–	–	–	16
S.20 → s.47	–	–	–	1	1	–	–	–	–	–	–	–	–	–	–	–	–	–	–	–	–	–	–	–	–	–	–	–	2
S.47 → common assault	–	–	–	–	–	–	–	–	–	–	2	–	–	–	–	–	–	–	–	–	–	–	–	–	–	–	–	–	3
Murder ⎫ manslaughter	–	–	–	–	–	–	–	–	–	–	–	–	–	–	–	–	–	–	–	–	–	–	–	–	–	–	–	–	
Att. murder ⎭	–	–	–	–	–	–	–	–	–	–	–	–	–	–	–	–	–	1	–	1	–	–	–	–	–	–	–	–	2
Manslaughter and cruelty to under 16 year old	–	–	–	–	–	–	–	–	–	–	–	–	–	–	–	–	–	–	–	1	–	–	–	–	–	–	–	–	1
S.20 wounding and cruelty to under 16 year old	–	–	–	–	–	–	–	–	–	–	–	–	–	–	–	–	–	1	–	–	–	–	–	–	–	–	–	–	1
Infanticide	–	–	1	–	–	–	–	–	–	–	–	–	–	1	–	–	–	2	–	–	–	–	–	–	–	–	–	1	1
Total	2	1	3	3	3	–	–	–	1	1	6	1	–	4	4	8	4	2	–	3	–	6	1	3	–	5	4	1	63

Key: → means 'reduced to'

their behaviour regarded as appropriate in the circumstances. Like McMurphy's rational yet violent response to Nurse Ratchet's psychological castration of Billy (see Kesey 1976), situations or social or health roles define first and foremost how conduct should be interpreted. Violent behaviour by women, whether in defence or retaliation, is not to be excused, even less considered and understood in its social and situational context.

In a sub-sample of thirteen social inquiry reports prepared in not-guilty pleas for offences of violence (sections 18 and 20 Offences Against the Person Act 1861) in three cases the defendants furnished accounts of their conduct. Of the remaining ten reports, in four of them officers tried to provide some explanation, two were supportive. Of the defendants' accounts two alleged provocation, one loss of control.

> Mrs L. has recounted to me two features she feels may have contributed to the incident. Firstly, her concern over her husband's blood pressure . . . she also tells me that she suffers quite badly from pre-menstrual tension which leaves her prone for some days prior to a period to a relative loss of control.

> She said she suffered harassment from the complainant on the day of visiting her boyfriend's parents. She threatened her with a knife so she picked up a glass and threw it at the complainant.

> She admits wounding, she did not intend to do it but was provoked.

In the remaining ten accounts where the defendants gave no account of conduct the report writers were more likely to make a judgment on the likelihood that the offence was committed.

> Doesn't seem a girl likely to cause trouble — not violent.

> She did not impress me as delinquently inclined in her attitude.

> She and her husband had both been celebrating on the night in question but it may be that the effect of alcohol consumed might have been worse because of being mixed with painkillers.

> Mrs C. has shown no emotional reaction to the fact that her son suffered from gangrene, frost bite, cigarette burns . . . Neither has she reacted to local authority institutional care proceedings and the absence of any reaction raises a series of questions over her maternal capability and state of mind.

Judicial utterances in the sentencing stage of the trial process often reveal the extent to which behaviour is considered inappropriate and a deviation from conventional behaviour. In one particular case in the sample a consolidated trial in which two women were eventually bound over to keep the peace the judge explained that this was a case 'where two middle-aged ladies should know better'. In another case, where the defendant who had been drinking in a public house picked up a broken glass with which she assaulted the complainant, the judge in his summing up said,

> . . . you used a glass on that man's face, it was not an accident, and twice . . . you told the police . . . you came to court and said not guilty – The matter has dragged on. You have a dreadful record. You are a dishonest person, you have been convicted of theft, disorderly behaviour – when you 'glassed' Mr C you were on probation.

Yet in some cases judges, in conceding that 'we are all human', excused defendants, though in such cases the crimes were committed in a domestic setting and perpetrated against those they loved the most (see Smith 1962, 1965; Klein and Kress 1981). In an argument resulting in a charge of wounding following a domestic incident, the judge because of what he considered to be exceptional circumstances took a lenient course. The defendant was of previous good character in what the judge described as an 'understandable family tiff', although again in another case where a broken bottle had been used the behaviour was inexcusable. In a case of unlawful wounding in a public house the fact that the defendant, in her own words, 'was pissed' and in the judge's view had had 'a vicious and evil weapon' reduced the plausibility or mitigating effect of her motive and she was sent without hesitation for Borstal training. In one particular case the defendant reported her experience elsewhere, in an impassioned claim that her bizarre conduct in arson attacks was because 'All I ever wanted was my son'. Her story carried with it a note of salutary caution to those mothers who, ardent for open discussion, disclose their baby-battering potentiality, to be met with 'policing' and 'containment' by para-legal agencies. Such was the plight of C. Bohanna, who claims that instead of being supported she became involved in a long, imbricated sequence of events which were eventually and almost irrevocably to separate her from her son and to bar her from access until the son was eighteen. This, the final straw, sent the mother on her escapade of offending in which she set fire to the area office's garage and subsequently was sentenced to twelve months' imprisonment Now released from prison, she is still separated from the son she so desperately wanted with her.[42]

Another arsonist before the Crown Court in 1981 was committed to Broadmoor under section 60 of the Mental Health Act 1959 (with no restriction). Charged on four separate counts, pleading guilty only to the fourth, her plea was accepted by the prosecution whilst the remaining three were ordered to lie on the file. In this case her accounting in its absurdity was taken as an indication of mental illness. She explained that the spirit of a dead girl had told her to do the thing and that this was in response to the dead girl's call.

In cases where atonement characterises the defendant's response to her conduct, even in untypical offences and however serious, if genuine remorse is seen then sentencing reflects this (see Chapter 6). In a rather unusual case of manslaughter where lack of sexual competence had provided the chief provocation the female defendant was sentenced to a term of three years. The judge was however not unmoved by the tragedy and passion of what had transpired, and whilst by no means condoning the offence, felt that in the face of such provocation anyone might have reacted with a spontaneous outburst, unaware that its consequence would lead to the death of the taunter. The judge remarked:

> I am quite satisfied, probably for the reason Mr H. has outlined. You consumed a large quantity of drink — drink led to this tragic and appalling affair. I accept you were taunted by Mrs B. Nobody knows better than you how appalling. I can only impose a sentence of imprisonment. I suspect for your part — in view that punishment ought to be imprisonment — to help you with a sense of guilt.

The greater the incongruity of conduct to action, the more likely that set rules and procedures will be marked in their absence, and discretion non-routinised. In the absence of even tacit guidelines, individual disparities in sentencing flourish. In this respect women convicted of arson and manslaughter of their children present the courts with indefatigable paradoxes. The recent case of Elizabeth Stevenson, who killed her two young children and tried to commit suicide, was motivated by the desire to save her family from the humiliation of eviction (*Guardian,* 10 November 1982). She was sentenced to three years' imprisonment in order, said Lord Wheatley, the Lord Justice Clerk, that she may get 'assistance and help'; this will stroke a bitter chord in the hearts of many who prefer to demand assistance and housing provision for families. The crime and shame highlights a society which should do more for the homeless.

However, where the offence, its seriousness, the method of commission used, the motivating rationale are all 'out of place' with traditional expectations, the more severe the sentence and the greater the likelihood that mental illness is suspected. Further systematic research is required to explore the relationship of untypicality of crime in the elements outlined above, judicial processing and sentencing.

Conclusion

Its main message is that crimes of aggression by women and crimes of resistance are assessed and judged in a sex-appropriate rather than situational context. This tendency is contrary to principles of justice and results in women often being sentenced more harshly than men for their crime, since they are sentenced too for contravening the appropriate behaviour of women. Women are thus doubly punished. Such crimes are rarely if ever considered legitimate responses to intolerable or threatening situations. And since judges, magistrates and the public utilise stereotypical characterisations in describing deviants it is not surprising that crimes of aggression by women are treated in a sex-appropriate context. As Swigert and Farrell (1977: 21) write, 'Social roles and expectations afford males greater exposure to illegal opportunity.'

8 · Individualised justice – Treatment, leniency or lessened responsibility or informal state control

For most women in prison the implication of psychiatric treatment is that she has committed an offence and is not fully responsible for her actions, and must be taught by others what is best for her. There are already signs that delinquent women and girls are resenting this suggestion, and seeing it as unfair discrimination As they see it, most women who commit crimes, or even minor offences, would certainly prefer to be considered bad than mad.

John Camp, *Holloway Prison,* 1974

Perhaps the most widely held assumption in studies of women on trial is the belief that the female defendant is likely to receive a more lenient sentence than her male counterpart, a view shared by amongst others Pollak (1950), Devlin (1970) and McClean and Wood (1969). This apparent leniency has been variously accounted for by the chivalry of men (Simon 1975, Anderson 1976, Chesney-Lind 1977), and by the position of women in society (Devlin 1970). It has also been said to arise because it is widely considered that certain forms of sentence are wholly inappropriate for women (Smith 1962, Giallombardo 1966) and more especially because sentences of imprisonment would separate women from their children (Sykes 1958, Goodman and Price 1967, Heidensohn 1969, 1975, Gibbs 1971). 'Prison and the prisoner', a 1977 Home Office publication, very much expressed the collective sentiment:

To send a woman to prison, or indeed to any residential institution – even a hospital – is to take her away from her family; her children, in particular, may suffer from this deprivation, which can lead to the break-up of the home even where there is a stable marriage. When a man is absent from home, it can be kept going by his wife if she is provided with sufficient money and support. But when it is the woman who is absent, the husband is often unable to cope and unless there are relations who can take on the housekeeping and care of the children, the home may have to be broken up and the children scattered either into the care of the local authority, or to different relatives. (para 185)

The belief that the law treats women with greater leniency than it does men is one that has been assumed and proclaimed throughout history. Women, it has been said, are the favourites of the law. Matilda Blake, a legal critic and feminist, writing in the nineteenth century exposed the insidious hypocrisy of such claims. In contrasting penalties for the crimes committed by and against women in focusing on brutality towards women she explained 'the male judges, appointed by a Government chosen by an exclusively male electorate, punish the offenders in a most inadequate manner, holding a woman's life at a less value than a purse containing a few shillings'.[1] Sachs and Hoff Wilson (1978) similarly questioned the genuiness of this claim to male chivalry and protectiveness, finding that in the nineteenth century it was no more than a myth. Mill told Parliament that he should like to have a Return of the number of women who were annually beaten, kicked or trampled to death by their male protectors, and to contrast the sentences imposed, if any, with the punishments by the same judges for thefts of small amounts of property. 'We should then have an arithmetical estimate', he declared, 'of the value set by a male legislature and male tribunals on the murder of a woman, often by torture continued through years' (p. 54, 78).

Carolyn Temin (1973), in her historical study of the sentencing of the female defendant in the United States, argued similarly that the entirety of law assumed a kind of 'need for the protection of women'. This need resulted in a number of ironies, one of which was longer sentences based on the divisive notion that women should be rehabilitated, which was in turn based on a belief that women's psychology made them more susceptible.[2] Gail Armstrong (1977) and Klein and Kress (1981) have similarly criticised the notion of the protection and chivalry of the law by exposing the way in which instead law controls women. Kate Millett exposes its underlying intent: 'While a palliative to the injustice of woman's social position, chivalry is also a technique for disguising it' (1970: 37). Preferential treatment for women was reported by Swigert and Farrell (1977) which, because of what they call the 'social pedestal' effect, resulted in women being less likely to be convicted of more serious charges.

The argument is more complex than these simplistic presentations. Visher (1983) in a study of police–suspect encounters with 785 men and women concluded:

Chivalrous treatment at the stage of arrest depends upon a larger set of gender expectations that exist between men and women. In encounters with police officers, those female suspects who violate typical middle-class standards of traditional female characteristics and behaviour (i.e. white, older, and submissive) are not afforded any chivalrous treatment deciding arrest decisions. (pp. 22–3)

The alleged reluctance on the part of the courts to imprison women arises largely, or so it is claimed, from a feeling of chivalry, women's role as wife and mother and the general nature of female crime. The Report of the Work of the Prison Department 1972 stated several well-worn assumptions:

> The public is on the whole less fearful of women: their crimes are fewer and generally less violent; when violent, they are more often directed against people known to them personally; sentences tend to be shorter; problems of their children are more immediately acute.[3]

In addition the impact on imprisonment on the lives of women is a factor which it is said deters sentencers from imposing prison sentences upon them unless there is absolutely no alternative. Alec Samuels expresses this sentiment when he writes, 'The impact of imprisonment is likely to be very severe especially if she has family responsibility',[4] a factor acknowledged in a Home Office circular which explained the need for social inquiries in the case of all women in these terms: 'the social consequences of imprisoning women tend to be more severe and background inquiries are therefore particularly valuable'.[5]

The belief that women receive more lenient treatment within the criminal justice system than do men is therefore one which should be regarded with some considerable caution (Walker 1965: 300). On the contrary the findings of Simon (1975), Foley and Rasche (1976)[6] and Bernstein, Kick, Leung and Schulz (1977)[7] reported more harsh sentences for women. Nagel (1981: 114), in her study of sex differences in judicial outcome, concluded that 'Females whose offence is more consistent with sex role expectations seem to experience less harsh outcomes than females whose offences is less traditional', – the conclusion reached by Temin (1973) in her historical study. Thus judicial outcome depended on the type of crime committed and the degree to which the crime was at variance with the female role. This was the conclusion drawn by Pat Carlen in her study of Cornton Vale, the women's prison in Scotland, where she found:

> In the main, Scottish women go to prison for trivial crimes. A woman prisoner is more likely to be a *persistent* offender than a *dangerous* offender. A woman who is still running a household and looking after children is more likely to be a candidate for a non-custodial penalty than is her sister who, in rebelling against marital tyranny, has also stepped outwith domesticity and motherhood. The latter goes to Cornton Vale – again and again and again. (1983: 70)

In the light of such conflicting views a study of sentencing practice of female defendants in both the Crown and City Magistrates' Courts in Manchester was contemplated. In this context, the sentencing of female defendants was considered a feature of a penultimate part of a sequential process outlined in the introductory passages. Sentencing decisions, how and why they were made, were examined for the degree to which role, gender and biological sex variables were seen to have an impact on the final sentence and the justificatory or motivatory rationale for such decisions. This was contemplated against a backdrop of unresolved countervailing penal tendencies within decision making. The extent to which these tendencies may unwittingly have had a decisive effect on men and women is also explored.

Developments during the last few years have pointed to a trend towards decarceration and individualised justice (Bottomley 1973: 130–2; Bean 1976: 96–8) where sentencers are increasingly tailoring sentences to 'fit' offenders, rather than tailoring them to the crimes which they had committed. Nevertheless the judiciary and magistracy, in passing sentence are presented with competing social and philosophical questions regarding the relative virtues of retributive as opposed to rehabilitative sanctions, public accountability being also of some central concern. They must then steer a steady course between the tariff system of punishment on the one hand and individualised justice on the other. In order that some balance may be struck between these competing interests, sentencers are given considerable discretion in the sentences they impose.

Whilst sentences imposed by judges and magistrates are subject to public scrutiny, another frequent criticism is that particular social groups are more or less likely to receive harsh or lenient treatment. This tendency owes more to the ideology of the sentencers (see Tarling 1979: 25) than to anything inherent in the sentencing structure, though certain administrative biases are apparent. Much of the argument in this respect during the last decades has eagerly focused on the disparity in sentencing outcome between the sexes (Devlin 1970). Not surprisingly perhaps the debate has centred on the ratio of men to women in custody, though the essential differences between the sentencing of men and women are more likely to be explained by focusing on types of disposal rather than concentrating exclusively on whether or not a term of imprisonment is imposed.

Nevertheless, until recently the custodial sentence has been taken as a measure of sentencing practice as it is applied to women, and here lies another misconception, since it has been widely assumed that women *per se* are sentenced in a particular way rather than as women in accordance with their gender role. Thus in the past explanations for the apparent leniency in sentencing displayed towards women have been all too often erroneous and simplistic. Earlier demonstrations of commutions of the death penalty to life imprisonment were seen as a 'natural reluctance' on the part of male sentencers, or so stated the Royal Commission on Capital Punishment 1949–53.[8] However, it must be conceded that sentencing decisions of judges are influenced by operational constraints – that is, the facilities available to women offenders. It has been recognised for some time that facilities for women are few and inadequate with particularly serious problems of overcrowding. In 1980 the population in Holloway at its peak was up to 78 per cent above the certified normal accommodation, in Styal up to 27 per cent and in Risley Remand Centre up to 135 per cent,[9] whilst more recently problems of over-crowding have contributed to outbreaks of violence in Bulwood Hall (*Times* 10 February 1982, *The Times* 23 March 1982). In addition certain judges consider girls' borstals counterproductive. One judge remarked that they were 'nasty and evil places'. In all there are three closed and four open prisons, three remand centres and two closed borstals; such limited facilities may contribute to the judicial reluctance to impose custodial sentences, thus the apparent leniency being also attributable to economic and political expediency. Rather more recent research has taken the view that women receive lighter sentences with considerably more cautions.[10]

On another level altogether what appears a most significant and striking difference in the sentencing practice of men and women is a predominant adherence to the application of principles of individualised justice in the sentencing of women, an adherence not so apparent where men are concerned. This essential difference emerges as a consequence of the ideology of the sentencers, the structure of the sentencing process itself, and the practical viability of certain forms of sentence for the female defendant in her gender role together with gender conceptions of female deviance (Phillips and DeFleur 1982: 433). For instance, the sentencer when considering the most appropriate form of sentence is invariably presented with a number of peculiar presumptions about female offending and the practicalities of certain forms of punishment. It is likely that, in sentencing women, judges and magistrates have already given some thought to the possible causes of crime. And because the idea that women too are capable of criminal behaviour is still a view regarded with some scepticism, then it is assumed that there is an automatic tendency to exculpate and exonerate when a woman appears before the court.

In this, the final chapter, it is concluded that the sentencing of female defendants is a sequential process especially guided by principles of individualised justice where women are more likely to be 'treated' for their errors rather than punished, a tendency that is being widely misread as an expression of leniency. In addition to which the individualised justice women receive in considering individual personality and social background characteristics contemplates these factors in a sex-role context that is in accordance with gender- or sex-class concepts, rather than within the confines of the individual context as claimed. This orientation of understanding motivation for crime is implicitly expressed not only within discretionary decision-making of personnel working within the criminal justice system, but is also a tendency given special credence within the more formalised guidelines of when and how information to the courts should be provided. In a study of women defendants, together with the trend towards individualised justice in assessing sentencing outcome the main concern is whether the sentencing process and outcome is influenced by notions of sex-class or gender-role membership which may result in a particular kind of justice which is concerned not simply with leniency but is treatment, resocialisation and rehabilitation orientated (Adler 1975), on the basis that criminal activity amongst a certain group is pathologically inspired and deviates from appropriate femininity. Thus women are reduced to 'subjects' within the criminal justice system's concept of motivation for crime, though appropriate treatment considers gender obligations.

In the process of the sentencing of women defendants, certain decisions are more likely to be made based on the underlying rationale that the woman defendant is in some way different. For instance, there is some evidence which suggests that requests for social and medical information are more likely to be made. And it is these requests which have a major impact on the realisation of sentencing. Mitigation too, particularly the invoking of gender role, has a major impact on sentencing. In addition to the individual bias of magistrates and the judiciary, within the sentencing process itself are built-in procedures which tend to result in a different treatment of women and treatment in accordance with conceptions of both sex and gender. Consider, for instance, that in 1968 the plans introduced by Mr Callaghan to build a new Holloway were guided by the notion that those few offending seriously enough to warrant imprisonment must be physically or mentally in need of therapy. 'Henceforward the female system was to be therapeutically oriented with the new Holloway at its centre' (Faulkner 1971).

Information for the court

It is true that in the process of the sentencing of women certain requests for social and medical information are more likely to be made and more likely to be honoured. These requests, routinely and non-routinely made, have a crucial impact on the sentencing outcome. The recent development of the provision of information to sentencers in the manner of social inquiry reports, medical reports and mitigation have all had a major impact on the realisation of sentencing. This being the case it is no longer realistic to talk solely of magisterial or judicial bias in the sentencing of men and women, but instead to examine each stage of the sentencing process. The discussion and analysis in the following pages is guided by the desire to ascertain what factors are relevant in sentencing, what impact they have on sentencing outcome, and if there are any factors which may lead to the differential treatment of men and women.

Social inquiries and sentencing

The practice of individualised sentencing, that of arriving at the most suitable sentence for a particular defendant, has been facilitated by the relatively recent introduction of the social inquiry report. As Hardiker and Webb (1979) explain, 'If sentencers are to consider the circumstances of individual offenders they need information which can be taken into account, either in mitigation of sentence (probation instead of custody) or as a pointer to a rehabilitative measure psychiatric treatment rather than borstal training).'And whilst 'At the beginning of the century, antecedents were the primary source of information for sentencers. Now, it is often social inquiry reports.' Social inquiries became mandatory under the auspices of the Criminal Justice Act 1948, section 5, where it was provided: 'It shall be the duty of probation officers to inquire into the circumstances or home surroundings of any person with a view to assisting the court in determining the most suitable method of dealing with these cases', providing also for the necessary adjournment in such cases. By 1961 the powers of the probation officer had widened considerably. The Report of the Interdepartmental Committee on the Business of the Criminal Courts (1961) stated that the probation officer's function was to provide information which will assist the court in sentencing and assessing the culpability of the offender. The probation officer 'can give a *useful opinion*' (para 339), 'a frank opinion on the likely effect on the offender of probation or other forms of sentence' (para 346). Thus officers' views were given a greater credibility and from the periphery of the court process they were given an increasingly central role.

But the recommendations expressed in the Streatfeild Committee report, as it was otherwise known, were not met with unanimous welcome. The Morrison Report of 1962 (Report of the Departmental Committee on the Probation Service) in a rejoinder took issue with certain of its recommendations. Paragraph 41 stated that probation officers were not trained nor were they equipped to give such an opinion. Yet it was on the advice of a Home Office Circular, 1963/84, that the real authorisation for officers to express opinions was provided. In this same document the value of pre-trial inquiries was expressed, later to be enshrined in the Criminal Justice Act 1967, section 57, which empowered the Secretary of State to require courts to consider social inquiries before sentence is passed. This requirement was followed by Home Office Circular 1971/159 and provided for in the Power of Criminal Courts Act 1973, section 45, though never brought into effect by the Home Secretary. A later Circular 1977/118 restated the need to prepare reports where the accused pleads not guilty.

Whilst the Criminal Justice Act 1948 stated that inquiries could be made on any person, since 1967 a rather special concern with providing antecedent histories of women defendants has been increasingly evident. This concern both implicit and explicit is based on the belief that women are law-abiding citizens and criminality must therefore be an expression constituted of biology, physiology and mentality (Rasche 1975). With this conceptualisation in mind, sentences are particularly cognisant of women's gender role – domestic commitment, obligations and family attachment bear significantly in sentencing decisions.

For instance a clear separatist treatment between the sexes was affirmed in the official guidelines on sentencing. In Home Office Circulars 1968/188, 189, 190, it was advised that social inquiry reports should be prepared before sentencing in the following instances:

(*a*) detention in a detention centre;
(*b*) borstal training;
(*c*) a sentence of imprisonment (including a suspended sentence) of two years or less where the offender has not received a previous sentence of imprisonment (including a suspended sentence) or borstal training;
(*d*) *any sentence of imprisonment on a woman* (my emphasis).

thereby displaying a special consideration for women in their gender role.

A similar special consideration is evident in the official guidelines for the provision of pre-trial reports. Home Office Circular 1971/59, paragraph 7, advised that officers should prepare pre-trial reports on an accused who consents, including '(vi) *Any other woman defendant*' (my emphasis). Already by the early 1970s from within these guidelines alone and for whatever rationale, women received special consideration. Pat Carlen (1983) and Chambers (1979) found that in Scotland 'sheriffs are generally much more likely to ask for a Social Inquiry Report on a woman than on a man' (Carlen 1983: 63). Moreover, the recommendations detailed in the Butler Report of 1975 for the preparation of social inquiry reports may unwittingly have had a disparate effect on reports prepared on men and women. The report outlined the role of the social inquiry report in these terms. Section 136: 'We propose that a greater use should be made of social inquiry reports as a screening process for mental disorder and to indicate the need for a full psychiatric report.'[12] The recommendations expressed in Butler reflected an already long-emergent trend in social inquiries, criticised by Sheppard (1980)[13] and Curnock and Hardiker (1979) who, amongst others, express a concern that reports were too frequently treatment-oriented and looked to isolate some pathologically intrinsic factor as the cause of crime, an orientation possibly exaggerated in reports prepared on women because of the already existent characterisation of their pathological nature.

But are there any special circumstances which are thought more likely to result in a request for a social inquiry report, for instance where the offence committed is thought likely to suggest disturbances of a psychological, medical or social nature? Crimes not normally committed by women, and therefore incongruous with the female role, appear to generate such requests, as in crimes of burglary and violence. Bean (1971)[14] noted that social inquiries were more readily sought by the court where there was a marked inconsistency in the type of offence committed and the type of offender.

In examining the relation, if any, between the defendant's sex and the type of crime committed, all social inquiry reports prepared for cases involving female defendants heard before magistrates at the City Magistrates' Court, Manchester, in 1981 were analysed according to the offence for which the report was prepared, and the sentencing outcome. Information in this instant was available in 397 reports on sentencing and offence. It was not possible to say whether the report was requested by the court or in fact requested by the defence. Reports were consulted on a weekly basis at the records office of the probation liaison department where reports were kept in duplicate on all cases. In the event of the defendant facing a number of charges and/or in cases where these involved different offences the principle category is recorded here as is the case in *Criminal Statistics*.

Table 8:1 indicates the number of social inquiries prepared in each offence category as a percentage of all appearances in that category for the year under inquiry. Two observations can be made from the data. First, there is a greater likelihood that a social inquiry report will be requested in the non-typical female crimes of burglary and violence than in the more typical female offences of theft, or DHSS deception. Consider for instance that in 56 per cent of all cases of burglary, and in 32 per cent of all violent crimes a report was prepared compared with 19 per cent in theft and a higher figure of 31 per cent in prostitution. These data lend support to the view that the more 'untypical' the crime, the greater the likelihood that pathological explanations are sought in social, psychological and personality factors. Second, as the primary object of the social inquiry report is to assess and recommend the most appropriate sentence together with an assessment of the defendant's suitability for probation it is to be noted with interest that the probation order constitutes 50 per cent of all disposals in offences of theft, 30 per cent in burglary, 25 per cent in violent offences and 36 per cent in offences of prostitution.

Recommendations and sentencing outcome

Much research investigation on the relationship of probation officers' sentencing recommendations to the final sentencing outcome has increasingly assumed that in the face of a significant correlation between the two, the relationship must of necessity be a causal one. Yet, counterindicative observations have otherwise concluded that the assumption that it is the officers' recommendations which have a direct influence on the court is unproven. Research conducted recently by Hine, McWilliams and Pease (1978) suggested that the reverse may also hold true – that

Table 8:1 *Social inquiry reports requested according to offence and sentencing outcome (Manchester City Magistrates' Court, 1981)*

	Committed to Crown Court for sentence/trial	BO	AD	CD	FINE	PO	CSO	SS	IMP	NK	Total reports prepared	Total defendants	Reports % of total
Prostitution	—	—	2	18	10	30	6	8	5	5	84	273	31
Burglary	1	—	—	2	1	5	2	2	1	—	14	25	56
Criminal damage	—	—	—	1	1	4	—	—	1	1	8	67	12
Drug offences	—	—	1	1	—	3	—	1	—	—	6	36	17
Drunkenness	—	—	2	6	3	—	—	—	—	—	11	297	4
Public order	—	2	—	1	1	1	—	—	—	—	5	43	12
Theft, deception and false representation	2	—	2	34	16	116	14	27	13	8	232	1241	19
Abstract: Electricity Taking without consent	—	—	—	4	1	12	—	1	—	—	18	—	—
Violent offences	1	1	1	2	3	3	—	—	—	1	12	37	32
Police assault	—	—	—	—	—	—	—	—	—	—	—	—	—
Robbery	—	—	—	—	—	—	—	—	—	—	—	—	—
Sexual offences	—	—	—	—	—	—	—	—	—	—	—	—	—
Other	—	—	—	—	—	—	—	—	—	7	7	—	—
Total	4	3	8	69	36	174	22	39	20	22	397		

is, officers may frequently anticipate the preferences of sentencers in their recommmendations.[15]

Whilst the correlation of recommendation to sentencing has nevertheless been closely scrutinised researchers have not always looked to the degree of correlation and diversity between specificity of recommendations and the direction of sentencing outcome.

Method

To this end, 397 reports were analysed with a view to discerning the possible impact which officers' recommendations have on the final sentencing outcome. In instances where a definite correlation between recommendation and sentencing outcome was evident the term 'followed' is applied so as not to imply any causality. In cases where magistrates appeared to impose a harsher or more punitive sentence than suggested by report writers the term 'severe' is used. And finally, where magistrates imposed a lighter sentence than that proposed the term 'lenient' appears to denote this diversity. Where a specific recommendation for instance a fine was proposed and magistrates fined the offender this was also recorded as 'followed'. In cases where officers recommended leniency (typically presented in reports in this format: 'I would suggest that this defendant is treated leniently') and a sentence in part A of the scale of disposals (in Figure 8:1) was considered then the recommendation was considered 'followed.'

The scale adopted for this purpose interpreted the following disposals as shown in Figure 8:1.

Figure 8:1   Scale of disposals

	Absolute discharge	Lenient ↑
	Conditional discharge*	
A	Fine	
	Probation order	
	Community service order	
B	Suspended sentence	
	Imprisonment	Severe ↓

* It has been argued that a conditional discharge is in fact akin to a suspended sentence: however for this purpose
it is regarded as lenient.
Deferred sentence is excluded from the study as final disposal can range enormously.

In 223 (56 per cent), magistrates concurred with recommendations of report writers (see Table 8:2, cols 1, 2, 3). In 66 (17 per cent), magistrates' choice of sentence proved to be more severe (see Table 8:2, cols 4, 6, 8, 10), and in 108 (27 per cent), were more lenient in their choice of disposal (see Table 8:2, cols 5, 7, 9). In 48 per cent where a specific recommendation was proposed it was 'followed' by magistrates (col 1), whilst officers made recommendations in 65 per cent of cases (cols 1, 4, 5), a similar proportion observed in other research (Perry 1974 observing recommendations in the region of 60–80 per cent, whilst Bean 1975 observed recommendations in 90 per cent of cases – significantly higher).[16] The Manchester study indicates that in 25 per cent of the cases no recommendation whatsoever was apparent (cols 7, 8, 9, 10), whilst it was suggested in 9 per cent of cases that magistrates take a lenient course (cols 2, 6).

There was some indication that certain offences seemed to generate a greater consistency of recommendations. For instance, in all four cases where a negative recommendation was given the defendants were charged with prostitution offences (see Table 8:2, col 3). And in a total of six out of fifteen cases where officers had specifically declared that clients would not co-operate with the terms of a probation order such an order was nevertheless made, this latter instance reflecting the degree of diversity in recommendations and sentencing.

It is perhaps of some significance that Hine, McWilliams and Pease recently found that 'probation officers' recommendations . . . were as likely to divert offenders INTO custody as away from it'.[17]

Pre-trial reports
In 1977 at their Annual General Meeting the National Association of Probation Officers passed a resolution agreeing not to prepare social inquiry reports in not-guilty pleas. A later policy paper p. 5/81, paragraph 13, outlined what lies at the kernel of this debate. 'If the social inquiry report's main emphasis is seen as

Table 8:2 *Agreement and diversity: probation officers' recommendations and magistrates' disposal (Manchester City Magistrates' Court, 1981)*

	Recommendation						No recommendation				
	1 Specific rec. followed	*2 Leniency rec. followed*	*3 Negative rec. followed*	*4 Specific rec.: magistrates severe*	*5 Specific rec.: magistrates lenient*	*6 Leniency rec.: magistrates severe*	*7 Rec. absent: magistrates lenient*	*8 Rec. absent: magistrates severe*	*9 Rec./absent, no co-op: magistrates lenient*	*10 Rec./absent, no co-op: magistrates severe*	*Total*
Number of reports	192	27	4	33	36	6	57	18	15a	9	397
as a % of the total	48	7	1	8	9	2	14	5	4	2	100
As a % of total where recommendation	64	9	1	11	12	2	–	–	–	–	100
As a % of total where no recommendation	–	–	–	–	–	–	58	18	15	9	100

(a) Offences relating to prostitution

evaluation and assessment, leading to the expression of a professional opinion, the inability to refer to the focal point of such an exercise namely the offence imposes great limitations on the usefulness of the document'. Samuels much earlier had pointed to this difficulty when he asked 'how can the character of the offender be assessed?' given that the defendant denies the offence.

Quite apart from this obvious difficulty, a much graver issue is at stake which relates to the quality of justice a defendant may be likely to receive in the event of such a report being prepared. Over this matter alone officers are deeply divided, some pressing most urgently for the total abolition of the pre-trial inquiry, others refusing to implement NAPO policy. The Inner London Probation and After-Care Service adopted the policy outlined by NAPO (p. 5/81), but left the final decision to individual officers, whilst the position adopted by the Greater Manchester Probation and After-Care Service was revealed in a recent consultation document: 'With regard to not-guilty pleas The Greater Manchester Probation and After-Care Service policy is the procedure outlined in HOC 118/1977' (indicating a departure from NAPO). Thomson in a recent article, in which he attempts to assess the effect of NAPO ruling, states: 'I suggest that all defendants regardless of mental, medical, social or family circumstances should be brought to trial without prior intrusion from the probation service.'[18] He sees the inconsistency from case to case, where in some reports are available and in others not, as the greatest obstacle to justice.

The preparation of social inquiry reports in not-guilty pleas is a highly controversial practice. Samuels' claim that the pre-trial report has virtually disappeared[19] cannot be substantiated in the light of this present research. Moreover Trepanier (1979) found the opposite was true; pre-trial inquiries, he discovered, have indeed become general practice in Crown Courts. The practice has for sometime been outlawed by NAPO on the basis that it persists only to prejudice a defendant's case, supported by Trepanier's finding that 'decision-makers are more likely to find the offender guilty if they know about his criminal past than if they do not'.[20]

So how can the continued preparation of such reports be justifiably sustained? The arguments in support of this practice are largely ones of administrative expediency, since in the event of a finding of guilt a report is immediately available allowing for sentence to be passed without the delay which would be incurred if a remand was necessary for inquiries to be made.

What is the argument against? In the preparation of such reports, because only the minimal antecedents can be referred to, it is argued that the nature of the report is so sparse as to be virtually no use at all. It has been widely argued that in reports where details and information of a more personal nature are attempted there is a clear danger of character assassination, though the primary objection is to the sentencer having access to the report before trial. In addition if 1971/59, paragraph 7, is applied the chances are that pre-trial social inquiry reports as well as post-trial reports are more likely to be prepared on women.

Method

All ninety-one pre-trial reports prepared on not-guilty pleas before the Crown Court, Manchester, were analysed first according to offence and whether a recommendation was given, and secondly the tenor of the report was examined for its neutrality, support or lack of support for the client. The variation in the range of supportive and unsupportive comments was tremendous, some writers stating that their clients were responsible, sensible and could not have committed the offence for which they had been charged, some stating that clients were uncooperative, whilst other officers made no comment on the offence whatsoever, nor passed any opinion on the social background or personality of the client, and others stated categorically that they were unable to make comment. The sample was derived from examining all court record sheets in trials, consulting probation records and social inquiry report duplicates available in order to ensure the complete sample of all pre-trial reports.

Out of the total of ninety-one reports prepared (169 requested) (see Table 8:3), the content of 73 per cent remained wholly factual (cols C, D). In 27 per cent of the remaining reports value judgments and personal prejudices of report writers as to the personality of the defendant, her leaning towards crime, bad behaviour and mode of life were evident (cols A, B). In 20 per cent of the grand total the comments of officers were generally supportive and positive (col. A), whilst in 7 per cent the comments contained were not merely unsupportive, negative and unequivocal, but indeed so prejudicial to the defendant that it was possible to conceive that the case could be condemned before it was even heard (col. B).

However throughout all categories of positive, negative and absent comment (cols A, B, C and D), officers nevertheless continued to make recommendations for leniency, indicating where a defendant could and would not respond to probation, and making specific recommendations. Such opinions were prefixed 'If a finding of guilt . . .'. The variation in officers' predilection to make recommendations and make personal assessments of the defendant may be extremely prejudicial. If pre-trial reports continue to be prepared then some policy guidelines must be clearly established regarding just what such a report may justifiably contain and whether personal prejudices of officers should be allowed to enter. In reports prepared where no comment or recommendation was given the information contained was little more than police antecedents, which may make a case for the revival of police antecedents in such cases and the abolition of the pre-trial report particularly if unsupportive and negative comments are a feature in reports

Table 8:3 *Pre-trial reports: according to offence, nature of comment and recommendation (Manchester Crown Court, 1981)*

Offence	A Supportive positive comment		B Unsupportive negative comment		C Comment absent		D Unable to comment		Total
	Rec.	No rec.	Rec.	No rec.	Rec	No rec.	Rec.	No rec.	
Brothel-keeping	–	–	–	–	–	1	–	–	1
Theft	5	6	3	3	8	10	4	10	49
Theft (false accounting	–	–	–	–	–	2	–	1	3
Affray	–	–	–	–	1	–	–	–	1
Cruelty to person under 16	–	–	–	–	–	–	–	1	1
DHSS F.A.	–	–	–	–	–	–	–	–	–
Drugs possession	2	–	–	–	–	3	–	–	5
Drugs theft	–	–	–	–	–	–	–	–	–
Deception/ forgery	–	–	–	–	–	–	–	–	–
Burglary	–	–	–	–	1	3	1	1	6
Robbery	1	1	–	–	–	1	–	–	3
Criminal damage	–	–	–	–	–	–	–	–	–
Arson	–	–	–	–	–	1	–	2	3
Wounding	–	–	–	–	–	–	–	–	–
Indecent assault	1	2	–	–	1	7	1	5	17
Manslaughter	–	–	–	–	–	–	–	–	–
S.47 assault	–	–	–	–	–	–	–	–	–
Wounding (GBH)	–	–	–	–	–	–	–	–	–
Allow self to be carried	–	–	–	–	–	–	–	1	1
Conspiracy	–	–	–	–	–	1	–	–	1
Total no. of reports	9	9	3	3	11	29	6	21	91
As a % of total	20		7		43		30		100

throughout the country and if officers refuse to comment, complying only with the need to prepare reports to keep in line with decisions made by Area officers.

In the remaining seventy-eight cases where a request had been made but a report was not forthcoming (see Table 8:4), in 15 per cent of the cases the officer refused to prepare a report. In 12 per cent officers referred to the policy of NAPO whilst flouting the guidelines of the Greater Manchester Probation and After-Care Service, otherwise in line with the Home Office Circular of 1977.

'Untypical' crimes and medical requests

I have already suggested in an earlier chapter that the nature of the offence for which a defendant is charged is likely to have a considerable impact on whether or not a medical report is requested. There is some evidence that the more incongruous the crime with the defendant committing it the greater the likelihood

Table 8:4 *Pre-trial social inquiry reports requested: reasons for non-preparation (Manchester Crown Court, 1981)*

	All offenders	1 NAPO	2 Defendant declines	3 No contact	4 Not-guilty plea comments	5 No report	6 Insufficient time	7 Solicitor bars access to report
Total absent	78	9	43	19	2	3	1	1
As a % of total absent	100	12	55	24	3	4	1	1
As a % of all pre-trial requests	46	5	25	11	1	2	1	1

that such a request will be made. Soothill and Pope (1974), and Gibbens, Soothill and Pope (1977) found in both studies that requests varied with this factor. 'The male sex offender was more frequently selected for a medical remand, whereas for rarer female offences (burglary, fraud, and forgery) the proportion of medical remands was comparatively high' (1977: 17). Not only did the authors find that particular offences resulted in medical requests but particular offence categories tended also to be associated with particular forms of treatment.

> In London, a small proportion of the women commiting offences of violence against the person were compulsorily detained by a hospital order . . . On the other hand, offences against property with violence when committed by females were likely to be regarded as a manifestation of psychiatric disturbance . . . Fraud and forgery was another category among female offenders where a medical disposal was higher than average. (1977: 20.)

The frequency with which a medical report was requested in typical and untypical offences and the implications this had for the final sentencing outcome were matters investigated in the Manchester study. Of a total of 2402 female defendants appearing before the City Magistrates' Court in Manchester in 1981, a medical report was requested in forty cases, a total of 2 per cent of all cases. In eight cases, constituting only 20 per cent of cases, medical treatment constituted part of the final disposal (see Table 8:5, cols 5 and 6).

It is not without some significance, despite the sample size, that medical reports were more likely to be requested in crimes of violence and criminal damage. It may be assumed then that women who commit violent crime are more likely to be considered 'sick' and the tendency to seek some explanation in pathological factors is greater than for the more typical crimes of prostitution and theft.

Table 8.5 Medical remands: number and percentage according to offence and disposal (Manchester City Magistrates' Court, 1981)

	1 AD	2 CD	3 F	4 PO	5 PO treatment	6 H.O.	7 SCO	8 SS	9 Imp	10 Comm. to Crown Court	11 Dismissed	12 Deferred sentence	Total	No. in court turnover	As a % of court turnover
1 Violence	–	1	–	1	1	–	–	–	–	–	–	1	4	121	3
2 Theft & handling	–	2	1	4	5	1	1	1	4	–	1	4	23	1112	2
3 Fraud & forgery	1	–	1	–	–	–	–	–	1	1	–	–	4	143	3
4 Criminal damage	–	–	–	–	1	–	–	–	2	–	–	2	5	81	6
5 Prostitution	–	1	–	–	–	–	–	–	–	–	–	1	2	299	1
6 S.5 POA	–	2	–	–	–	1	1	–	–	–	–	–	2	86	2
Total	1	6	2	5	7	1	1	–	7	1	1	8	40	1546	–

(a) All but one were offences of shoplifting.

Mitigation and sentencing outcome

Mitigation and its visibility in the sentencing process is only of recent advent; it is dependent on legal representation and thus facilitated by recent developments in legal aid (see Table 8:6). Since the advent of legal aid and duty solicitor schemes, mitigation is an increasingly viable factor in the sentencing process with its own impact on sentencing outcome. Shapland (1981) has recently made a study of this process and the particular factors presented in mitigation of sentence. Shapland sibility and although not confining her study to a particular offence recognised that problems of accounting may be linked to particular offences (Shapland, p. 55).

Table 8:6   Representation and sentence (Manchester City Magistrates' Court, 1981)

Sentence	Plea and representation					R Elsewhere	Age			Age unknown	Total
	NG R	NG NR	G R	G NR	NG to Ga R		<20	21-39	40+		
Absolute discharge	5	–	31	55	5	–	16	45	35	0	96
Conditional discharge	41	10	260	309	28	–	171	284	142	51	648b
Fine	65	13	213	598	36	–	276	445	166	38	925b
Probation order	13	1	144	52	6	–	68	111	21	16	216b
Hospital order	–	–	1	–	–	–	–	1	–	–	1b
C.S. order	2	–	21	2	4	–	9	18	2	–	29b
Suspended sentence	6	–	68	11	5	–	15	56	12	7	90b
Imprisonment	3	–	50	4	7	–	13	36	12	3	64b
Total	135	24	788	1031	91	–	568	996	390	115	2,069b
Comm. Crown Court –Trial	–	–	–	–	–	114	18	74	19	3	114
Comm. Crown Court –Sentence	1	–	14	1	–	1	12	5	–	–	17
Deferred sentence	5	–	34	16	3	–	28	28	–	2	58
Case withdrawn Case dismissed	133	20	4	28	1	16	58	108	36	–	202
Grand total	269	44	806	1,060	92	131	656	1,183	445	118	2,402

(a) Plea change
(b) This number excludes the DHSS figures in the age category as not known.
    Grand total excludes deferred sentence total as already incorporated.

Method

A total of fifty cases of loitering for the purpose of prostitution were observed where there was an admission of a finding of guilt and notes taken. Particular attention was given to the factors invoked by advocates in mitigation of sentence. Five factors were invoked in one form or another. In some cases they were presented as the sole factor in mitigation whilst in other instances several factors were invoked collectively, two on average (see Table 8:7). In each case information was collected on mitigation in relation to sentencing outcome.

Table 8:7 *Mitigation and its influence on sentencing in offences of loitering for the purposes of prostitution (Manchester City Magistrates' Court, 1981)*

| Form of disposal | *Mitigatory factors* | | | | | | | | | | *Total* | |
| | *1 Social security* | | *2 Financial difficulty* | | *3 One-parent family* | | *4 Family bkgd.* | | *5 Medical problems* | | | |
	No.	*As a % of sub-total*	*No.*	*As a % of sub-total*	*No.*	*As a % of sub-total*	*No.*	*As a % of sub-total*	*No.*	*As a % of sub-total*	*Factors*	*Persons*
Conditional discharge	5	16	7	31	5	21	1	11	1	25	19	11
Fine	13	40	10	45	8	34	3	33	3	75	37	19
Probation order	2	6	1	4	1	4	—	—	—	—	4	2
Community service order	1	3	—	—	1	4	—	—	—	—	2	2
Suspended sentence	6	18	3	13	6	26	2	22	—	—	17	8
Imprisonment	3	9	1	4	2	9	2	22	—	—	8	4
Deferred sentence	2	6	—	—	—	—	1	11	—	—	3	2
Dismissed	—	—	—	—	—	—	—	—	—	—	0	2
Sub-total	32		22		23		9		4		90	50
% of persons	64		44		46		18		8			

Explanatory note: Factors 1–5 may be invoked collectively or singly in mitigation.

In 64 per cent of all cases the fact that defendants were in receipt of social security was invoked (col. 1). In 40 per cent of these cases despite the fact that financial hardship was acute a fine was imposed, whilst in 6 per cent defendants were given probation orders (col. 1). Where financial difficulty was given in mitigation (44 per cent of all cases), (col. 2), in 45 per cent of this sub-sample a fine was imposed (col. 2). The fine as a disposal diminished slightly where defendants were one-parent families to 34 per cent (col. 3). However, this particular offence category is perhaps especially problematic because of the limited range of realistic sentencing possibilities, particularly so since the probation order is not a typical disposal. As I have indicated previously prostitutes do not regard themselves in need of guidance, support or rehabilitation, all objectives of probation supervision. And those given probation orders can be seen frequently to breach them.[21]

The offences for which women are prosecuted

It has been widely argued that women are prosecuted for very different offences than are men, or else for similar offences but in differing proportions. Traditionally women's crimes have been those of theft, prostitution, assault and social welfare fraud, the more serious offences of robbery, burglary and violence being a male preserve (Hoffman-Bustamante 1973). In examining the types of crime women commit all defendants before the City Magistrates' Court and Crown Court in Manchester (excluding appeals against conviction or sentence) were recorded (see Tables 8:8, 8:9 and 8:10). As such the information contained is a reflection of the offences for which women are prosecuted. The information was derived from the Magistrates' Court from details obtained in the court register which was consulted daily. In the Crown Court the numbers of all defendants were noted and the details consulted by examining court record sheets. In the lower courts out of a sub-total of 2069 offences where a guilty plea was entered or case proven, 49 per cent of all offences committed by women were for theft and handling, 14 per cent for drunkenness, 13 per cent for offences of prostitution, 6 per cent for offences of fraud and forgery and 6 per cent of offences of DHSS deception, whilst in 2 per cent women were charged with violence, drug offences, breach of the peace, criminal damage 3 per cent and burglary 1 per cent.

In the Crown Court, out of a total of 275 defendants found guilty, 16 per cent were for offences of violence, 0.3 per cent for sexual offences, 14 per cent for burglary, 4 per cent for robbery, 42 per cent for theft and handling, 16 per cent for fraud and forgery, and 3 per cent for criminal damage (see Table 8:10). These proportions compare with the following percentages of defendants found guilty in each offence category in England and Wales for 1981: 0.6 per cent for violent offences, 0.15 for sexual offences, 4 per cent for burglary, 0.03 per cent for

Table 8:8 All offences committed by women according to sentence
(Manchester City Magistrates' Court, 1981)

	Violence	Sexual offences	Burglary	Robbery	Theft and handling	Fraud and forgery	Criminal damage	Prostitution	Drug offences	Drunkenness	Assault	DHSS offences	Breach of peace and s.5 POA	Possession of offensive weapon	Harbouring escaped prisoner	Wasting police time and obstruction	Grand total	% of all disposals
Absolute discharge	3	–	1	–	34	2	6	11	–	30	5	–	4	–	–	–	96	5
Cond. discharge	12	1	5	–	338	45	26	61	10	73	9	51	12	1	2	2	648	31
Fine	15	–	4	1	430	38	27	109	20	193	19	38	23	5	–	3	925	45
Probation order	5	–	5	–	127	18	5	33	5	1	–	16	1	–	–	–	216	10
Hospital order	–	–	–	–	1	–	–	–	–	–	–	–	–	–	–	–	1	–
C.S. order	–	–	2	–	16	–	–	11	–	–	–	–	–	–	–	–	29	1
Suspended sentence	–	–	5	–	36	7	–	31	1	–	–	7	2	1	–	–	90	4
Imprison-ment	2	–	3	–	26	8	3	17	–	–	1	3	1	–	–	–	64	3
Sub-total	37	1	25	1	1008	118	67	273	36	297	34	115	43	7	2	5	2069	
As a % of all offences sentenced	2	a	1	a	49	6	3	13	2	14	2	6	2	a	a	a		
Comm. to Crown Court: trial	17	1	15	9	40	13	5	–	9	–	–	3	–	1	1	–	114	
Comm. to Crown Court: sentence	1	–	2	–	10	1	1	1	1	–	–	–	–	–	–	–	17	
Case withdrawn	9	–	–	–	6	11	2	–	–	1	1	–	38	–	–	–	68	
Case dismissed	17	–	8	3	48	–	6	25	4	9	5	1	5	1	1	1	134	
Adj. sine die	–	–	–	–	1	–	–	–	–	–	–	–	1	–	–	–		
Deferred sentence	1	–	1	–	34	1	1	18	–	–	–	2	–	–	–	–	58	
Grand total	81	2	50	13	1,112	143	81	299	50	307	40	119	86	9	4	6	2,402	

(a) Less than 0.5

robbery, 73 per cent for theft and handling, 8 per cent for fraud and forgery, and 1 per cent for offences relating to criminal damage (see *Criminal Statistics* 1981, Table 5.1, 90).

Gender role is certainly a significant feature in the choice of sentence, some research studies concluding that women are more likely to receive a particular kind of disposal than are men, for example Devlin (1970: 214). Mawby (1975) found that women were more likely to receive probation order than were men for similar offences. Thomas (1979: 212) argues that family considerations have a

Table 8:9 *Committals for sentence by type of offence and outcome (at Manchester Crown Court from a number of magistrates' courts including city Magistrates' Court, 1981)*

	1 Borstal	2 Probation Order	3 Imprisonment	4 Supervision Order	5 Conditional Discharge	6 C.S. Order	7 Hospital Order	8 Absolute Discharge	9 Suspended Sentence	Total
(1) Violence against the person	2	—	1	1	—	—	—	—	—	4
(2) Sexual offences	—	1	—	—	—	—	—	—	—	1
(3) Burglary	6	1	1	—	—	—	—	—	—	8
(4) Robbery	3	—	—	—	—	—	—	—	—	3
(5 Theft and handling	7	13	8	2	2	1	1	—	2	36
(6) Fraud and forgery	—	1	1	1	1	—	—	—	—	4
(7) Criminal damage	—	—	—	—	—	—	—	—	—	—
(8) Other	—	1	3	—	1	—	—	—	1	6
Total	18	17	14	4	4	1	1	0	3	62

Note: A total of 40 per cent of those committed to the Crown Court for sentence on the basis that the higher court has greater powers were given sentences which could have been given by magistrates under statutory restriction (Powers of Criminal Courts Act 1973) see cols 2, 4, 5. The assumption that judicial sentencing of offenders is more severe is not borne out (see Tarling 1979).

mitigating effect on sentence particularly in the case of an offender who is a mother of young children. In *Charles,* the defendant was convicted of unlawful wounding another. The court suspended her sentence of nine months, partly because 'she is the mother of a number of small children'. Certainly in this respect further research is required to look at differences in sentencing between women who are mothers and women who are childless, to see to what extent sentencing varies with sex or gender role.

Gender considerations in appeals against sentence and/or conviction

Gender role has influenced appeal decisions and provided the justificatory rationale for varying sentence (see 1972 CLR 447; Thomas 1979: 213). In *Arnold* for instance the appellant received sentences for three years for bankruptcy offences which had caused losses amounting to thousands of pounds. The court said that there was 'absolutely nothing wrong' with such sentences for deliberate offences committed over a period of two years, but in view of the uncertain future of the appellant's children, from whose father she had been divorced some years earlier, the court reduced the sentence to eighteen months as 'some contribution towards keeping the family together as a unit' (Thomas 1979: 213). Similarly, in *Parkinson* the Court of Appeal declared that although sentences totalling nine months for a young woman uttering forged banknotes were properly imposed the sentences were reduced because of the effect on her two young children (Thomas 1979: 212). Similarly, in *Owen* (1972 CLR 324), the defendant stabbed her husband in his chest following a quarrel. She was sentenced to four years' imprisonment. The Court of Appeal took into special consideration that the appellant had

Table 8:10 *Sentencing of female defendants according to offence (Manchester Crown Court, 1981)*

	Violence	Sexual Offences	Burglary	Robbery	Theft and Handling	Fraud and Forgery	Criminal Damage	Other	Total
Absolute discharge	1	–	–	–	–	–	–	–	1
Conditional discharge	6	–	2	–	8	7	–	–	23
Fine	3	1	–	–	30	1	–	1	36
Supervision order	–	–	2	2	1	–	–	–	5
Community service order	–	–	2	–	2	–	–	–	4
Hospital order	–	–	–	–	–	–	1	–	1
Probation order	7	–	5	–	22	5	1	1	41
Probation order/ cond. of treatment	5	–	–	–	4	–	–	–	9
Borstal	4	–	7	3	3	2	2	–	21
Suspended sentence	8	–	11	2	22	14	–	8	65
Imprisonment	9	–	7	3	24	16	3	5	67
Transferred to juv. ct. for sentence	–	–	2	–	–	–	–	–	2
Sub-total	43	1	38	10	116	45	7	15	275
NOT GUILTY RECORDED									
Found N.G. by jury	6	–	–	–	27	1	–	–	34
Prosecution offers no evidence	1	–	2	–	11	4	–	1	19
N.G plea accepted	3	–	–	–	–	2	–	–	5
Found N.G bound over	5	–	–	–	–	–	–	–	5
N.G., lie on file	4	2	3	2	6	1	–	1	19
N.G. by direction	1	–	2	–	11	–	–	1	15
Total	63	3	45	12	171	53	7	18	372
Conviction rate	68	33	84	83	68	85	100		

five children: 'having regard to the interests of the children, and the birth of her latest child, the court thought that the public interest would be adequately served if, as an act of mercy, the sentence was varied to thirty months'.

Such considerations may not have such a mitigating impact in offences of a rather more serious nature. In *Ayoub* for example the sentence of six years was upheld on a West African woman for fraudulently importing a large amount of cannabis, though the appellant had six children (Thomas 1979: 212).

Family considerations may weigh even more heavily when the appellant is a single parent. In *Fels* the appellant, a single parent, had received five years for importing cannabis. This was later on appeal reduced to three because her five-year-old son was suffering greatly in her absence.

In the Manchester appeal sample a total of seventy-one cases against sentence and/or conviction were examined for the reasons recorded for allowing, varying or dismissing the appeal (see Table 8:11). Whilst the majority of appeals were tendered on some legal technicality, a significant number of cases were allowed on matters strictly outside the legal administration of justice.

Table 8:11   Appeals: according to offence and outcome (Manchester Crown Court, 1981)

	Appeal against conviction allowed	Appeal against conviction/ sentence varied	Abandoned	Dismissed	Remitted to magistrates	Total
Violence	1	–	–	1	–	2
Sexual offences (prostitution)	–	1	–	–	–	1
Burglary	1	2	–	–	–	3
Robbery	–	–	–	–	–	–
Theft and handling	12	9	7	11	2	41
Fraud and forgery	–	5	–	–	–	5
Criminal damage	–	–	–	–	–	–
Other	8	3	2	6	–	19
	22	20	9	18	2	71

In forty-two cases the appeal was allowed or varied (a total of 60 per cent). In twenty-nine of those cases the reasons for allowing or varying the appeal were recorded (see Table 8:12). A question of some considerable interest was whether appeals were allowed solely on the basis of gender role and whether gender role was particularly influential in cases where the original sentence imposed was one of imprisonment. In eight of these twenty-nine cases (28 per cent) the decision of the court was based on gender-role considerations of women in the family context. In the remaining 72 per cent wholly technical matters decided. As McLean has indicated, 'The Crown Court primarily exists, in its appellate jurisdiction, to deal with disputed questions of fact' (1980: 1).

In all of the cases where gender was invoked a sentence of imprisonment had originally been imposed. The reasons recorded for varying the appeal were of this nature: 'To lock up this appellant would be destructive to the mother–child relationship . . .', 'defendant said to be a good mother and could lose custody of her children . . .'. In all of the cases the women concerned had children and in two of the cases the fact that appellants were single parents seemed to be an additional factor influencing the judge's decision.

Regional differences in sentencing

The use of discretion in sentencing decisions is very often reflected in regional disparities, the result of decisions of magistrates' committees, the viability of particular disposals as much as the bias of individual sentencers. In pursuit of the nature and extent of diversity in sentencing information on all those appearing on

Table 8:12   Reasons for allowing or varying appeal

	Allowed	Varied
Not enough evidence to convict	9	–
Too severe/wrong in law	1	4
Not opposed by respondent	3	1
Court concern for family	3	5
Previously not represented	1	–
Time-lag between offence and prosecution	–	1
Recent good character	–	1
Total	17	12

charges of loitering or soliciting for the purpose of prostitution at the city magistrates' courts in Manchester, Sheffield, Liverpool and Birmingham and at an Inner London Court was selected for 1981. First, information relating to the courts' use of a particular disposal was sought. Second, a comparison of those pleading guilty in three of the five areas selected was possible. Third, additional information regarding the relationship between sentencing and previous convictions was sought for individual biographies on the assumption that custodial sentences could be used only on or after a third conviction, following the dictate of the Street Offences Act 1959.

Table 8:13 shows the regional variation in the use of particular disposals for 1981. Absolute discharge was used significantly more in Manchester at 4 per cent constituting only 1 per cent of all sentences in the other areas, Liverpool excepted. Conditional discharge was highest in London, constituting 31 per cent of all disposals, lowest in Sheffield at 8 per cent. Probation was used significantly more in Liverpool at 37 per cent; it was lowest in London at only 6 per cent and low in Manchester at only 11 per cent of all disposals. London favoured the use of the fine as a means of disposing with prostitutes (52 per cent), lowest at Sheffield at 24 per cent. Community service orders were not particularly popular in any of the areas, highest in Sheffield at 24 per cent and lowest in London at 2 per cent. As to the use of suspended and prison sentences each area was consistent. Both London and Liverpool only occasionally used either of these disposals, London 3 per cent and 5 per cent for the suspended and prison sentence respectively, whilst Liverpool was the lowest at 1 per cent and 4 per cent. By contrast, Birmingham was highest in its use of these disposals at 15 per cent each for the suspended and prison sentences (see Table 8:14 for additional information on England and Wales).

Second, information was collated in three of the five areas relating to the use of the guilty plea. Manchester was lowest, contested cases constituting 16 per cent of all cases, whilst in London this figure was 22 per cent and in Sheffield higher still at 28 per cent (see Table 8:13). The variations here may well have been the result

Table 8:13 Inter-urban variations in the sentencing of prostitutes

	No. of defendants	No. of appearances on separate charges	No. of guilty pleas	Proportion of guilty pleas	Total found guilty	Absolute discharge	%	Conditional discharge	%	Probation	%	Fine	%	Community service order	%	Suspended sentence	%	Prison	%	Other
Manchester: City Magistrates'	172	299	46	16.0	273	11	4.0	61	20.0	33	11.0	109	36.0	11	4.0	31	10.0	17	6.0	26
London: Highbury Corner	96	130	29	22.0	118	1	1.0	36	31.0	7	6.0	62	52.0	2	2.0	4	3.0	6	5.0	12
Sheffield: City Magistrates'	44	82	23	28.0	72	1	1.0	6	8.0	13	18.0	17	24.0	18	25.0	8	11.0	9	13.0	10
Liverpool: City Magistrates'	32	59	–	–	51	1	2.0	7	14.0	19	37.0	14	27.0	7	14.0	1	2.0	2	4.0	8
Birmingham: City Magistrates'	85	124	–	–	122	1	1.0	12	10.0	28	23.0	35	29.0	9	7.0	19	15.0	18	15.0	2
England and Wales	–	–	–	–	4,127	39	1.0	686	17.0	379	9.0	2,389	58.0	115	3.0	288	7.0	205	5.0	26

Table 8:14 All women aged 17 and over proceeded against at magistrates' courts for loitering for the purposes of prostitution, by result, 1981 (England and Wales)

Age	Total proceeded against	%	Discontinued	%	Outcome of proceedings Dismissed	%	Found guilty	%	Totals
17–21	1,582		4		55		1,523		1,582
21+	2,706		11		124		2,571		2,706
Total	4,288		15		179		4,094		4,288

Age	Abs. disc.	%	Recog.	%	Cond. disc.	%	Hosp. order s.60	%	Prob. order	%	Disposal Fine	%	Comm. serv. order	%	Susp. sent.	%	Prison	%	Comm. for sent	%	Otherwise dealt with	%	Totals
17–21	17		–		267		–		155		889		32		90		66		6		1		1,523
21+	22		1		409		1		224		1,490		83		198		138		–		5		2,571
Total	39	0.9	1	0.02	676	16.5	1		379	9.2	2,379	60	115	2.8	288	7.0	204	4.9	6	0.1	6	0.1	4,094

Source: Criminal Statistics, England and Wales: Supplementary Tables, 1981, Vol.1, pp.136–7, 176–7.

of availability of duty solicitor schemes and representation or police cautioning procedure as evidence, a matter already discussed in Chapter 2.

Thirdly, since custodial sentences for this offence can only be imposed on or following a third conviction (following the Street Offences Act 1959), then it is necessary to establish whether there is a pattern of imposing custodial sentences after a given number of convictions, and whether the influence of previous convictions on present sentence may also be considered differently between four of the five regions, London excepted. Concerning the relationship of sentence to previous convictions complete details on the biographies of all prostitutes before the Manchester Magistrates' Court in 1981 were obtained from police records, this presenting the most accurate picture of past convictions, some convictions dating as far back as 1960. Table 8:15 shows the pattern of disposals for Manchester. The purpose of this exercise was to determine whether imprisonment was used after three convictions and whether it increased in its usage with the number of convictions.

In Manchester, after six convictions, the chance of being given a prison sentence does not decrease. The proportion given a fine decreases after six convictions from about one-half to one-third.

Information on previous convictions prior to 1981 of those appearing for charges related to prostitution in the areas of Birmingham, Sheffield and Liverpool respectively (Tables 8:16a, b, c) is based on information derived from probation records; such antecedents may not be complete and should should be treated extremely cautiously. In the Birmingham sample there is little change in probation over time, suspended sentence and prison are high, and conditional discharge low, whilst in Sheffield the chance of prison increases steadily with the number of convictions and in the Liverpool sample prison only becomes a viability after six convictions.

In 1982 after much pressure, the offence of loitering and soliciting for the purposes of prostitution was made a non-imprisonable offence (section 71 of the Criminal Justice Act), a reform made effective as from 31 January 1983 (Home Office Circular 2/1983). However this amendment will not remove the power to imprison for non-payment of fines for this offence, a shortcoming well recognised by the Standing Committee in debating this amendment in March 1982 at the Bill stage. The effect of the abolition of direct or indirect imprisonment by means of a suspended sentence for this offence will undoubtedly have the effect of sending many more women to prison for this offence who are in default of fine payments (see figures for 1981, Table 8:17). In view of this inevitable consequence there is a need for an immediate review of the law relating to imprisonment for fine defaulters particularly in those instances where imprisonment is not viable as a sanction for the original offence. A total of 1107 women were received into prison

Table 8:15 *Effect of number of previous convictions for offences of loitering for the purposes of prostitution on sentencing outcome (Manchester City Magistrates' Court, 1960–1981)*

No. of convictions	Absolute discharge	Conditional discharge	Fine	Probation order	Community service order	Borstal training	Suspended sentence	Imprisonment	Deferred sentence	Care order	Bound over	Adjourned sine die	Total
1	8	65	70	24	–	–	1	1	2	1	–	–	172
2	4	30	94	20	2	–	–	1	3	–	–	–	154
3	6	19	66	20	2	–	9	2	7	–	–	1	132
4	2	16	50	17	1	1	5	4	14	–	–	–	110
5	2	7	50	14	1	–	8	8	9	–	–	–	99
6	6	22	28	8	–	1	10	8	11	–	–	–	94
7	4	12	24	10	4	–	13	6	8	–	–	–	81
8	1	10	20	5	3	–	10	10	9	–	–	–	68
9	3	9	12	4	1	–	11	8	9	–	–	–	57
10	2	11	8	8	1	–	8	10	3	–	1	–	52
11	3	9	11	6	3	–	7	3	4	–	–	–	46
12	2	7	8	3	–	–	5	9	5	–	–	–	39
13	1	5	10	4	1	–	5	8	1	–	–	–	35
14	–	5	9	2	2	–	5	6	3	–	–	–	32
15	2	4	9	1	4	–	2	5	2	–	–	–	29
16	–	7	4	5	–	–	8	2	1	–	–	–	27
17	2	2	4	2	2	–	2	5	1	–	–	–	20
18	1	2	5	–	–	–	4	4	2	–	–	–	18
19	–	4	3	2	–	–	1	5	2	–	–	–	17
20	–	5	2	2	–	–	4	4	–	–	–	–	17
21	–	3	6	1	1	–	1	3	1	–	–	–	16
22	–	6	2	1	1	–	2	1	2	–	–	–	15
23	2	1	1	4	1	–	1	2	1	–	–	–	13
24	–	2	2	1	–	–	3	3	–	–	–	–	13
25	–	–	1	1	–	–	4	2	–	–	–	–	8
26	–	1	1	1	–	–	1	–	2	–	–	–	6
27	–	–	3	–	–	–	1	–	2	–	–	–	6
28	–	–	1	2	–	–	–	–	2	–	–	–	5
29	–	–	1	–	–	–	1	1	1	–	–	–	4
30	–	–	1	1	–	–	–	1	–	–	–	–	3
31	–	1	–	–	–	–	1	–	–	–	–	–	2
32	–	–	–	–	1	–	–	–	–	–	–	–	1
33	–	–	–	–	1	–	–	–	–	–	–	–	1
34	–	–	1	–	–	–	–	–	–	–	–	–	1
35	–	–	–	–	–	–	–	1	–	–	–	–	1
36	–	–	–	–	–	–	–	1	–	–	–	–	1
37	–	–	–	–	–	–	–	–	1	–	–	–	1
38	–	–	–	–	–	–	–	–	1	–	–	–	1
39	–	–	–	–	–	–	1	–	–	–	–	–	1
40	–	–	–	–	–	–	–	1	–	–	–	–	1
41	–	–	–	1	–	–	–	–	–	–	–	–	1
42	1	–	–	–	–	–	–	–	–	–	–	1	1
43	–	–	–	–	1	–	–	–	–	–	–	–	1

Note: Information from Greater Manchester Police

in 1981 for non-payment of fines.

Whilst decarceration is to be welcomed, it seems already clear that it may lead to other forms of control, particularly those of close supervision and surveillance (Conrad 1980: 197).

Table 8:16a,b,c, *Percentage distribution of sentencing of prostitutes in relation to previous convictions*
a: *Birmingham City Magistrates*

No. of convictions	AD	CD	Fine	Prob.	CSO	Bors.	SS	Prison	DS	Other		All
1	–	10.6	45.9	32.9	1.2	–	4.7	1.2	–	3.5	–	85
2	–	5.8	55.1	17.4	2.9	1.4	8.7	5.8	–	2.9	–	69
3,4,5	0.7	7.5	29.9	18.7	3.7	–	19.4	16.4	1.5	2.2	–	134
6–10	1.0	11.4	0.2	17.1	5.7	–	21.0	22.9	–	1.0	–	105
11 +	–	9.7	22.6	29.0	9.7	–	16.1	12.9	–	–	–	31
Total	2	38	145	92	17	1	63	55	2	9	–	424
All %	0.5	9.0	34.2	21.7	4.0	0.2	14.9	13.0	0.5	2.1	100	–

b: *Sheffield City Magistrates*

No. of convictions	AD	CD	Fine	Prob.	CSO	Bors.	SS	Prison	DS	Other		All
1	–	6.8	29.5	47.7	2.3	–	4.5	6.8	–	2.2	100	44
2	–	2.8	22.2	36.1	22.2	–	2.8	13.9	–	–	100	36
3,4,5	–	5.6	25.4	21.1	25.4	–	7.0	14.1	–	1.4	100	71
6–10	–	5.1	18.6	6.8	16.9	–	13.6	22.0	6.8	–	100	59
11+	–	4.8	4.8	19.0	23.8	–	–	38.1	–	9.5	100	21
Total	–	12	51	63	42	0	16	39	4	4	–	231
All %	–	5.2	22.1	27.3	18.2	0	6.9	16.9	1.7	1.7	–	

c: *Liverpool City Magistrates*

No. of convictions	AD	CD	Fine	Prob.	CSO	Bors.	SS	Prison	DS	Other		All
1	–	18.8	34.4	43.8	–	–	–	–	–	–	–	–
2	–	17.4	56.5	26.0	–	–	–	–	–	–	–	–
3,4,5	2.2	20.0	31.1	20.0	8.9	4.4	4.4	2.2	6.7	–	–	26
6–10	–	16.3	30.2	16.3	7.0	–	11.6	18.6	–	–	–	43
11+	–	19.2	7.7	23.4	15.4	–	15.4	15.4	38	–	–	26
Total	1	31	53	42	11	2	11	13	5	–	–	169
All %	0.6	18.3	31.4	24.9	6.5	1.2	6.5	7.7	3.0	–	–	

Women on trial – what kind of justice?

The recent trend towards individualised justice has been discussed extensively in the works of Box (1971), Bottomley (1973), Bean (1976), Halmos (1978), Hardiker and Webb (1979) and Cohen (1979) amongst others. It has been examined and monitored for its impact at various stages of the criminal justice process. Curnock and Hardiker (1979) and Hardiker and Webb (1979) have explored the impact this judicial trend has had on the preparation content and recommendations in social inquiry reports. Despite the wealth of discussion on this debate one fundamental consideration has been overlooked and that is the exaggerated effect the

Table 8:17   Receptions of adult women (21 and over) by age and offence and fine default

	Immediate imprisonment							In default of payment of fine: total
	Total	21–24	25–29	30–39	40–49	50–59	60+	
All offences	2087	627	478	589	277	99	17	825
Violence against person	216	69	54	68	17	8	–	22
Murder	6	–	–	4	1	1	–	–
Manslaughter	12	4	4	3	1	–	–	–
Other homicide	3	1	1	1	–	–	–	–
Wounding	119	38	33	33	10	5	–	5
Assaults	58	19	13	21	4	1	–	14
Cruelty to child	5	3	1	1	–	–	–	–
Other violence	13	4	2	5	1	1	–	3
Sexual offences	5	1	–	3	1	–	–	–
Rape	1	–	–	1	–	–	–	–
Gross ind. child	2	1	–	1	–	–	–	–
Other	2	–	–	1	1	–	–	–
Burglary	134	45	41	26	17	5	–	25
Robbery	26	10	4	8	4	–	–	–
Theft, handling, fraud, forgery	1209	340	255	341	187	72	14	386
Theft of vehicle	–	–	–	–	–	–	–	1
Taking and driving	6	3	1	2	–	–	–	1
Other	859	243	179	234	133	57	13	190
Handling stolen goods	84	35	20	16	12	1	–	15
Frauds	237	49	50	83	40	14	1	170
Forgery	23	10	5	6	2	–	–	9
Other offences	497	162	124	143	51	14	3	391
Arson	15	5	2	4	4	–	–	2
Criminal damage	65	15	18	20	7	5	–	41
Drugs	133	30	36	51	12	3	1	8
Imm. Act 1971	1	–	1	–	–	–	–	2
Drunk in charge	5	1	1	1	2	–	–	4
Other motoring	5	1	2	1	–	–	1	35
Prostitution	127	70	31	20	6	–	–	44
Drunkenness	—	–	–	–	–	–	–	64
Vagrancy	6	3	–	2	1	–	–	4
Other	140	37	33	44	19	6	1	187

Source: Prison Statistics: England and Wales 1981, Cmnd. 8654 (Table 5:1, p.76).

practice of individualised justice has on the processing and sentencing of the female defendant. This trend has been paralleled by the tendency to define deviant behaviour committed by either sex in medical terms (see Bottoms and McWilliams 1979) and this medicalisation of deviancy also contains special consequences for female defendants. In this context Conrad (1980: 196) argued that 'The medicalisation of deviance has become in effect a *de facto* social policy.'

Female defendants are processed within the criminal justice system in accordance with the crimes which they commit and the extent to which the commission of the act and its nature deviates from appropriate female behaviour; Gibbens, Soothill and Pope (1977: 20) found that a relationship existed between particular offences and persons labelled mentally disordered. And whilst criminal conduct is generally assessed according to motivation, its commission, and the social context which provides a background to the pattern of offending, all crimes committed by women are invariably pathologised. At this particular juncture women as defendants are examined and their behaviour analysed in much the same manner as the behaviour of non-deviant politically active or simply 'normal' women (Hutter and Williams 1981: 16). In one way or another the crimes women commit are considered to be the final outward manifestation of an inner medical inbalance or social disability, but never a response to an oppressive social situation.

This particular construction of female deviance has its conceptual origins in the wider private image of women, and this has exaggerated as the recent trend across sex lines in the criminal justice system is towards personalisation, with its attendant consequence of the depoliticisation of social problems (Halmos 1978). This tendency has been examined rather more recently by Cohen (1979) and Conrad (1980: 96); the latter suggests that there have been changes in the formal social control apparatus over the last decade in the direction of 'community-based programs of social control' which have been equally as intrusive and punitive.

Central to this proclivity is the view that women are by nature private and personal, a sentiment echoed in a recent court case by Judge Ewart James (Brundson 1978: 18) and discussed for its social and political consequences by Elshtain (1981). The consequence of this personalisation is constantly to overlook women's challenges to oppressive structures and to understand such opposition as evidence of a private disability. Struggles in the public sphere for enfranchisement, for political, educational and occupational equality, and within the domestic sphere for a more balanced distribution of domestic labour and child-care tasks have been similarly misunderstood. It is by no means an accident, therefore, that more women than men define themselves as mentally ill and are so defined by others. Procek (1981: 22) examines the role psychiatric ideologies play in shoring up the belief that depression in women emanates from a personal mental illness, a distinction made in another context between depression and clinical depression (see Brian Clarke's play *Who's Life Is It Anyway?*). Lipshitz (1978: 93) similarly examines the way in which 'implicit beliefs about women contribute to the diagnosis and treatment of their illnesses by western doctors, psychiatrists and therapists'.

Whilst during the last decade there has been much criticism of the pathologisation of wider social and political contradictions the criminal justice system continues to adhere to a particular pathological construction of the female defendant. Consider for instance that R. D. Laing, in his book *Sanity, Madness and the Family*, stated that although the eleven women whose experiences formed the basis of his study were originally defined as psychotic, if analysed in the context of the social situation which produced them they would appear as intelligible, rational and responsible. Thus particular ideologies, psychoanalytical theory and popularised versions of psychoanalysis, not unlike medical approaches to mental instability, tend to discredit political solutions to practical problems in living in favour of an individual or pathological approach.

Within the criminal justice system this interpretative construction of criminal manifestation has particular pragmatic consequences for sentencing, treatment, rehabilitation and resocialisation. Rehabilitation practices are often doubly oppressive since their intention is the resocialisation of women into traditional female roles which many women, deviant and non-deviant alike, reject. Probation supervision can be stifling and unsupportive, particularly if the officers attempt to impose a particular gender model. Women feel punished not only for breaking the law but for their nonconformity to traditional gender models. Moreover their deviance is generally regarded as an expression of some intrinsic problem, reflected in the trend within social inquiry reports towards treatment and therapy (Hardiker and Webb 1979, Curnock and Hardiker 1979, Bottoms and McWilliams 1979, Menzies 1980, Taylor 1981: 91 and Van Dijk and De Wit 1982).

Rehabilitation within the custodial setting is, similarly, primarily concerned with the enforcement of a traditional gender role (Smart 1976: 140–4, Adler 1975), where typical days may be spent in traditional female tasks such as sewing, cooking and washing, rather than learning these skills along with others in a rather different context of self-sufficiency. This tendency is also found throughout all institutions of incarceration. Rowett and Vaughan (1981: 137–8), in their excellent discussion on Broadmoor, write,

> Current visitors to the female wing of Broadmoor are often shown the room of one patient as an example of what can be achieved in a difficult setting. The room, decorated in pale yellow and pinks, with shelves of vanity goods and cosmetics, contains a sizeable collection of elaborately dressed dolls. Perhaps the room symbolises what is still seen as a significant factor in 'recovery' — pride in one's 'feminine' appearance and ability to fulfil a stereotype.

This tendency is very much reminiscent of the S. Weir Mitchell method, used widely during the latter half of the nineteenth century, for the 'cure' or more appropriately resocialisation of recalcitrant female patients. His famous 'rest cure' depended for its success on the tyrannical dictatorship of the physician, who demanded that the patient be totally isolated from family, friends and any kind of stimulation whatever, and through subtle persuasion, physical massage and a diet of bland food brainwashed the patient into her appropriate role when her resistance had been totally eroded and her healthy criticism finally subdued (Ehrenreich and English 1979: 118–20).

Similarly, treatment reflected an assumption that women criminals were socially inadequate and invariably mentally ill. As Rafter and Natalizia (1981: 91) write, women as offenders demonstrate that they are sick and in need of rehabilitation, a view reaffirmed by Nigel Walker who amongst others has pointed out that 'Women offenders have a higher chance of being dealt with as mentally abnormal.'

Table 8:18 *Proportionate comparison between males and females aged 17 and over: subject to hospital order under Mental Health Act, 1959 (England and Wales).*

	S.60 hospital order(a)						S.65 restriction order						Total number of defendants found guilty (in thousands)		Total number given hospital order	
	17–21		21+		Sub-total		17–21		21+		Sub-total					
	M	F	M	F	M	F	M	F	M	F	M	F	M	F	M	F
Violence against person	7	1	129	24	136	25	3	–	51	7	54	7	46.8	4.0	190	32
Sexual offences	7	1	16	1	23	2	1	–	5	–	6	–	6.9	0.1	29	2
Burglary	5	–	48	3	53	3	1	1	1	1	2	2	73.8	2.6	55	5
Robbery	2	–	2	2	4	2	–	–	–	–	–	–	3.9	0.2	4	2
Theft and handling stolen goods	5	2	97	20	102	22	–	–	–	–	–	–	184.0	48.2	102	22
Fraud/forgery	1	2	25	12	26	14	–	–	–	–	–	–	20.1	5.5	26	14
Criminal damage	3	2	52	19	55	21	5	1	18	9	23	10	11.0	0.8	78	31
Other offences	–	–	10	1	10	1	–	–	–	–	–	–	25.9	–	10	1
Total indictable	30	8	379	82	409	90	10	2	75	17	85	19	26.8	3.1	594	103
Summary offences	11	6	132	25	143	31	–	–	2	1	2	1	1,464.5	0.9	145	34
Total	41	14	511	107	552	121	10	2	77	18	87	20	1,863.6	65.5	639	141

(a) In 14–17 age groups total of seven males given a s.60 hospital order, as against one female.

Source: Criminal Statistics, England and Wales: Supplementary Tables, 1981, Vol.4 (Table S4.8A, p.58).

Women defendants are on trial both for their legal infractions and for their defiance of appropriate femininity and gender roles. Their punishment is aimed principally at treatment and resocialisation, the key concern being the 'individual adjustment of erring women to their natural feminine role' (Snäre and Stang Dahl 1978: 22). Punishment in the guise of treatment or community rehabilitation is chiefly concerned with resocialisation of recalcitrant women, the intrusion of treatment, punishment and rehabilitative agencies is experienced by offenders at every level of the personal. Women defendants find themselves, their families, life styles and essentially their everyday conduct scrutinised, on trial, up for judgment, constantly surveyed by the various informal state mechanisms of welfare and the para-legal agencies. Scrutinisation and therefore control is more insidious, more complete and more debilitating for the offender. This is the reality of women's so-called 'lenient' treatment in the sentencing process, and the reality of individualised justice.

Notes and references

Introduction

1. E. Goffman, *Stigma*, Harmondsworth, 1970, p. 11
2. H. J. Walls, *Expert Witness*, London, 1972, pp. 29–46. See also R. Wright, G. Geis and R. Geis, 'Police officer or doctor? Police surgeons' attitudes and opinion about rape, forthcoming, in edition by June Hopkins.
3. A. Worrall, 'Out of place: female offenders in court'. *Probation Journal*, XXVIII, 1981, pp. 90–3.
4. J. A. Scutt, 'Criminal investigation and the rights of victims of crime', *University of Western Australia Law Review*, XIV, 1979, pp. 1–29.
5. J. Weeks 'Discourse, desire and sexual deviance: some problems in a history of homosexuality', in K. Plummer (ed) *The Making of the Modern Homosexual* London 1981 p.95.
6. J. Brophy and C. Smart, 'From disregard to disrepute: the position of women in family law', *Feminist Review*, IX, 1981, p. 12.
7. Brophy and Smart, 'Women in family law'.
8. P. Hewitt, *The Abuse of Power*, London, 1981, p. 3
9. L. Wilkins, 'The measurement of crime', *British Journal of Criminology*, III, 1963, 3, p. 321.
10. D. J. Newman, 'The effects of accommodation in justice administration on criminal statistics,' *Sociology and Social Research*, XLVI, 1962.
11. M. King (assisted by Christine Jackson), *Bail or Custody*, London, 1971.
12. See Memorandum to the House of Commons Expenditure Committee (Education, Arts, Home Office Sub-Committee), Enquiry into Women and the Penal System, National Association for the Care and Resettlement of Offenders, December 1978.
13. 'Women in the penal system', NACRO Briefing, 1981.
14. 'Women in the penal system', pp. 10–11.
15. J. P. Martin and D. Webster, *The Social Consequences of Conviction*, London, 1971.
16. P. Hardiker, 'The role of probation officers in sentencing' in H. Parker (ed.), *Social Work and the Courts*, London, 1979 pp. 117–34.
17. M. Cohen, 'Soliciting by men,' *Criminal Law Review*, 1982, pp. 349–62.
18. B. Berger, P. Berger and H. Kellner, *The Homeless Mind*, Harmondsworth, 1974, p. 91.

Chapter 1

1. P. N. P. Wiles, 'Criminal statistics and sociological explanations of crime', in W. G. Carson and P. N. P. Wiles (eds), *The Sociology of Crime and Delinquency in Britain*, London, 1971, pp. 216–7.
2. D. Gorham, 'A "maiden tribute of modern Babylon" re-examined: child prostitution and the idea of childhood in late-Victorian England', *Victorian Studies*, XXI, 1978, pp. 353–79.
3. D. H. Bracey, *Baby Pros*, Criminal Justice Center Monograph No. 12, New York, 1979, p. 60.
4. T. L. Newman, *Miscellanies*, III, *Essays, Tracts or Addresses, Political and Social*, London, 1899, p. 254.
5. Metropolitan Police Act 1839, Town Police Clauses Act 1847, Manchester Police Regulation Act 1844.

6. Cf. L. E. Rozovsky and F. A. Rozovsky, *Legal Sex,* Toronto, 1982. See also Martin's Criminal Code, s. 195.
7. 'Solicitation for the purpose of prostitution: a discussion paper', *Law and Government Division, Research Branch, Library of Parliament, Ottawa.* Prepared for the House of Commons Sub-Committee on Justice and Legal Affairs, 1982.
8. I. McColl Kennedy, 'Transsexualism and single-sex marriage', *Anglo-American Law Review,* II, 1973, p. 112.
9. Report of the Royal Commission Upon the Duties of the Metropolitan Police, Cd. 1141, 1908, 21.
10. M. Cohen, 'Soliciting by men', *Criminal Law Review,* 1982, pp. 349–62.
11. Sir Robert Peacock, *City of Manchester Police Instruction Book,* 1923, p. 580.
12. Medical Women's Federation, Submission to the Criminal Law Revision Committee on Prostitution and Allied Offences, 1982.
13. Manchester City Magistrates' Court, Abstract of transcript, 1981.
14. S. French, *Crime Every Day,* London, 1976, p. 120.
15. Law Commission Report (No. 33), 'Family law: Report on the nullity of marriage', Cmnd. 164, XXI, 1973, pp. 15–16.
16. Nullity of Marriages Act 1973, Matrimonial Causes Act 1973, s. 11. See also H. A. Finlay, 'Sexual identity and the law of nullity', *Australian Law Journal,* LIV, 1980, p. 124.
17. Hansard, 814, 1971, col. 1827.
18. D. K. Smith, 'Transsexualism, sex reassignment surgery and the law', *Cornell Law Review,* LVI, 1971, pp. 963–1009, at pp. 1005–9.
19. S. Poulter, 'The definition of marriage in English law'. *Modern Law Review,* XLII, 1979, pp. 424–5.
    See also M. Roth, 'Transsexualism and the sex-change operation', *Medico-Legal Journal,* XLIX, 1981, pp. 5–19.
20. See E. Crawley, *The Mystic Rose,* London, 1965.
21. A. S. Diamond, *Primitive Law, Past and Present,* London, 1971, p. 250.
22. See U. Wikan, 'Man becomes woman: transsexualism in Oman as a key to gender roles', *Man,* XII, 1977, pp. 304–19.
23. D. B. Billings and T. Urban, 'The socio-medical construction of transsexualism: An interpretation and critique', *Social Problems,* XXIX, 1982, p. 266.
24. Council of Europe, International Bulletin on Legal Affairs, 10 November, 1981, Application No. 7654/76 (D. Van Oosterwijck).
25. April Ashley's application to the Council of Europe, still undecided.
26. See K. C. Horton, 'The law and transsexualism in West Germany', *Family Law,* 1978, pp. 191–2.
27. C. A. Mercier, 'Vice, crime and insanity', in T. C. Allbutt, *A System of Medicine,* VIII, London, 1899, pp. 248–94.
28. See Ruth Hall, *Marie Stopes: A Biography,* London, 1978.
29. E. J. Tilt, *On Uterine and Ovarian Inflammation,* London, 1802, p. 234. W. Thomas, *Diseases of Women,* London, 1884, G. Hewitt, *Diseases of Women,* London, 1872, p. 533.
30. I. Baker Brown, *On the Curability of Certain Forms of Insanity, Epilepsy, Catelepsy and Hysteria in Females,* London, 1866. See also J. Scoffern, *The London Surgical Home,* London, 1867, p. 6.

31. F. Engels, *The Origins of the Family, Private Property and the State*, New York, 1972, p. 83.
32. Kingsley Davis, The sociology of prostitution', in S. Dinitz, R. R. Dines and A. C. Clarke (eds), *Deviance*, New York, 1969, p. 386.

Chapter 2
1. *Shield*, 9 May, 1870.
2. W. Acton, *The Functions and Disorders of the Reproductive Organs, in Youth, in Adult Age, and in Advanced Life*, London, 1857, p. 62.
3. See Select Committee on Prostitution, 1869.
4. J. G. Smith, *The Principles of Forensic Medicine*, London, 1824.
5. W. R. Greg, 'Prostitution', *Westminster Review*, No. 53, 1850, p. 457.
6. Report of the Metropolitan Police, London, 1857.
7. Hansard, 1883, CCLXXX, col. 1399.
8. Hansard (Lords), 1884, CCLXXXIX, col. 1219.
9. A. D. Desbruslais, 'The "common prostitute" – an acquired status', *Justice of the Peace*, CXLI, 1977, pp. 639–41.
10. Hansard, 1967, CCLXXXVIII, col. 1286.
11. A. Sanders, 'Guilt, innocence, and jury acquittals', *Howard Journal*, XVIII, 1979–80, p.13.
12. See *Social Trends*, No. 13, 1983, for waiting time for trials (p. 164, Chart 12·7), Central Statistical Office, London.
13. E. Burney, *Magistrate Court and Community*, London, 1979.
14. G. Williams, 'The mathematics of proof', *Criminal Law Review*, 1979, pp. 297–308.
15. Greg, 'Prostitution'.

Chapter 3
1. Rape defendants are frequently understood as the 'victims' of uncontrollable urges, or social or sexual inadequacy. See D. J. West, C. Roy and F. L. Nichols, *Understanding Sexual Attacks*, London, 1978, and L. Taylor, 'The significance and interpretation of replies to motivational questions; the case of the sex offender', *Sociology*, 6, 1972, pp. 23–37.
2. For a consideration of the 'drive reduction' theory, see W. Simon and J. H. Gagnon, *Sexual Conduct*, 1973. S. Jackson, 'The social context of rape: sexual scripts and motivation', *Women's Studies, International Quarterly*, I, 1978, pp. 27–38.
3. J. Weeks, *Sex, Politics and Society*, London, 1981 (see Chapter 2).
4. A. R. Lindesmith and Y. Levin, 'The Lombrosian myth in criminology', *American Journal of Sociology*, XLII, 1937, p. 669.
5. H. H. Ploss, M. Bartels and P. Bartels, *Woman, An Historical, Gynaecological and Anthropological Compendium*, London, 1935, p. 154.
6. R. von Krafft-Ebing, 'Psychosis Menstrualis', cited in *Australian Law Journal*, LVI, 1982, p. 99.
7. S. Icard, *La Femme pendant la periode menstruelle*, Paris, 1890, pp. 270–5.
8. S. Ross, 'Menstruation and insanity', *Journal of Mental Science*, LX, pp. 78–80.
9. C. Lombroso and W. G. Ferrero, *The Female Offender*, London, 1895.
10. Ploss, Bartels and Bartels, *Woman*, I, p. 154.
11. H. H. Ellis, *Studies in the Psychology of Sex*, Philadelphia, I, 1928, p. 100.

12. H. H. Ellis, *Man and Woman* London, 1899, pp. 254–5.
13. Ellis, *Psychology of Sex,* pp. 296 and 284.
14. G. H. Savage, *Insanity and Allied Neuroses,* London, 1884, pp. 16, 360 and 371.
15. *Medico-Legal and Criminological Review,* IV, 1906–7, p. 60.
16. E. J. Tilt, *The Change of Life in Health and Disease,* London, 1882.
17. J. D. McClean and J. C. Wood, *Criminal Justice and the Treatment of Offenders,* London, 1969, p. 259.
18. K. Devlin, *Sentencing Offenders in the Magistrates' Court,* London, 1970, p. 213.
19. *Monthly Journal of Medical Science,* 1845, pp. 632–5.
20. P. Bennett, 'Pre-menstrual tension: excuse or reason,' *Police Review,* XC, 1982, Issue no. 4642, p. 169.
21. J. Mitchell, *Women's Estate,* Harmondsworth, 1971.
22. K. Dalton, *Once a Month,* London, 1978, pp. 115–6.
23. J. Delaney, M. J. Lupton and E. Toth, *The Curse,* New York, 1976.
24. C. Damme, 'Infanticide: the worth of an infant under law', *Medical History,* XXII, 1978, pp. 1–24. See also G. K. Behlmer, 'Deadly motherhood: infanticide and medical opinion in mid-Victorian England', *Journal of the History of Medicine,* XXXIV, 1979, pp. 403–27; and W. L. Langer, 'Infanticide: a historical survey', *Historical Childhood Quarterly,* I, 1979, 353–66.
25. The Homicide Law Amendment Bill 1872 (Bill 289); see the Homicide Law Amendment Bill Committee 21 July 1874, p. 19.
26. J. A. Paris and J. Fonblanque, *Medical Jurisprudence,* London, 1823.
27. Report of the Appeal of Ethel Harding, *Journal of Mental Science,* LV, 1909, p. 347.
28. Report of the Committee on Mentally Abnormal Offenders, Cmnd. 6244, 1974–5, para. 19.8.
29. N. Walker, 'Butler *v.* The CLRC and Others', *Criminal Law Review,* 1981, pp. 597–8.
30. Gordon Bourne, *Pregnancy,* London, 1979, pp. 422, 447.
31. A. Oakley, *Women Confined,* London, 1981.
32. D. J. West, *Murder Followed by Suicide,* London, 1965, p. 147.
33. C. Dean and R. E. Kendell, 'The symptomatology of puerperal illness', *British Journal of Psychiatry,* CXXXIX, 128–33.
34. S. Maddison, 'Mindless Militants? Psychiatry and the university', in I. Taylor and L. Taylor (eds), *Politics and Deviance,* Harmondsworth, 1973, p. 123.
35. A. Oakley, 'Normal motherhood: An exercise in self-control', in B. Hutter and G. Williams (eds.), *Controlling Women: The Normal and the Deviant,* London, 1981, p. 84.
36. Oakley, 'Normal motherhood', p. 97.
37. A. Coote and B. Campbell, *Sweet Freedom: The Struggle for Women's Liberation,* London, 1982, p. 40.

Chapter 4

1. R. Brazier, 'Reform of sexual offences', *Criminal Law Review,* 1975, pp. 421–9.
2. S. Brownmiller, *Against our Will,* London, 1975, p. 256.
3. Hansard, 1982, XXXIII/IV, col. 285–6; cf. *The Times,* 15 December 1982.
4. Rape Bill [48] 19 January 1982, col. 166.

5. T. Clifton, 'The case against rape', in L. Blom-Cooper and G. Drewry (eds.), *Law and Morality*, London, 1976.
6. Z. Adler, 'Rape – the intention of Parliament and the practice of the Courts', *Modern Law Review*, XLV, 1982, p. 665.
7. C. Simpson, *The Cleveland Street Affair*, London, 1978.
8. I. Bloch, *Sexual Life in England*, London, 1965, p. 125.
9. C. Bishop, *Women and Crime*, London, 1931.
10. Women's Report, 'Reclaiming the night', October-November 1978.
11. Eva Hunter, *Scottish Woman's Place*, Edinburgh, 1978, p. 113.
12. A. Sedley and M. Benn, *Sexual Harassment at Work*, London, 1982.
13. Case heard before magistrates at Highbury Corner Magistrates' Court, January 1982.
14. R. Walmsley and K. White, 'Sexual offences, consent and sentencing', Home Office Research Study No. 54, 1979.
15. H. Giarretto, 'A comprehensive child sexual abuse treatment program', in P. B. Mrazek and C. H. Kempe (eds.), *Sexually Abused Children and Their Families*, Oxford, 1981.

Chapter 5

1. A. V. Cicourel, *The Social Organisation of Juvenile Justice*, New York, 1968; H. E. Pepinsky, 'Police patrolmen's offence reporting behaviour', *Journal of Research in Crime and Delinquency*, 1976, pp. 33–47. D. A. Smith and C. A. Visher, 'Street-level justice: situational determinants of police arrest decisions', *Social Problems*, XXIX, 1981, p. 167.
2. P. A. Roby, 'Politics and criminal law: revision of the New York State penal law on prostitution', *Social Problems*, XVII, 1969, pp. 83–109.
3. V. Swigert and R. Farrell, 'Normal homicides and the law', *American Sociological Review*, XLII, p. 17.
4. D. Powis, *The Signs of Crime*, London, 1977, p. 73.
5. G. H. Lewis and J. F. Lewis, 'The dog in the night time: negative evidence in social research', *British Journal of Sociology*, XXXI, 1980, p. 544.
6. E. M. Lemert, 'The concept of secondary deviation', in *Human Deviance, Social Problems and Social Control*, Englewood Cliffs, 1967, p. 53.
7. J. Young, 'The role of the police as amplifiers of deviancy, negotiators of reality and translators of fantasy', in S. Cohen (ed.), *Images of Deviance*, Harmondsworth, 1971, p. 39.
8. E. Bittner, 'The police on skid row: a study of peace keeping', *American Sociological Review*, XXXII, 1967, pp. 699–715.
9. I. Piliavin and C. Werthman, 'Gang members in the police', in D. Bordua (ed.), *The Police*, New York, 1967, pp. 56–98.
10. Thomas F. Adams, 'Field interrogation', *Police*, March-April 1963, p. 28.
11. Powis, *The Signs of Crime*, pp. 111, 65–6.
12. Piliavin and Werthman, 'Gang members', pp. 68–9.
13. Cicourel, *Juvenile Justice*, p. 173.
14. Piliavin and Werthman, 'Gang members', p. 84.
15. M. Barrett, *Women's Oppression Today*, London, 1980, p. 236.

16. D. McBarnet, 'The police and the state: arrest, legality and the law', in G. Littlejohn, B. Smart, J. Wakeford and Nira Yuva Davis (eds), *Power and the State*, London, 1978, pp. 196–216.
17. See E. A. Rooney and D. C. Gibbons, 'Societal reaction to crimes without victims', *Social Problems*, XIII, 1966, pp. 400–10.
18. Interview at Manchester City Magistrates' Court, 1981.
19. Z. Adler, 'Rape – the intention of Parliament and the practice of the Courts', *Modern Law Review*, XLV, 1982, pp. 664–75.
20. S. Edwards, 'Contributory negligence in compensation claims by victims of sexual assault', *New Law Journal*, 1982, pp. 1140–2.
21. G. V. Poore, *A Treatise on Medical Jurisprudence*, London, 1901.
22. D. Miers, *Responses to Victimisation*, Abingdon, 1978.
23. K. Millett, *The Prostitution Papers*, London, 1975.
24. W. Lecky, *A History of European Morals*, 2 vols, London, 1911.
25. F. Engels, *The Origin of the Family, Private Property, and the State*, New York, 1972.
26. Report of the Committee on Obscenity and Film Censorship. Cmnd. 7772, London, 1979.
27. Ibid, pp. 80–3.
28. Susan H. Gray, 'Exposure to pornography and aggression toward women: the case of the angry male', *Social Problems*, XXIX, 1982, pp. 387–98. See also R. Coward, 'Sexual violence and sexuality', *Feminist Review*, XI, 1982, pp. 9–22. Angela Carter, *The Sadeian Woman*, London, 1979, p. 1.
29. Engels, *Origin*.
30. A. Gouldner, *Patterns in Industrial Bureaucracy*, New York, 1954.
31. Young, 'Role of the police'.
32. Z. Progl, *Women of the Underworld*, London, 1964.

Chapter 6

1. H. Garfinkel, 'Studies of the routine grounds of everyday activities', in *Studies in Ethnomethodology*, Englewood Cliffs/London, 1967.
2. L. Wilkins, 'The relative nature of deviance', in L. Radzinowicz and M. Wolfgang (eds), *The Criminal Society*, I, New York/London, 1971, pp. 46–50.
3. For further discussion see H. A. Prins, 'Diminished responsibility and the Sutcliffe case: legal, psychiatric and social aspects (a layman's view)', *Medicine, Science, Law*, XXIII, 1983, pp. 17–24.
4. G. H. Mead, *Mind, Self and Society from the Standpoint of a Social Behaviourist*, Chicago, 1934.
5. J. J. Sirica, *To Set the Record Straight: The Break-In, the Tapes, the Conspirators, the Pardon*, New York, 1979.
6. H. Becker, *The Outsiders*, New York, 1963, p. 42.
7. M. Weber, *The Theory of Social and Economic Organisation*, New York, 1964.
8. A. Schutz, *The Phenomenology of the Social World*, London, 1972, p. 86.
9. H. H. Gerth and C. W. Mills, *Character and Social Structure*, London, 1970, p. 116.

10. M. Phillipson, *Sociological Aspects of Crime and Delinquency,* London, 1971, pp. 39–40.
11. C. W. Mills, 'Situated actions and vocabularies of motive', *American Sociological Review,* 1940, V, pp. 439–52.
12. Schultz, *Phenomenology,* p. 91.
13. Ibid., pp. 89–90.
14. Mills, 'Situated actions', p. 117.
15. W. Whyte, 'A slum sex code', in *Street Corner Society,* Chicago, 1955.
16. M. B. Scott and S. M. Lyman, 'Accounts', *American Sociological Review,* XXXIII, p. 53.
17. P. Hardiker and D. Webb, 'Explaining deviant behaviour: the social context of "action" and "infraction" accounts in the probation service', *Sociology,* XIII, 1979, pp. 1–18.
18. A. F. Blum and P. McHugh, 'The social ascription of motives', *American Sociological Review,* XXXVI, 1971, p. 103.
19. Mills, 'Situated actions', pp. 113–118.
20. Blum and McHugh, 'Motives', p. 107.
21. L. Taylor, 'The significance and interpretation of replies to motivational questions', *Sociology,* VI, 1972, pp. 23–37. See also 'Vocabularies, rhetorics and grammar problems in the sociology of motivation', in O. Downes and P. Rock (eds), *Deviant Interpretations,* London, 1979, pp. 145–61.
22. D. Sudnow, 'Normal crimes: sociological features of the penal code in a public defender officer', *Social Problems,* XII, 3, 1965, pp. 255–76.
23. Blum and McHugh, 'Motives'.
24. N. Foote, cited in P. Rock, *Deviant Behaviour,* London, 1973.
25. P. W. Blumstein *et al.,* 'The honouring of accounts', *American Sociological Review,* XXXIX, 1974, pp. 551–66.
26. G. Williams, 'The theory of excuses', *Criminal Law Review,* 1982, p. 732.
27. Ibid., p. 735.
28. Hardiker and Webb, 'Deviant behaviour', 1979, p. 7.

Chapter 7
1. C. Wolff, *Bisexuality,* London, 1977, p. 60.
2. H. Garfinkel, *Studies in Ethnomethodology,* New York, 1967, p. 118.
3. D. Spender, *Man-Made Language,* London, 1980.
4. S. Trombley, 'All the summer she was mad', *Society for the Social History of Medicine,* XXVIII, 1981.
5. G. H. Mead, *Mind, Self and Society,* Chicago, 1934.
6. D. R. Cressey, 'Criminological research and the definition of crimes', *American Journal of Sociology,* LXI, 1951, p. 548.
7. L. Shacklady-Smith, 'Sexist assumptions about female delinquency: an empirical investigation', in C. and B. Smart (eds), *Women: Sexuality and Social Control,* London, 1978.
8. See also S. Myers, Why are crimes underreported?', *Social Science Quarterly,* LXI, 1980.
9. Z. Adler, 'Rape – the intention of Parliament and the practice of the Courts', *Modern Law Review,* XLV, 1982, pp. 664–75.

10. Three women were proceeded against and convicted of 'rolling' in 1981 in Manchester. As A. D. Smith points out, 'The victims of thefts by prostitutes seldom contact the police, or attempt to recover their property' (*Women in Prison*, London, 1962, p. 13).

11. G. Pearson, *The Deviant Imagination*, London, 1975, p. 175.

12. Criminal Justice Bill 1982.

13. M. A. Walker, *Crime*, Oxford, 1981.

14. P. N. P. Wiles, 'Criminal statistics and sociological explanations of crime', in P. N. P. Wiles and W. G. Carson (eds), *Crime and Delinquency in Britain*, London, 1971, pp. 174–92.

15. C. W. Mills, 'The professional ideology of social pathologists', *American Journal of Sociology*, XLIX, 2, 1942, pp. 165–80.

16. Hansard 1978, XCXLVI, cols 833–923.

17. D. A. Ward, M. Jackson and R. E. Ward, 'Crimes of violence', in F. Adler and R. J. Simon (eds), *The Criminology of Deviant Women*, Boston, Mass., 1979.

18. C. Smart, 'The new female criminal, myth or reality?', *British Journal of Criminology*, XIX 1969 pp. 50–9.

19. R. Levin, 'Women and crime today, *The Prison Journal*, 1979, 3.

20. Mills, 'Professional ideology'.

21. E. Cummings, 'Suicide as an index of role strain', *Canadian Review of Sociology and Anthropology*, XII, pt. 1. R. R. Korn and L. M. McCorkle, 'Social roles: linking individuals to criminal and delinquent behaviour', in C. Bersani (ed.), *Crime and Delinquency*, London, 1970, pp. 223–39.

22. W. R. Gove and J. Tudor, 'Sex differences in mental illness', *American Journal of Sociology*, LXXVIII, 1977.

23. D. Klein, 'The etiology of female crime: a review of the literature', *Issues in Criminology*, VIII, 2, 1973. See also R. Mawby, 'Sex and crime: the results of a self report study', *British Journal of Sociology*, XXXI, pp. 525–43; A. Morris and L. Gelsthorpe, 'False cues and female crime', in A. Morris and L. Gelsthorpe (eds), *Women and Crime*, Cropwood Conference Series, No. 13, Cambridge, 1981.

24. R. Cloward and L. Ohlin, *Delinquency and Opportunity*, New York, 1960.

25. B. O'Donnell, *Should women hang?* London, 1956, p. 88.

26. *Chronicles of Crime*, I, London, 1891, p. 398.

27. M. A. Betrand, 'Self-image and delinquency', *Acta Criminologica*, 1969, p. 81.

28. W. Bonger, *Criminality and Economic Conditions*. Bloomington/London, 1969.

29. Ibid.

30. L. Duffin, 'Prisoners of progress' in L. Duffin and S. Delamont (eds), *The Nineteenth Century Woman*, London, 1978.

31. Hansard 4th series col. 1283 (1856).

32. Hansard, 1868, CXCII, col. 1355.

33. L. Colebrook, *Sir Almroth Wright: Provocative Doctor and Thinker*, London, 1954.

34. R. Levin, 'Women and Crime Today', *The Prison Journal*, 1979, p. 3. See also W. I. Thomas, *The Unadjusted Girl*, London, 1924, p. 85.

35. S. Chibnall, *Law and Order News: An Analysis of Crime Reporting in the British Press*, London, 1977. Tavistock 1972.

36. S. Cohen, *Folk Devils and Moral Panics*, St Albans.

37. D. J. Steffensmeier, 'Assessing the impact of the Women's Movement on sex-based differences in the handling of adult criminal defendants', *Crime and Delinquency,* XXVI, 1980, pp. 344–57.
38. Hansard 1978, CMXLVI, col. 833–923.
39. W. Bacon and R. Lansdowne, 'Women who kill husbands: the battered wife on trial', in *Family Violence in Australia* C. O'Donnell and J. Craney (eds) Melbourne 1982 pp. 67–93.
40. Ibid., p. 85.
41. Ibid., pp. 91–2.
42. C. Bohanna, 'All I ever wanted was my son' New Society, February 17 1983, pp. 254–6.

Chapter 8

1. Matilda M. Blake, 'Are women protected?', *The Westminster Review,* CXXXVII, 1892, p. 44.
2. C. Temin, 'Discriminatory sentencing of women offenders', in S. K. Datesman and F. R. Scarpitti (eds), *Women, Crime and Justice,* New York/Oxford, 1980, pp. 255–76.
3. Report of the Work of the Prison Department, London, 1972, Cmnd. 5375, para. 145.
4. A. Samuels, 'The social inquiry report: the law and the practice', *Justice of the Peace,* 1980, p. 350.
5. Home Office circular 1959.
6. L. Foley and C. Rasche, 'A longitudinal study of sentencing patterns of female offenders'. Paper presented at the American Society of Criminology, Tucson, Arizona, 1976.
7. I. Bernstein, E. Kick, J. Leung and B. Schulz, 'Charge reduction: an intermediary stage in the process of labelling criminal defendants', *Social Forces,* LVI, pp. 362–84.
8. The Royal Commission on Capital Punishment, 1949–53, Cmd. 8932, London.
9. *Women in the Penal System,* NACRO Briefing, 1981, p. 2.
10. *Criminal Statistics,* England and Wales, 1981, Cmnd. 8668, London, p. 83.
11. P. Hardiker and D. Webb, 'Explaining deviant behaviour: the social context of "action" and "infraction" accounts in the probation service, *Sociology,* XIII, 1979, pp. 1–18.
12. The Report of the Committee on Mentally Abnormal Offenders, 1974–5, Cmnd. 6244, London, section 136.
13. B. Sheppard, 'Research into aspects of probation', Home Office Research Bulletin No. 10, 1980, p. 23.
14. P. Bean, 'Social enquiry reports and the decision-making process', *Family Law,* VI, 1971, pp. 174–8.
15. J. Hine, W. McWilliams and K. Pease, 'Recommendations, social information and sentencing', *Howard Journal,* XVII, 1978, pp. 91–100.
16. J. Thorpe, 'Social inquiry reports: a survey', Home Office Research Study No. 48, London, 1979.
17. Ibid.
18. J. Thomson, 'Pre-trial reports', *Justice of the Peace,* 1982, p. 144.
19. Samuels, 'Social inquiry report'.
20. J. Trepanier, 'Pre-trial social inquiry reports on defendants pleading not guilty: are they acceptable?', *Probation Journal,* XXVII, 1979, pp. 9–15.

21. *Probation and After-Care Statistics,* 1981, Table 2:11, p. 25. *Criminal Statistics, England* 1981, Cmnd. 8668, Table 3:32, p. 180.

Select bibliography

Acton, W. (1857) *Prostitution* (1968 edn) London.

Adams, P. (1979) 'A note on the distinction between sexual differences', *m/f* no. 3, 1979, pp. 51–7.

Adler, F. (1975) *Sisters in Crime: The Rise of the New Female Criminal,* New York.

Adler, F. and Simon, R.J. (eds) (1979) *The Criminology of Deviant Women,* Boston

Adler, Z. (1982) 'Rape – the intention of Parliament and the practice of the courts', *Modern Law Review,* XLV, pp. 664–75.

Anderson, E. A. (1976) 'The "chivalrous" treatment of the female offender in the arms of the criminal justice system: a review of the literature', *Social Problems,* XXIII, pp. 349–57.

Armstrong, B. K. (1977) 'The role of diet in human carcinogenesis with special reference to endometrial cancer', in H. Hiatt, J. D. Watson and J. A. Winsten (eds), *Origins of Human Cancer,* New York.

Armstrong, G. (1977) 'Females under the law – "protected" but unequal', *Crime and Delinquency,* XXIII, pp. 109–20.

Austin, R. L. (1982) 'Women's Liberation and increases in minor, major and occupational offences', *Criminology,* XX, pp. 407–30.

Baldwin, J. and Bottomley, A. K. (1978) *Criminal Justice: Selected Readings,* London.

Baldwin, J. and McConville, M. (1977) *Negotiated Justice,* London.

Barker-Benfield, G. J. (1976 *The Horrors of the Half-Known Life,* New York.

Barrett, M. (1980) *Women's Oppression Today,* London.

Barrington Baker, J. *The Matrimonial Jurisdiction of Registrars* (SSRC, London, 1977).

Bean, P. (1976) *Rehabilitation and Deviance,* London.

Becker, H. (1963) *Outsiders,* New York.

Becker, H. (ed.) (1964) *The Other Side,* New York.

Bedford, A. (1974) 'Women and parole', *British Journal of Criminology,* XIV, pp. 106–17.

Bennett, H. M. (1968) 'Shoplifting in midtown', *Criminal Law Review:* 413–425.

Bernstein, I. N., Cardascia, J. and Ross, C. E. (1979 'Defendants, sex and criminal court decisions', in R. Alvarez *et al.* (eds), *Discrimination in Organisations,* San Francisco, pp. 329–54.

Bishop, C. (1931) *Women and Crime,*London.

Bordua, D. (1967) *The Police,* New York.

Bottoms, A. E. and McClean, D. (1976) *Defendants in the Criminal Process,* London.

Bottoms, A. E. and McWilliams, W. (1979) 'A non-treatment paradigm for probation practice', *British Journal of Social Work,* IX, 2, 159–201.

Bottomley, A. K. (1973) *Decisions in the Penal Process,* London.

Bottomley, A. K. (1977) *Criminology in Focus,* London.

Bowker, L. (1978) *Women, Crime and the Criminal Justice System,* Lexington, Massachusetts.

Box, S. (1971) *Deviance, Reality and Society,* London.

Box, S. and Hale, C. (1983) 'Liberation and female criminality in England and Wales', *British Journal of Criminology,* XXIII, pp. 35–49.

Brahams, D. (1983) 'Pre-menstrual tension and criminal responsibility', *The Practitioner,* CCXXVII, pp. 807–13.

Brodsky, A. (ed.) (1975) *The Female Offender*, London.

Brownmiller, S. (1975 *Against our Will: Men, Women and Rape*, New York.

Brundson, C. (1978) 'It is well known that by nature women are inclined to be rather personal', in *Women Take Issue*, London, pp. 18–34.

Bujra, J. M. 1982 , 'Women "entrepreneurs" of early Nairobi', and 'Postscript: prostitution, class and the state', in C. Sumner (ed.), *Crime, Justice and Underdevelopment*, London.

Bullough, V. (1976) *Sex, Society and History*, New York.

Burman, S. (ed.) (1979) *Fit Work for Women*, London.

Carlen, P. (1983) *Women's Imprisonment*, London.

Carlen, P. and Collison, M. (eds) (1980) *Radical Issues in Criminology*, London.

Chambers, G. A. (1979) *Social Work with Adult Offenders*, Edinburgh Scottish Home and Health Department, Social Research Branch.

Chapman, J. R. and Gates, M. (eds) (1978) *The Victimization of Women*, London/Beverly Hills.

Chesler, P. (1972) *Women and Madness*, New York.

Chesney-Lind, M. (1977) 'Judicial paternalism and the female status offender', *Crime and Delinquency*, XXIII, pp. 121–30.

Cicourel, A. V. (1968) *The Social Organisation of Juvenile Justice*, New York.

Cloward, R. and Ohlin, L. (1960) *Delinquency and Opportunity*, New York.

Cohen. S. (1979) 'The punitive city: notes on the dispersal of social control', *Contemporary Crises*, III, pp. 339–63.

Comfort, A. (1967) *The Anxiety Makers*, London.

Conrad, P. (1980) 'Implications of changing social policy for the medicalization of deviance', *Contemporary Crises* IV(a), pp. 195–205.

Conrad, P. and Schneider, J. W. (1980) *Deviance and Medicalization*, St Louis/Toronto/London.

Cousins, M. (1980) 'Mens rea: a note on sexual difference, criminology and the law', in P. Carlen and M. Collison (eds), *Radical Issues in Criminology*, London, pp. 109–22.

Coward, R. (1983) *Patriarchal Precedents: Sexuality and Social Relations*, London.

Cranfield, R. and E. (1983) 'Female circumcision: an assault' *The Practitioner*, CCXXVII, 1379, pp. 816–17.

Cressey, D. R. (1962) 'Role theory, differential association and compulsive crimes', in A. M. Rose (ed.), *Human Behaviour and Social Processes*, London, pp. 443–67.

Criminal Law Revision Committee (1974) Working Paper on Vagrancy and Street Offences.

Criminal Law Revision Committee (1976) Working Paper on Offences Against the Person.

Criminal Law Revision Committee (1976) Working Paper on Vagrancy and Street Offences.

Criminal Law Revision Committee (1980) Working Paper on Sexual Offences.

Criminal Law Revision Committee (1982) Working Paper on Offences Relating to Prostitution and Allied Offences.

Crites, L. (1978) *The Female Offender*, Lexington.

Cunnington, S. (1980) 'Some aspects of prostitution in the West End of London in 1979', in D. J. West (ed.), *Sex Offenders in the Criminal Justice System*, Cambridge, pp. 121–30.

Curnock, K. and Hardiker, P. (1979) *Towards Practice Theory*, London.

Daly, M. (1978) *Gyn/Ecology*, London.

Datesman, S. K. and Scarpitti, F. R. (1980) *Women, Crime and Justice*, New York/Oxford.

Delaney, J. (1976) *The Curse*, New York.

Dell, S. (1978) 'Inconsistent pleaders', in J. Baldwin and A. K. Bottomley (eds), *Criminal Justice: Selected Readings*, London, pp. 106–15

Deming, R. (1977) *Women: The New Criminals* , Nashville.

Department of Justice (1968) *Crime in New Zealand*, Wellington, New Zealand.

Devlin, K. M. (1970) *Sentencing Offenders in Magistrates' Courts*, London.

Dijk Van, G. and De Wit, A. (1982) 'Lady Justice or Lady Hysteria? Notes on the psychiatrization of female crime', *Proces*, LXI, 7, 188–97.

Dinitz, S., Dynes, R. R. and Clarke, A. C. (eds) (1969) *Deviance*, New York.

Ditton, J. (1978) 'Alibis and aliases: some notes on the "motives" of fiddling bread salesmen', *Sociology*, XI, pp. 233–55.

D'Orban, P. T. (1972) 'Female Crime', *The Criminologist*, VII, p. 104–16.

D'Orban, P. T. (1971) 'Social and psychiatric aspects of female crime', *Medicine, Science and the Law*, II, pp. 104–16.

Douglas, M. (ed.) (1971) *Rules and Meanings*, Harmondsworth.

Edwards, S. S. M. (1979) 'Sex crimes in the nineteenth century', *New Society*, 13 September.

Edwards, S. S. M. (1981a) *Female Sexuality and the Law*, London.

Edwards, S. S. M. (1981b) 'Femina sexualis: medico-legal control in Victoriana', *The Society for the Social History of Medicine Bulletin*, No. 28, pp. 17–20.

Edwards, S. S. M. (1982a) 'The medical control of female sexuality in the nineteenth century', *British Journal of Sexual Medicine*, VIII, 80, pp. 46–9.

Edwards, S. S. M. (1982b) 'Sex or gender: the prostitute in law', *British Journal of Sexual Medicine*, IX, 81, pp. 5, 6, 11.

Edwards, S. S. M. (1982c) 'Rape: a consideration of contributory negligence, police procedures and the mandatory sentence', *Justice of the Peace*, CXLVI, 8, pp. 108–10.

Edwards, S. S. M. (1982d) 'Indecent assault: is *Faulkner* v *Talbot* a watershed?', *Justice of the Peace*, CXLVI, 17, pp. 244–5.

Edwards, S. S. M. (1982e) 'Imprisonment is not for prostitutes', *Justice of the Peace*, CXLVI, 22, pp. 325–7.

Edwards, S. S. M. (1982f) 'Pre-menstrual tension: no defence in law', *Justice of the Peace*, CXLVI, 32, pp. 476–8.

Edwards, S. S. M. (1982g) 'Henry Maudsley: his views on mental health', *British Journal of Sexual Medicine*, IX, 89, pp. 32–8.

Edwards, S. S. M. (1982h) 'No man's land: the transsexual and the law', *Justice of the Peace*, CXLVI, 34, pp. 510–11.

Edwards, S. S. M. (1982i) 'Everybodys talking 'bout ma baby', *The Leveller*, No. 89 pp. 22–3.

Edwards, S. S. M. (1983a) 'The law relating to prostitution: a case for immediate reform', *Justice of the Peace*, CXLVII, 3, pp. 38–40.

(1983b) 'Pre-menstrual "syndrome": a medico-legal conundrum', *Psychiatry in practice*, II,14, pp. 24–9.

Edwards Hiller, A. (1982) 'Women crime and criminal justice: the state of current theory and research in Australia and New Zealand', *Australia and New Zealand Journal of Criminology*, 15, 2, pp. 69–89.

Ehrenreich, B. and English, D. (1979) *For Her Own Good*, London.

Ellis, H. H. (1901) *The Criminal*, London.

Elshtain, B. (1981) *Public Man, Private Woman*, London.

Fallon, P. (1975) *Crown Court Practice: Sentence*, London.

Faulkner, D. (1971) 'The redevelopment of Holloway Prison', *Howard Journal*, XIII, 2, pp. 122–32.

Figes, E. (1972) *Patriarchal Attitudes*, London.

Firestone, S. (1972) *The Dialectic of Sex*, London.

Foote, N. N. (1951) 'Identification as the basis for a theory of motivation', *American Sociological Review*, XVI.

Friedan, B. (1965) *The Feminine Mystique*, Harmondsworth.

Foucault, M. (1977) *Discipline and Punish*, Allen Lane.

Foucault, M. (1978) *The History of Sexuality: An Introduction*, New York.

Foucault, M. (1980) *Heculine Barbin*, Sussex.

Giallombardo, R. (1966) *Society of Women: A Study of Women's Prison*, New York.

Gibbens, T. C. N. (1962) *Shoplifting*, London.

Gibbens, T. C. N. (1971) 'Mental health aspects of shoplifters', *British Medical Journal*, CXI, p. 612.

Gibbens, T. C. N., Palmer, J. and Prince, J. (1971) 'Mental health aspects of shoplifting'. *British Medical Journal*, III, p. 612–5.

Gibbens, T. C. N., Soothill, K. L. and Pope, P. J. (1977) *Medical Remands in the Criminal Court*, Oxford.

Gibbs, C. (1971) 'The effect of imprisonment of women on their children', *British Journal of Criminology*, II, pp. 113–30.

Gilman, C. P. (1911) 'Charlotte Perkins Gilman's Dynamic Social Philosophy', *Current Literature*, July.

Goffman, E. (1963) *Behaviour in Public Places*, New York.

Goffman, E. (1970) *Stigma*, Harmondsworth.

Goffman, E. (1971) *Relations in Public*, London.

Goffman, E. (1972) *Interaction Ritual*, London.

Goffman, E. (1977) 'The arrangement between the sexes', *Theory and Society*, IV, pp. 301–31.

Goodman, N. and Price, J. (1967) *Studies of Female Offenders*, London, pp. 63–78.

Gouldner, A. V. (1954) *Patterns of Industrial Bureaucracy*, Glencoe.

Graham, H. (1950) *Eternal Eve*, London.

Greenwald, H. (1969) 'The social and professional life of the call girl', in S. Dinitz, R. Dynes and A. Clarke (eds), *Deviance*, New York, pp. 400–11.

Greenwood, V. (1981) 'The myths of female crime', in Morris and Gelsthorpe, *Women and Crime*, pp. 73–84.

Gross, E. (1911) *Criminal Psychology*, London.

Haft, M. 'Hustling for rights' in L. Crites (ed.), *The Female Offender*, Lexington 1969, pp. 207–28.

Halmos, P. (1978) *The Personal and the Political*, London.

Hancock, L. (1980) 'The myth that females are treated more leniently than men', *Australia and New Zealand Journal of Sociology*, XVI, pp. 4–13.

Hardiker, P. (1979) 'The role of probation officers in sentencing', in H. Parker (ed.), *Social Work and the Courts*, London, pp. 117–34.

Hardiker, P. and Webb, D. (1979) 'Explaining deviant behaviour: the social context of "action" and "infraction" accounts in the probation service', *Sociology*, XIII, 1979, pp. 1–18.

Harris, A. (1977) 'Sex and theories of deviance: towards a functional theory of deviant type-scripts', *American Sociological Review*, XLII, pp. 3–16.

Heidensohn, F. (1969) 'Prison for women', *Criminologist* IV, 12, pp. 113–22.

Heidensohn, F. (1975) 'The imprisonment of females', in S. McConville (ed.) *The Use of Imprisonment*, London, pp. 43–56.

Heidensohn, F. (1981) 'Women and the penal system', in Morris and Gelsthorpe, *Women and Crime*, pp. 125–39.

Henry, S. (1976) 'Fencing with accounts: the language of moral bridging', *British Journal of Law and Society*, III, pp. 91–100.

Hill, J. B. (1981) 'Prostitution – is sex important?', *Justice of the Peace*, CXLV, pp. 215–17.

Hoffman-Bustamante, D. (1973) 'The nature of female criminality', *Issues in Criminology*, VIII, pp. 117–36.

Hollway, W. (1981) 'I just wanted to kill a woman, Why? The Ripper and male sexuality', *Feminist Review*, IX, pp. 33–40.

Home Office (1981) *Criminal Statistics*, England and Wales Cmnd. 8668, London, (Supplementary Tables 1–4).

Home Office (1981) *Prison Statistics*, England and Wales, Cmnd. 8654, London.

Home Office (1981) *Probation and After-Care Statistics*, England and Wales, London.

Honore, T. (1978) *Sex Law*, London.

Hood, W. C. (1850) 'Criminal lunatics: a letter to the Chairman of the Commissioners in Lunacy' (British Museum 6095 blo).

Hutter, B. and Williams, G. (eds) (1981) *Controlling Women*, London.

Illich, I. (1976) *Medical Nemesis*, London.

Jaget, C. (ed.) (1980) *Prostitutes, Our Life*, Bristol.

James, A. (1979) 'Sentenced to surveillance', *Probation Journal*, XXVI, pp. 15–20.

James, J. (1978a) 'Motivations for entrance into prostitution', in L. Crites (ed.), *The Female Offender*, New York.

James, J. (1978b) 'The prostitute as victim', in J. R. Chapman and M. Gates (eds), *The Victimization of Women*, London/Beverly Hills, pp. 175–201.

James, J., Davis, N. J. and Vitaliano, P. (1982) 'Female sexual deviance: a theoretical and empirical analysis', *Deviant Behaviour*, III, pp. 175–95.

James, T. E. (1951) *Prostitution and the Law*, London.

Jones, A. (1980) *Women Who Kill*, New York.

Kesey, K. (1976) *One Flew Over the Cuckoo's Nest*, London.

Kitsuse, J. I. (1964) 'Societal reaction to deviant behaviour: problems of theory and method', in H. Becker (ed.), *The Other Side*, Glencoe, pp. 87–102.

Klein, D. (1973) 'The etiology of female crime: a review of the literature', *Issues in Criminology*, VIII, pp. 3–30.

Klein, D. and Kress, J. (1981) 'Any woman's blues: a criminal overview of women, crime and the criminal justice system', in T. Platt and P. Takagi (eds), *Crime and Social Justice,* London, pp. 153–83.

Kruttschnitt, C. (1981) 'Social status and sentences of female offenders', *Law and Society Review,* XV, pp. 247–61.

Kruttschnitt, C. (1982) 'Women, crime and dependency: an application of the theory of law', *Criminology,* XIX, pp. 495n

Land, H. (1978) 'Sex-role stereotyping in the social security and income tax system', in J. Chetwynd and O. Hartnett (eds), *The Sex Role System,* London, pp. 127–42.

Lemert, E. (1951) *Social Pathology,* New York.

Lewis, D. K. (1981) 'Black women offenders and criminal justice', in I. Warren (ed.), *The Sex Role System,* London, pp. 89–105.

Lipshitz, S. (1978) 'Women and psychiatry', in J. Chetwynd and O. Hartnett (eds), *The Sex Role System,* London, pp. 93–108.

Lombroso, C. and Ferrero, W. (1895) *The Female Offender,* London.

Lytton C., *Prison and Prisoners* (reprinted by E. P. Publishers, London, 1976).

McBarnet, D. J. (1976) 'Pre-trial procedures and the construction of convictions', in P. Carlen (ed.), *The Sociology of Law,* Keele, pp. 172–99.

McClean, J. D. and Wood, J. C. (1969) *Criminal Justice and the Treatment of Offenders,* London.

McIntosh, M. (1978) 'The state and the oppression of women', pp. 254– 89, in A. Kuhn and A. M. Wolpe (eds), *Feminism and Materialism,* London.

Mackesy, A. N. (1956) 'The criminal law and the woman seducer', *Criminal Law Review,* pp. 446–56 and 529–41.

McLean, I. (1980) *Criminal Appeals: A Practical Guide,* London.

McLeod, E. (1981) 'The street prostitutes' campaign against control', in Hutter and Williams, *Controlling Women,* pp. 61–77.

McLeod, E. (1982) *Women Working: Prostitution Now,* London.

Mannheim, H. (1965) *Comparative Criminology,* London.

Matza, D. (1964) *Delinquency and Drift,* Berkeley.

Matza, D. (1969) *Becoming Deviant,* Englewood Cliffs, N.J.

Mawby, R. (1977) 'Sexual discrimination and the law', *Probation Journal,* XXIV, pp. 38–43.

Mawby, R. (1980) 'Sex and crime: the results of a self-report study', *British Journal of Sociology,* XXXI, pp. 525–43.

Menzies, R. J. (1980) 'Law, politics and madness: on the pathologisation of deviance', *Canadian Criminology Forum,* II, 2, 11–28.

Mercier, C. (1918) *Crime and Criminals Being the Jurisprudence of Crime,* London.

Merrick, B. (1970) 'Shoplifting: a microcosm', *The Criminologist,* V, 18, pp. 68–81.

Millett, K. (1971) *Sexual Politics,* New York.

Millett, K. (1975) *The Prostitution Papers,* London.

Mills, C. Wright (1943) 'The professional ideology of social pathologists', *American Journal of Sociology,* XLIX, 2, pp. 165–80.

Mitchell, J. (1971) *Women's Estate,* Harmondsworth.

Morris, A. and L. Gelsthorpe (1981) *Women and Crime,* Cropwood Conference Series No. 13, Cambridge.

Morton, J. H. (1953) *International Record of Medicine,* no. 166.

Mukherjee, S. K. and W. Fitzgerald (1981) 'The myth of rising female crime', in Mukherjee and Scutt, *Women and Crime.*

Mukherjee, S. K. and Scutt, J. A. (eds) (1981) *Women and Crime,* Australia.

Nagel, I. (1981) 'Sex differences in the processing of criminal defendants', in Morris and Gelsthorpe, *Women and Crime.*

Newman, D. J. (1962) 'The effects of accommodations in justice administration of criminal statistics', *Sociology and Social Research,* XLVI, p. 144.

Norland, S. and Shover, N. (1977) 'Gender role and female criminality: some critical comments', *Criminology,* XV, pp. 87–104.

O'Donovan, K. (1979) 'The male appendage: legal definitions of women', in S. Burman (ed.), *Fit Work for Women,* London, pp. 134–99.

Oleck, H. L. (1955) 'Legal aspects of pre-menstrual tension', pp. 492–501 in J. H. Morton, *International Record of Medicine,* no. 166.

Omodei, R. (1981) 'The myth interpretation of female crime', in Mukherjee and Scutt, *Women and Crime.*

Pearson, G. (1975) *The Deviant Imagination,* London.

Pearson, R. (1976) 'Women defendants in magistrates' courts', *British Journal of Law and Society,* III, pp. 265–73.

Pepinsky, H. (1976) 'Police patrolmen's offence reporting behaviour', *Journal of Research in Crime and Delinquency,* XIII, pp. 33–47.

Perry, F. (1974a) 'Reports for the courts', *Justice of the Peace,* CXXXVIII, pp. 589–90.

Perry, F. (1974b) *Information for the Courts,* Cambridge.

Phillips, D. M. and DeFleur, L. B. (1982) 'Gender ascription in the stereotyping of deviants', *Criminology,* XX, pp. 431–48.

Piliavin, I. and Briar, S. (1964) 'Police encounters with juveniles', *American Journal of Sociology,* LXX, pp. 260–74.

Platt, T. and Takagi, P. (1981) *Crime and Social Justice,* London.

Pollak, O. (1950) *The Criminality of Women,* Philadelphia.

Price, R. R. (1977) 'The forgotten female offender', *Crime and Delinquency,* XXIII, pp. 101–08.

Prison and the Prisoner (1977) Home Office.

Procek, E. (1981) 'Psychiatry and the social control of women' in Morris and Gelsthorpe, *Women and Crime.*

Rafter, N. H. and Natalizia, E. M. (1981) 'Marxist feminism: implications for criminal justice', *Crime and Delinquency,* XXVII, pp. 81–98.

Rasche, C. (1975) 'The female offender as an object of criminal research', in Brodsky, *Female Offender.*

Reckless, W. (1957) *The Female Offender.*

Reiman, J. H. (1979) 'Prostitution, addiction and the ideology of liberalism', *Contemporary Crises,* III, (January) pp. 53–68.

Report of the Street Offences Committee 1928, Cmd. 3231.

Report of the Royal Commission Upon the Duties of the Metropolitan Police 1908.

Report of the Committee on Homosexual Offences and Prostitution 1957, Cmnd. 247.

Roby, P. A. (1969) 'Politics and criminal law: review of the New York State penal law on prostitution', *Social Problems,* No. 17, pp. 83–109.

Rock, P. (1973) *Deviant Behaviour,* London.

Rosenblum, K. E. (1975) 'Female deviance and the female sex role: a preliminary investigation', *British Journal of Sociology*, XXVI, pp. 173–8.

Rothman, M. L. and Gandossy, R. P. (1982) 'Sad tales: the accounts of white-collar defendants and the decision to sanction', *Pacific Sociological Review*, XXV, pp. 449–73.

Rowett, C. and Vaughan, P. J. (1981) 'Women and Broadmoor: treatment and control in a special hospital', in Hutter and Williams, *Controlling Women*, pp. 131–53.

Royal Commission on Criminal Procedure (1981) 'The investigation and prosecution of criminal offences in England and Wales: the law and procedure', Cmnd. 8092–1, London.

Royal Commission on Police (1962).

Sachs, A. and Wilson, J. Hoff (1978) *Sexism and the Law*, Oxford.

Sacks, H. (1972) 'Notes on police assessment of moral character' in Sudnow (ed.), *Studies in Social Interaction*, New York.

Sadaawi, N. E. (1980) *The Hidden Face of Eve*, London.

Sayers, J. (1982) *Biological Politics*, London/New York.

Scheff, T. J. (1966) *Being Mentally Ill*, Chicago.

Schur, E. M. and Bedau, A. A. (1974) *Victimless Crimes*, Englewood Cliffs, N.J.

Schutz, A. (1970) *The Phenomenology of the Social World*, London.

Scutt, J. (1978) 'Towards the liberation of the female lawbreaker', *International Journal of Criminology and Penology*, VI, pp. 5–18.

Scutt, J. (1981) 'Sexism in the Law', in Mukherjee and Scutt, *Women and Crime*.

Scutt, J. A. (1979) 'The myth of the "chivalry" factor in female crime', *Australian Journal of Social Issues*, XIV, pp. 3–20.

Seaborne Davis, D. (1937) 'Child killing in English law', Modern Law Review, I, pp. 203–17.

Sedley, A. and Benn, M. (1982) *Sexual Harrassment at Work*, London.

Shacklady Smith, L. (1978) 'Sexist assumptions and female delinquency', in B. Smart and C. Smart (eds), *Women, Sexuality and Social Control*, London, pp. 74–86.

Shapland, J. (1981) *Between Conviction and Sentence*, London.

Shaw, C. R. and McKay, H. D. (1942) *Juvenile Delinquency and Urban areas*, Chicago.

Simon W. and Gagnon, J. H. (1973) *Sexual Conduct*, Chicago.

Simon, R. J. (1975) *Women and Crime*, Lexington, Massachusetts.

Simon, R. J. and Sharma, N. (1978) 'Women and crime: does the American experience generalise', in F. Adler and R. J. Simon (eds), *The Criminality of Deviant Women*, Boston, Mass., pp. 391–400.

Skolnick, J. H. (1966) *Justice Without Trial: Law Enforcement in Democratic Society*, New York.

Smart, B. and Smart, C. (1978) *Women, Sexuality and Social Control*, London.

Smart, C. (1976) *Women, Crime and Criminology: A Feminist Critique*, London.

Smart, C. (1981) 'Law and the control of women's sexuality: the case of the 1950s', in Hutter and Williams, *Controlling Women*, pp. 40–60.

Smith, A. D. (1962) *Women in Prison*, London.

Steffensmeier, D. (1978) 'Crime and the contemporary woman: an analysis of changing levels of female property crime: 1960–75', *Social Forces*, 57, 566–84.

Smith, A. D. (1965) 'Penal policy and the woman offender', in Sociological Review Mongraph No. 9, Keele, pp. 111–32.

Smith, D. A. and Visher, C. A. (1981) 'Street-level justice: situational determinants of police arrest decisions', *Social Problems*, XXIX, 2, pp. 167–77.

Smith, D. E. (1978) 'K is mentally ill: the anatomy of a factual account', *Sociology*, XII, pp. 23–57.

Sñare, A. and Stang-Dahl, T. (1978) 'The coercion of privacy', p. 8–26, in Smart and Smart, *Women, Sexuality and Social, Control*, London.

Smith, J. C. and Hogan, B. (1965), (1978) *Criminal Law* (4th ed), London.

Soothill, K. L. and Pope, P. J. (1974) *Medical Remands in Magistrates' Courts*, Cambridge.

Spender, D. (1980) *Man-made Language*, London.

Steffensmeier, D. (1980) 'Sex differences in the pattern of adult crime 1967–1977: a review and assessment', *Social Forces*, LVIII, pp. 1080–1108.

Steffensmeier, D. and Cobb, M. J. (1981) 'Sex differences in urban arrest patterns, 1934–1979', *Social Problems*, XXIX, pp. 37–50.

Sudnow, D. (1965) 'Normal crimes: sociological features of the penal code in a public defender office', *Social Problems*, XII, pp. 255–76.

Sudnow, D. (1972) *Studies in Social Interaction*, New York.

Sumner, C. (ed.) (1982) *Crime, Justice and Undervelopment*, London.

Sumner, M. (1980) 'Prostitution and the position of women: a case for decriminalisation', in Morris and Gelsthorpe, *Women and Crime*, pp. 88–99.

Swigert, V. and Farrell, R. (1977) 'Normal homicides and the law', *American Sociological Review*, XLII, pp. 16–32.

Sykes, G. (1958) *The Society of Captives*, Princeton.

Sykes, G. and Matza, D. (1957) Techniques of neutralisation: a theory of delinquency', *American Sociological Review*, XX, pp. 664–70.

Szasz, T. S. (1963) *Law, Liberty and Psychiatry (and Psychiatric Justice)*, London.

Szasz, T. S. (1970) *The Manufacture of Madness*, London.

Tarling, R. (1979) 'Sentencing practice in magistrates' courts', Home Office Research Study No. 56, London.

Taylor, Buckner, H. (1978) 'Transformations of reality in the legal process', in T. Luckmann (ed.), *Phenomenology and Sociology*, Harmondsworth, pp. 311–23.

Taylor, I. (1981) *Law and Order: Arguments for Socialism*, London.

Taylor, I. Walton, P. and Young, J. (1973) *The New Criminology*, London.

Taylor, L. (1972) 'The significance and interpretation of replies to motivational questions: the case of sex offenders', *Sociology*, No. 6, pp. 23–39.

Taylor, L. and Dalton, K. (1983) 'Pre-menstrual syndrome: a new criminal defence', *California Western Law Review*, XIX, pp. 269–87.

Temin, C. (1973) 'Discriminatory sentencing of women offenders: the argument for ERA in a nutshell', *American Criminal Law Review*, XI, pp. 355–72.

Thomas, D. A. (1979) *Principles of Sentencing*, London.

Thomas, W. I. (1923) *The Unadjusted Girl*, New York.

Vennard, J. (1981) 'Acquittal rates in magistrate's courts', Home Office Research Bulletin No. 11, London, pp. 21–3.

Vennard, J. (1982) 'Contested trials in magistrates' courts', Home Office Research Study No. 71, London.

Victimology: An International Journal, 1983 (papers presented to the Second International Institute on Victimology, Italy 1982).

Visher, C. A. (1983) 'Gender, police arrest decisions and notions of chivalry', *Criminology*, XXI, pp. 5–27.

Walker, M. (1981) *Crime: Reviews of United Kingdom Statistical Sources*, XV, London.

Walker, N. (1965) *Crime and Punishment in Britain*, Edinburgh.

Walker, N. (1981) 'Feminists' extravaganzas', *Criminal Law Review*, pp. 379–86.

Walker, N. (1977) *Behaviour and Misbehaviour*, Oxford.

Walkowitz, J. R. (1980) *Prostitution and Victorian Society: Women, Class and the State*, London.

Wallach and Rubin (1971) 'The pre-menstrual syndrome and criminal responsibility', *UCLA Law Review*, XIX, pp. 210–310.

Walmsley, R. and White, K. (1979) 'Sexual offences, consent and sentencing', Home Office Research Study No. 54, London.

Ward D. A., Jackson, M. and Ward, R. E. (1979) 'Crimes of violence', in F. Adler and R. J. Simon (eds), *The Criminology of Deviant Women*, Boston, Mass., 1978.

Warren, M. Q. (ed.) (1981) *Comparing Female and Male Offenders*, London.

Weeks, J. (1981) *Sex, Politics and Society*, London/New York.

Weis, J. (1976) 'Liberation and crime: the invention of the new female criminal', *Crime and Social Justice*, 6, 17–27.

Werthman, C. and Piliavin, I. (1967) 'Gang members and the police', pp. 56–98, in D. Bordua (ed.), *The Police: Six Sociological Essays*, New York.

Wilkins, L. (1965) *Social Deviance*, London.

Williams, G. (1978) *A Longman Textbook of Criminal Law*, London.

Wilson, E. (1980) 'Feminism and social work', in R. Bailey (ed.), *Radical Social Work and Practice*, London.

Women Endorsing Decriminalization (1973) 'Prostitution: a new victim crime', *Issues in Criminology*, VIII, pp. 137–62.

Wilcox, A. F. (1972) *The Decision to Prosecute*, London.

Yablonsky, L. (1962) 'The role of law and social science in the juvenile court', *Journal of Criminal Law, Criminology and Police Science*, XXXV, pp. 426–36.

Young, J. (1971) 'The role of the police as amplifiers of deviancy, negotiators of reality and translators of fantasy: some consequences of our present system of drug control as seen in Notting Hill', pp. 27–61, in S. Cohen (ed), *Images of Deviance*, London.

Name index

Acton, Dr W., 53–4
Adams, P., 1, 9, 10
Adams, T. F., 124
Adler, F., 163, 168
Adler, Z., 105–6, 133, 165, 175

Bacon, W., 176
Baldwin, J., 21, 70, 75
Bartels, M., 83
Becker, H., 2, 77, 146, 151, 164
Bedford, A., 17
Benn, M., 49, 111
Bohanna, C., 99, 180
Blake, M., 183–4
Blum, A., 149–50, 151
Bottomley, A. K., 14, 70
Box, S., 14, 164, 168
Bowker, L., 33
Brahams, D., 85
Brophy, J., 6
Bull, M., 16, 95
Bujra, J. M., 50, 51

Camp, J., 183
Carlen, P., 7, 20, 185, 190
Cicourel, A., 126
Cohen, S., 5, 98, 163, 173, 212
Cousins, M., 9, 10, 11, 13
Cressey, D., 162
Cunnington, S., 121

Dalton, K., 86–9, 90
Daly, M., 49, 102
Damme, C., 91
De Fleur, L. B., 3, 187
Dell, S., 17, 69, 70
Denning, Lord, 6–7, 11, 15, 165
Devlin, K., 84
Ditton, J., 153
D'Orban, P., 173

Ellis, H. H., 83
Engels, F., 50
Evans, K., 89

Fallon, P., 7
Farrell, R., 2, 4, 121, 142, 182, 184
Foote, N., 151
Foucault, M., 81

Garcia, I., 4, 176
Garfinkel, H., 143, 161–2
Gelsthorpe, L., 3
Gibbens, T., 16, 173
Goffman, E., 1, 12, 13, 126, 138, 152
Gorham, D., 29
Greenwood, V., 3
Greg, W. R., 54, 78

Hardiker, P., 189
Hale, G., 168
Halmos, P., 20, 99, 214
Harris, A., 2
Hogan, B., 94
Honoré, T., 33

Icard, S., 83

Jones, A., 170

Klein, D., 3, 80, 99, 180, 184
Krafft-Ebing, R. von, 82
Kress, J., 3, 99, 170
Kruttschnitt, C., 4

Lansdowne, R., 176
Levin, R., 168
Little, J., 4, 176
Lombroso, C., 81–2, 170, 171
Lyman, S., 150
Lytton, C., ii

McBarnet, D., 141
McClean, J., 84, 206
McConville, S., 21, 70, 75
McHugh, P., 149, 151
McLeod, E., 25, 50, 133
Martin, J., 16
Massett, L., 92
Matza, D., 122, 126, 162

Mawby, R., 3, 170
Mercier, C., 47, 48, 84
Mill J. S., 148, 184
Millett, K., 25, 50, 56, 134, 184
Mills, C. Wright, 147, 149, 169
Mitchell, J., 90
Mitchell, S. Weir, 215
Mooney, B., 175
Morris, A., 3

Nagel, I., 4, 185
Natalizia, E. M., 100

Oakley, A., 95, 98
O'Donovan, K., 5, 10, 12
Ormrod, Justice, 44–5, 50

Phillips, D. M., 3, 187
Piliavin, I., 125, 135
Ploss, H. H., 83
Pope, P., 16
Powls, D., 124

Rafter, N. H., 100
Rock, P., 165
Rowett, C., 2, 18, 215

Sachs, A., 14, 184
Sacks, H., 122, 126
Savage, G., 84
Scales, J., 48
Schur, E., 26
Schutz, A., 143, 146, 162
Scutt J., 98–9
Scott M., 150

Sedley, A., 49, 111
Skolnick, J., 2, 123,125, 127, 131
Smart, C., 6, 11, 51, 95, 130
Smith, A., 3, 81, 163
Smith, D., 140–41
Soothill, K., 16
Steffensmeier, D., 168, 174
Sudnow, D., 147, 150–51, 162
Swigert, V., 2, 4, 121, 142, 182, 184
Sykes, G., 148, 152–3, 162

Taylor, I., 154
Taylor, L., 150, 223 n.
Temin, C., 184
Thomas, D., 204
Tilt, E. J., 84
Trimmer, E., 88

Vaughan, P. J., 2, 18
Visher, C., 184

Walker, N., 15, 94, 151
Walkowitz, J., 53
Weber, M., 145–6, 162
Webster, D., 16
Weeks, J., 6, 49, 81
Werthman, C., 125, 135
West, D. J., 95
Wiles, P. N. P., 26, 167
Williams, G., 91, 103, 114–16
Wilkins, L., 15
Wilson, J. Hoff, 14, 184
Worrall, A., 3
Wright, Sir A. E., 172

Young, J., 78, 123, 125

Subject index

age of consent, 112–17
arrest, 168, 184

bail, 15, 16–17, 25
  fixed abode, 17
  legal representation, 17
Bail Act 1976, 17
biological positivism, 9, 10, 81
brothel-keeping, 107–8
Bulwood Hall, 187
Butler Committee, 94

chivalry, 184
Contagious Diseases Act, 29, 39
crime:
  typical, 1, 8, 14, 117, 148, 163, 175–82
  untypical, 8, 163, 197
criminal characterisations, 1–2, 121, 141–2
Criminal Injuries Compensation Board, 133
Criminal Justice Act 1948, 189
Criminal Justice Act 1967, 189
Criminal Law Revision Committee, 51–3, 128

decision to prosecute, 15, 164–5
defences to crime:
  automatism, 87
  PMT, 85–90
discretion, 14, 19, 20
division of labour, 1, 6, 7
drive reduction theory, 9, 148, 219 n.
due process, 85, 86

English Collective of Prostitutes, 50, 52, 57

family:
  ideology, 7, 98, 99, 100, 174–5
  parole, 8
  regulation of heterosexuality, 44–5, 49–50
  single parents, 96
female crime:
  differential opportunity, 169–70

emancipation thesis, 167–9, 171–5
  positivism, 80–83, 170–71
female sexuality:
  active, 9, 11, 102
  passive, 9, 102, 112
forensic experts, 2–3

gender characterisations, 6, 9, 10
Greenham Common women, 162
Guardianship of Infants Act, 6

Holloway, 16, 94, 187–8
Homicide Act, 94–5
homosexuality, 33, 34–5, 135
  AIDS, 48

importuning, 38–43
imprisonment:
  effect of, 183
  effect of on family, 185
Indecency with Children Act 1960, 113, 116
indecent assault:
  by male, 110, 112
  by female, 102, 109, 110, 112–18
individualised justice, 99, 145, 212–13
infanticide, 2, 4, 5, 84, 91–6
Infanticide Act, 4, 5, 7, 93–5
Infanticide Bill, 92, 93

kerb crawlers, 31–5, 52, 74–5

lactation and crime, 80, 91, 93, 94
lesbianism, 48, 111
laws, 'sex-specific', 5, 37

male:
  chivalry, 184
  protectiveness, 183–4
marriage and heterosexuality, 5, 44–5
Married Women's Property Bill, 6, 12
medical reports, 16, 27, 197–8
medical therapy, 183, 188

mitigation:
  family, 7, 202–4
  financial circumstances, 201
  medical problems, 69, 201
  motherhood, 7–8, 13, 205–6
  one-parent family, 62, 201
  social security, 201
moral crusaders, 47–8
'moral panics', 167–74
motivational accounts, 8, 145, 147–53
  action, 152
  aliases, 152
  crime-specific, 144–5
  excuses, 148, 155–8
  in the law, 153
  infraction, 149, 152
  justifications, 64, 148, 154, 158–9
  'remedial work', 66, 144, 152
  sex-specific, 148
  sexual, 109
  techniques of neutralisation, 148

NACRO, 12
NAPO, 19–20, 26, 193, 195, 197
'normal' crime, 144, 150, 163

pathology, 3, 8
plea bargaining, 21, 69, 70
  inconsistent, 70, 106
  prevaricate, 71, 106–7
  sentencing discount, 22, 76
police, 28
  apprehension, 131
  arrest, 27, 30, 122, 131
  bail, 15
  lay sociology of crime, 123
  prosecution, 15, 29
  reasonable suspicion, 15–30, 121,
    122–6, 129–30, 135, 137–8
  recording, 165
  violence, 110
pornography, 109, 110, 134
post-natal stress, 94, 96
pregnancy, 84
pre-menstrual tension:
  and crime, 83–4, 86–91
  in law, 85, 86–91

PROS, 517
prostitutes:
  'active', 11
  as a sex class, 25
  as victims, 133, 134
  cautioning of, 30, 37, 128
  'common', 28, 32, 53, 54, 55, 56,
    57–9, 75
  known, 58, 63, 130
  male, 33
  'passive', 11
  unequal before law, 78, 132
prostitution:
  'accepting unlawful solicitation', 35, 36
  prosecution, 28, 31
  sentencing, 207
prison:
  custodial remand, 18
  overcrowding, 187
probation, 128, 189
puerperal psychosis, 79, 91

rape:
  adult victims, 2, 9, 103, 105–6
  child victims, 8–9, 103
  contributory negligence, 9
  conviction, 105
  of prostitutes, 54
  sentencing, 104–5
'Reclaiming the Night', 110, 221 n.
'rolling', 165

sentencing:
  appeals against, 8, 13, 205–6
  committals for resocialisation, 216
  committals for treatment, 216
  of single parents, 205
sexual behaviour, control of:
  AIDS, 48
  cancer of cervix, 49
  cancer of uterus, 48
  clitoridectomy, 49–50, 102
  glossodoctomy, 49
sexual harassment, 110, 111
Sexual Offences Act, 26, 28, 30, 36
Sexual Offences Amendment Act, 132
social inquiry reports, 144, 188–91
  post-trial, 193

pre-trial, 193
recommendations, 191–6
sentencing, 191–6
soliciting, 35
store detectives:
evidence in court, 139–41
suspicion, 137–9
Street Offences Act, 9, 15, 35, 30–31, 56, 83

theft, 1, 8, 18, 122, 124, 137–41, 153, 155–8
transsexuals, 161, 165
civil status, 46
legal status, 37, 46
marriage, 37, 44–6
prostitutes, 37–43

victimisation, 102, 132–4
violent crime:
against wives, 133
and the media, 167–8
and women, 164, 167, 175
provocation, 178
pathology, 198
self-defence, 175–7

Wolfenden Committee, 25, 30, 31, 51
women:
arrest of, 168
as a 'sex class', 25
Working Paper on Sex Offences, 25
Working Party on Vagrancy and Street Offences, 194, 58

Yorkshire Ripper, 73, 77, 133